THE BLACK BOX OF BHOPAL

A CLOSER LOOK AT THE WORLD'S DEADLIEST INDUSTRIAL DISASTER

THEMISTOCLES D'SILVA

Order this book online at www.trafford.com/06-0167
or email orders@trafford.com

Most Trafford titles are also available at major online book retailers.

Proceeds from the book will be donated to charitable and educational institutions in India.

Cover Design and map by Carl J. D'Silva

Note for Librarians: A cataloguing record for this book is available from Library
and Archives Canada at www.collectionscanada.ca/amicus/index-e.html

Printed in Victoria, BC, Canada.

ISBN: 978-1-4120-8412-3

 www.trafford.com

North America & international
toll-free: 1 888 232 4444 (USA & Canada)
phone: 250 383 6864 ♦ fax: 250 383 6804 ♦ email: info@trafford.com

The United Kingdom & Europe
phone: +44 (0)1865 722 113 ♦ local rate: 0845 230 9601
facsimile: +44 (0)1865 722 868 ♦ email: info.uk@trafford.com

10 9 8 7 6 5

CONTENTS

PREFACE

In February 2001, Union Carbide Corporation (UCC) ceased to exist as an independent entity as the company merged with Dow Chemical Company, its longtime industry competitor. While the name may no longer be listed on Wall Street, Union Carbide and its widely recognized hexagonal logo will be remembered on Main Streets around the world for years to come, if only for one reason: the Bhopal tragedy. The name conjures feelings and reactions on a level comparable to Exxon *Valdez*, Three Mile Island, and Chernobyl. The reason for this notoriety may appear to be self-evident – a giant American multinational corporation, motivated by profits and share value, used outdated technology in a developing country and did not take precautions to ensure the safety and health of the people surrounding its industrial operations. The fact that the victims were among the poorest of India's poor and that the environment was the urban slums of Bhopal seems to make the case even more black and white. Everyone, from the media to environmentalists to governments, started from this assumption, before the cause of what actually happened was investigated and confirmed.

The facts are horrifying indeed. Just after midnight on December 3, 1984, a gas leak occurred at the Union Carbide pesticide plant in Bhopal, India. A vigorous chemical reaction inside a tank that stored methyl isocyanate (MIC) caused most of the material to vaporize and escape. Within days, over two thousand nearby residents were confirmed dead and tens of thousands exposed to toxic gases, which would cause them untold pain and health problems for years to come. News of the tragedy sent shock waves throughout the world, as Bhopal was soon characterized as the worst industrial disaster in history.

The disaster occurred just a month after the assassination of longtime Indian Prime Minister Indira Gandhi by her two Sikh bodyguards. With the communal backlash, rioting and curfews that ensued, the tragedy became part of a political vortex, as campaigning candidates scrambled to gain momentum before national elections later that month. Caught up in this whirlwind were hundreds of individual and class action lawsuits worth tens of billions of dollars.

Political, medical, environmental, and socioeconomic fallout from Bhopal dominated the headlines of national and international media for months. From the outset, accusing fingers were being pointed in every direction. Residents of the affected slums accused plant personnel for failing to activate the emergency siren as soon as the gas leak was discovered. Plant employees, in turn, blamed faulty equipment and poor maintenance practices by Union Carbide management. Government officials also blamed Union Carbide and its Indian subsidiary for faulty plant design, poor siting of the plant, and overall negligence. Senior management of Union Carbide Corporation blamed its subsidiary for noncompliance with standard safety and operating procedures. The tort lawyers were preparing to blame whomever and whatever would be the most profitable for them. Faced with such confusion and a lack of factual and credible information in the months following the incident, speculation became the order of the day. Politicians, lawyers, and both national and international media took on private investigator roles without truly understanding even the most basic details of the Bhopal plant and its history. The result was a number of investigations, findings, parliamentary hearings, and court cases that transpired without the benefit of a disclosure of all the relevant facts.

Twenty-one years after the Bhopal tragedy, I have yet to come across an objective, comprehensive account of the disaster, its causes, and its consequences. All too often, opinions and conclusions are not grounded in facts, but rather influenced by emotions and other agendas. Following my retirement in 1993, I decided to write this book in an attempt to bring together all the pertinent facts from the mountains of documentation that arose from the various investigations. In the course of researching these documents, which included U.S. court proceedings that had previously been viewed only by lawyers, the scope of this book was expanded to include new findings and insight. In the interest of preserving the colloquialism and authenticity of interviews and the previously unpublished documents, I have incorporated large sections of them into the text as appropriate. Selected complementary documents have been included in the appendix in their entireties for those who wish to review them more thoroughly.

In this book I will analyze a number of issues that are essential to understanding why and how "Bhopal" occurred and the investigations that followed. The first part of the book will probe into the history of the Bhopal plant with an in-depth look into the extent of involvement by UCC, Union Carbide India Limited (UCIL), and the central government, and the *modus operandi* of these organizations in managing the Indian company. It will review the industrial policies and the laws enacted by the Indian Parliament and how they impacted foreign companies doing business in India; how decisions were made with regard to Bhopal plant's design, construction and operation; and who technically owned and operated the plant.

Previously unpublished correspondence between the various agencies of the central government and UCIL will help explain a number of these unanswered issues. Documents will also show that Indian engineers built the plant according to government guidelines and met the country's manufacturing standards. The Bhopal plant operated successfully, though not without problems, for five years.

The new disclosures will also reveal that when UCIL's pesticide business began to falter, due to technical problems in manufacturing alpha-naphthol (another intermediate required to produce the pesticide) and competing market forces, the management considered various proposals to reduce losses, including closing and dismantling the facility. The decision had to be made by the end of December 1984, as the foreign collaboration agreement was set to expire on January 1, 1985. Tragedy struck a month earlier.

In the third chapter, I will focus on the investigations that followed the gas eruption. The Indian government's participation in these investigations was contentious and unprecedented in its control. I will also expound on how Union Carbide investigators used the residue – the brownish dirt-like material recovered from the MIC storage tank, now analogous to an airplane's "Black Box"- to determine the cause of the tragic event. Complete chemical analyses of the residue, and the extensive laboratory studies undertaken to reproduce the residue, provided the first clues that a large quantity of water had entered the tank, which triggered a chemical reaction. While this fact was not disputed, the controversy has persisted over how so much water got in, as well as other contributing factors.

Two possible routes were advanced to explain the entry of water. The Indian government scientists upheld the hypothesis first proposed by the plant operators to the media, commonly referred to as the "water washing of the plugged filter and leaking valves" route. This rationale assumes that since the operator did not take adequate precautionary measures during the water washing of a plugged filter tube, separated by about four hundred feet of piping from the storage tank, water freely flowed through the system and entered the tank. This route also assumes that all the valves along the pipeline leaked badly or were fully open. UCC investigators did not consider this explanation as plausible and a year later produced their evidence to indicate that water was introduced directly into the tank. The opposing views will be presented and compared.

The in-depth chemical studies also shed new light on the activities of the employees just before the eruption and into the nature of other possible gaseous materials that might have escaped along with MIC. Since the air in the affected areas was not sampled and analyzed soon after, the findings should help the medical research community, who have thus far attributed all the ill effects solely to MIC.

Finally, in the chapter on litigation, I will highlight the posturing by the various parties and lawyers in the early phase of the litigation, and significant judicial pronouncements in the U.S. and Indian courts which led to the final settlement ordered by the Supreme Court of India. Since there was no formal trial to determine culpability, the real cause of the tragedy has not been revealed to the public.

This book is an independent study that relies primarily on archival court documents, laboratory investigations, newspaper reports and interviews – personal as well as the ones published in the media. Union Carbide declined to provide any privileged information that might be in their possession and was not presented to the courts. The two top managers of the pesticide plant, who are still facing trial at the Bhopal Magistrate Court, declined to comment about factual information from that night and the early hours after the incident.

After completing my postdoctoral research, I joined Union Carbide's Agricultural Chemicals Division as a chemist in discovery research for novel pest control agents and worked for the company from 1967 to 1987. During that time, I synthesized hundreds of active molecules in the general class of carbamate insecticides. MIC is normally used to produce carbamates, and so I had extensive experience with this chemical and its properties. On three occasions prior to the 1984 tragedy, I visited the Union Carbide India Technical Research Center in Bhopal as a member of a team to assist in the establishment of a modern research and development facility. Following the tragedy, I was a member of Union Carbide's Scientific Investigation Sub-Team charged with the task of replicating the composition of the residue left inside the fateful tank and determining the cause of the gas leak from the study of its chemistry. Laboratory studies by UCC scientists to replicate the tank residue have helped to precisely identify the materials and the quantities that had to be present in the tank immediately prior to the gas leak. The chemical details were later published in two

4

peer-reviewed international chemical journal articles, of which I was the principal author.

I have presented this brief summary in order to acknowledge up front my association with Union Carbide. I am aware that those who rushed to judgment in 1984 could very well do so once again with the mistaken assumption that I have a hidden agenda and bias for writing this book. This is simply not the case. I feel that a disservice has been done to the families of the Bhopal victims, who until now have not heard the whole truth, and that misinformation has been disseminated to the public and the scientific community at large. Given my own first-hand experiences and access to previously unpublished documents, I feel an obligation to share as much as I know about this truth so that the past can finally be understood. This analysis will also help the chemical industry understand the underlying causes of this tragedy and hopefully prevent similar incidents in the future.

During the preparation of this book I have had constant encouragement and support from my wife Rose Marie and children Marisa, Karena, Carl and Marc. Marc, my first critic and editor, initially helped me to organize the massive amount of information. I also thank all of them for reviewing the manuscript and for their numerous suggestions and constructive comments. My thanks also to Warren Woomer, former plant manager, for explaining some of the subtle aspects of the MIC plant, and for sharing documents of historical importance, and some photographs. I am grateful to Jay Mukund, former works manager of the MIC plant, who in spite of legal constraints provided several documents and information; Sri Sridhar, Gordon Rutzen, Ernie Marshall, formerly of UCC, and Steve Weisman of *the New York Times* for information and sharing their experiences. My thanks to Sonia Jamal, a member of the family of former nawab of Bhopal, for a rare photograph of the former palace; and William (Bill) Ilgen, bibliographer at the University of North Carolina, Chapel Hill, for directing me to sources of information.

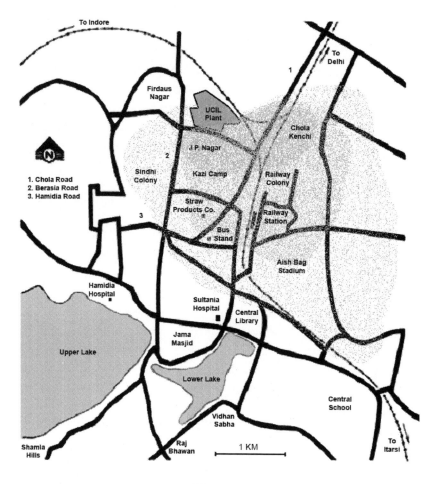

Figure A.
Section of the old city of Bhopal most affected by the gaseous cloud.

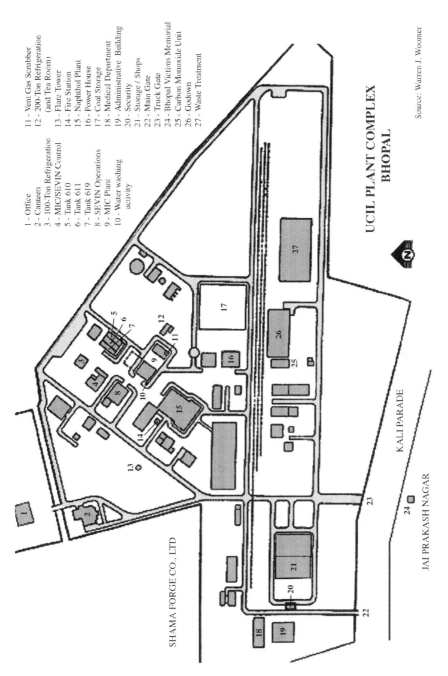

1 - Office
2 - Canteen
3 - 100-Ton Refrigeration
4 - MIC/SEVIN Control
5 - Tank 610
6 - Tank 611
7 - Tank 619
8 - SEVIN Operations
9 - MIC Plant
10 - Water washing
      activity
11 - Vent Gas Scrubber
12 - 200-Ton Refrigeration
      (and Tea Room)
13 - Flare Tower
14 - Fire Station
15 - Naphthol Plant
16 - Power House
17 - Coal Storage
18 - Medical Department
19 - Administrative Building
20 - Security
21 - Storage / Shops
22 - Main Gate
23 - Truck Gate
24 - Bhopal Victims Memorial
25 - Carbon Monoxide Unit
26 - Godown
27 - Waste Treatment

UCIL PLANT COMPLEX
BHOPAL

Source: Warren J. Woomer

SHAMA FORGE CO., LTD

KALI PARADE

JAI PRAKASH NAGAR

Figure B.
Layout of UCIL'S Plant Complex in Bhopal

7

Anytime we find interest groups in conflict, whether the rich against the poor, one nation against another, or environmentalists against corporations, we find inconsistent accounts of the situation, with each version serving the interests of its subscribers. We must discriminate when these claims represent separate realities, subjectively valid for each side, and when there is a single factual reality, with one side correct and the other wrong. Unless we sort out testable from untestable assertions and, where feasible, attempt to find an objective truth, we will be lost in an irresolvable morass of claims and counterclaims.

Allan Mazur (*A Hazardous Inquiry: The Rashomon Effect at Love Canal*)

Chapter One

THE CATASTROPHE AND ITS AFTERMATH

Nowhere else in the world did the year 1984 fulfill its apocalyptic portents as it did in India. Separatist violence in the Punjab; the military attack on the great Sikh temple of Amritsar; the assassination of the Prime Minister, Mrs. Indira Gandhi; riots in several cities; the gas disaster in Bhopal – the events followed relentlessly on each other.[1]

Nineteen eighty-four was indeed an extraordinary year for Union Carbide India, Limited. Publicly, it was celebrating its fiftieth anniversary as a company. Privately, its management was seriously questioning the future of its Agricultural Products Division, long before the disastrous event that killed thousands of people and vilified the corporation.

Shortly after midnight on December 3, 1984, a massive cloud of noxious vapors began spewing out of storage tank E-610. This tank was part of Union Carbide's agricultural chemicals manufacturing plant in Bhopal, the capital city of the central Indian State of Madhya Pradesh. Within minutes the vapors made their way through the plant's one hundred-foot emissions stack and entered the atmosphere. The cool night temperatures kept this heavy haze of poisonous gases close to the ground as northwesterly winds gradually swept it across the plant compound and into the nearby shantytowns of Jai Prakash Nagar, Kazi Camp, Indira Sahayata Nagar, Chola Kenchi, and Railway Colony, located to the south and southeast. The gases are believed to have traveled as far as eight kilometers (five miles) in this direction before being diluted and dissipated into the atmosphere.

The resulting scene outside the plant immediately became one of confusion, panic, and mass hysteria. As they began inhaling the toxic fumes, sleeping residents awoke to uncontrollable choking and burning sensations. Unaware of what was happening, people began to run in different directions in an effort to escape this unknown assailant. As families fled their homes, parents and children were separated in the dark of the night. In the confusion, infants and the elderly were forgotten and left behind. Many died in their beds.

---

[1]   Amitav Gosh, "The Ghost of India," *The New Yorker*, July 17, 1995.

Jai Prakash Nagar, a poor neighborhood of about eight hundred houses, was the closest to the plant and, as a result, suffered the most. Over two hundred residents from this neighborhood are believed to have died, mostly children, the elderly, and others in weak physical condition. These poor residents were either Muslims or Hindus from the lowest caste. Most were illiterate and scratched out a meager living working as menial laborers. Their dwellings could hardly be called houses, as they were often comprised of little more than recycled scrap sheets of metal, wood, cloth, plastic, and other used materials. Furniture was limited to the most basic, as families slept in the same room as their goats, cows, and other animals.

Rahis Bano awoke when she found it difficult to breathe. Later she recalled that "'all around me my neighbors were shouting, and then a wave of gas hit me'...she fell down, vomiting. Her two sons rolled in agony beside her. She grabbed the nearer child and ran outside before collapsing again in the street. She would survive, but the son she left behind would be lost." Other witnesses recalled "nightmarish scenes in which sobbing, half-blinded people stumbled and even trampled over one another in the streets.... There were cars, trucks, buses, auto rickshaws, anything that would move on the road trying to get up to the hill in the center of the city...people just collapsing by the side of the road..."[2]

Sayed Khan, a resident of a one-room tenement in Jai Prakash Nagar, had returned from a film show at 12:30 a.m. and just as he got into his bed his eyes started to burn "as if someone had flung chilies into a fire." The irritation became more acutely painful when he went out of his room. Forced to make an instant decision, he decided to flee, leaving his family behind. Sayed never saw them alive again.[3] Dozens of nearby residents went through similar, devastating experiences. For Sajida Khan, the nightmare of losing her five-year-old son Arshad that night only compounded her family's tragedy – three years earlier, her husband Ashraf Khan had died from exposure to phosgene gas from the same plant.[4] Mangla Ram, another resident of the shantytown, lost his wife that night, as vividly described in the following newspaper report:

---

[2]   "The Disaster in India: How a City Became Engulfed in a Cloud of Lethal Gas," *New York Times,* December 16, 1984, p. 4.

[3]   "Bhopal: City of Death," *India Today,* December 31, 1984, p. 4.

[4]   Darryl D'Monte, "Report From Bhopal," *Legal Aftermath of the Bhopal Disaster: A Collection of Press Clippings and other materials,* University of Wisconsin, 1985 -1986, pp. 1014-5.

Pregnant women stumbled and fell on the ground crying in pain and bleeding profusely.... Children got separated from their parents, husbands from their wives and brothers from their sisters, in the mad rush to run away from the clouds. Many were trampled to death.... When he arrived at the hospital it was 2.30 a.m....the hospital had received more people than it could accommodate.... When a young doctor lifted his wife's hand to feel the pulse, it was already stiff and cold. The doctor covered her face with the sheet she was wrapped in and walked away. Down the corridor so many corpses lay one next to the other that Mangla Ram forgot to weep.[5]

Anees Chishti was one of the first reporters to reach the scene of disaster. He had arrived in Bhopal three days earlier to cover the upcoming state elections. At Hotel Nalanda, in the heart of the old city, he felt the sting of the spreading gas:

...at about 2.30 a.m...I felt some choking in my throat.... There was burning sensation in the eye.... When I came out, I saw hordes of people moving towards some direction. I was new to Bhopal city, I didn't know all the routes.... I saw ladies, almost undressed, straight out of the bed in petticoats, children clinging on to their breasts, all wailing, weeping, some of them vomiting, some of them vomiting blood, some falling down...and when I was passing through ...Kamala Park it was a very bad situation, people trying to enter temples...they were falling dead, family members were leaving their own family members behind and running for safety.... My own rationality was challenged for the first time in my life – on that stretch of four kilometers.... My eyes were burning. In that condition I reached the Indian Express office. This was around 3.30 [a.m.].... Nobody knew what was happening...[6]

At the time, the Bhopal railway station was being used by some of city's homeless as a dry place to spend the nights. Due to the station's proximity to the plant, at least twenty-five porters and homeless were reported to have died that night, with an additional two hundred fifty left unconscious.[7] Many more deaths were prevented by a handful of heroic

---

5   *Sunday Magazine,* Calcutta, India: December 16-22, 1984.
6   Anees Chisti, *A Night in Hell, Dateline Bhopal – A newsman Diary of the Gas Disaster,* Criterion Publications, New Delhi: 1986, pp. 7-8.
7   "Poisonous Gas Tragedy due to leak from factory tank," *The Times of India,* December 4, 1984, p. 1.

station employees who managed to warn several incoming trains and stop them before their scheduled arrival at the station. These courageous efforts came at the cost of the lives of the stationmaster and his senior booking clerk, who succumbed to the toxic fumes. Later, a colleague wrote in homage to his friend:

> On the fateful night of gas disaster, my friend from college days Harish Dhurve was at Bhopal. He was informed of the leak at his residence close by. He immediately rushed to the station, and from his room contacted the Station Masters of Vidisha and Itarsi, telling them not to send any train to Bhopal. He collapsed in his chair and died.[8]

Efforts were also underway to evacuate the other affected settlements. Workers at the J.K. Straw Products Company, located on Chola Road to the south of the plant, smelled the gas early on and contacted the local army base, Sultania Infantry Lines, for assistance. Army personnel immediately started the evacuation process, which began at 3:00 a.m. and lasted until 6:00 p.m. on December 4. Army vehicles were also used to transport the sick and dying to nearby hospitals.[9] Two officers from the base, Brigadier M.K. Mayni and Major C.S. Kanojha are credited with having risked their lives to evacuate around ten thousand people, until they fell unconscious from the fumes.[10] While army personnel were praised for their sacrifices, it was also reported that the municipal police were hardly seen anywhere before ten the next morning, and organized relief by municipal authorities was virtually nonexistent.

With their eyes squinting and throats nearly choked, Chisti and three of his colleagues – Suresh Mehrotra of the *Free Press Journal,* Vijay Tiwari of the *Navabharat Times*, and Pushp Raj Purohit of the *Hindustan Samachar* – reached the plant at 4:00 a.m. Jagannathan (Jay) Mukund, the plant's works manager, told them that the leak had been controlled within thirty minutes, and that the District Magistrate informed him at his resi-

---

[8]   On the 7th anniversary of the disaster, Arvind Datar wrote in praise of the heroic effort by the station master. "Homage to Ex-friend," Letter to the Editor, *Madhya Pradesh Chronicle,* Bhopal, 3/12/1991, p. 4. and also cited by P.S. Chauhan, *Bhopal Tragedy, Socio-legal Implications,* Rawat Publications, New Delhi, 1996, p. 16.

[9]   P.S. Chauhan, pp. 16, 89.

[10]   "Bravery of two army officers in Bhopal," *The Times of India,* December 18, 1984, p. 4.

dence around 2:00 a.m. The next morning, the chief minister of Madhya Pradesh announced that J. Mukund and other members of the plant's senior management – R.B. Roy Choudhury, S.P. Choudhary, K.V. Shetty, and Shakil Ibrahim Qureshi – were taken into custody under section 304(A), "for causing death by negligence or any rash act." The government also announced the closure of the plant, stating that no more production would be allowed until a complete investigation had been launched and concluded. Spearheading this investigation would be India's equivalent to the FBI – the Central Bureau of Investigation (CBI), which took immediate control of the plant. Teams from India's Council of Scientific and Industrial Research (CSIR) would also later participate in the investigation. All information emanating from the plant was henceforth controlled by and filtered through either the CBI or the CSIR.

Thousands of victims overwhelmed Hamidia Hospital and its sister health institutions in town, quickly exhausting the limited medical supplies in stock. At least 250 doctors from other parts of India rushed to Bhopal to assist the city's beleaguered 500-650 doctors and medical students. Nurses, social workers, and members of non-governmental organizations such as religious and civic groups volunteered their services. Even politicians were on the scene. A candidate from the opposition political party Bharatiya Janata party (BJP), engaged in a heated argument with the ruling Congress party's state minister for health over how the scarce medical supplies should be used. Unfortunately, such political interference only increased in the following days, leading to about 200 doctors walking out of Hamidia Hospital to protest this inappropriate behavior. Given the impending local elections, slogans and posters soon appeared. One read: "Congress musclemanship is deadlier than MIC."[11] Even though additional medicines arrived later, in the early stages doctors lacked sufficient knowledge and understanding of the poisonous gases. As such, they were unable to administer the appropriate treatments in many cases.

The heroic efforts of the doctors, volunteers, and nongovernmental organizations, nevertheless, won praise and admiration both nationally and internationally. Dr. M.N. Nagoo, director of medical services for Madhya Pradesh, described the scene at the hospital from his vantage point.

---

[11]   "Doctor's strike adds to Bhopal agony," *The Times of India,* December 12, 1984, pp. 1, 9.

People running away from Bhopal, volunteers coming in with needed supplies, schoolboys and girls looking after the victims, giving them water, tea, bread.... With the help of volunteer organizations, scouts, students, we organized medical treatment and arranged for water, medicines, food. There was tremendous cooperation. We have 500 doctors here now, five major hospitals, 22 clinics, and we called 500 more doctors from the outside, plus 200 more nurses and 700 paramedics. Besides the treatment in hospitals, we organized 25 teams to give treatment in the affected areas.... We have kept six clinics open around the clock, besides the 35 units already working and the 30-bed hospital we started at the former residence of the police superintendent next to the Union Carbide plant. Seven more clinics have been opened, four of which perform blood and urine tests.[12]

On December 4, the state government confirmed that 269 people had died as a result of the gas leak, with an additional 2,000 requiring hospital care from exposure to the fumes. Survivors from the affected shantytowns immediately challenged these numbers, claiming that countless bodies still remained scattered throughout these areas. That same day, two of India's leading newspapers, *The Times of India* and the *Statesman*, reported the figure at 410. By the next day, the reported death count had risen to 1,200, climbing to over 2,000 over the next few days.

Soon after, the government also announced a 24-hour period of mourning as authorities began preparations for mass burials and cremations. Starting the next day, 530 men and women were cremated at the Chola Road cremation site and 110 children buried in accordance with Hindu customs. At the main Muslim cemetery, Firdaus Manzil Saifa Colony, 350 victims were buried. Another 300 bodies were either cremated or buried at four smaller locations.[13]

The toxic fumes also killed hundreds of domestic animals. The army was given the unenviable job of locating and removing these carcasses. As time passed, some of the bloated carcasses found inside the abandoned dwellings were so large that the walls and doorways of houses had to be broken in order to remove them. According to the army officer in charge of the operation, "twenty dumpers and six cranes...were detailed to carry

---

12   Wil Lepkkowski, "People of India Struggle Toward Appropriate Response to Tragedy, Bhopal," *Chemical & Engineering News,* Special Issue, vol. 63, No.6, 1985, pp. 19 -23.

13   "Gas poisoning toll mounts to 1,600," *The Times of India,* Dec. 6, 1984, p. 1.

out…the task of removing 790 buffalos, 270 cows, 483 goats, 90 dogs and 23 horses" which lay strewn throughout the shantytowns.[14]

Two weeks after the disaster, a team of Indian and British doctors carried out a community sampling survey of 379 people in eight exposed clusters and 119 from two nonexposed clusters of households of similar socioeconomic status south of the factory.

Based on this data, they estimated that about 1,850 deaths occurred in and around the eight exposed clusters in the vicinity and to the south of the plant, which covered about 70 percent of the exposed area. While many residents living north of the factory sought treatment for burning eyes and coughing that night, no deaths were reported from these areas, as the slight north wind allowed them to escape the gas cloud.[15] Four and a half months later, Mr. V. Patil, the Minister of Chemicals and Fertilizers, reported to the *Lok Sabha* (India's Lower House of Parliament) that the number of deaths totaled 1,430, but that this number was subject to revision.[16]

However, another survey conducted by students and staff members of ten institutions from various parts of the country and coordinated by the Tata Institute of Social Sciences in Bombay – the Family Profile Survey – arrived at a different count. The six-week survey (from Jan. 1 to Feb. 12, 1985) of 25,300 households in the gas-affected areas recorded 1,021 deaths leaving 150 orphans and 168 women widowed.[17] The results differed from the unofficial estimates at the time, which ranged between 2,000 and 2,500 dead.

The final figures of those who died and were injured are still the subject of debate, given the simple fact that the official record is incomplete. To describe the confusing state of affairs, one observer has offered the following explanation:

> During the emergency all semblance of control over admissions and releases was lost. Consider only that patients by the thousands were camped on the grounds outside. All control over burials at the Muslim cemeteries and the mass cremations by the Hindus was lost. (A man, thought dead, climbed down from his own funeral pyre)…

---

[14] *India Today,* December 31, 1984, p. 16.

[15] N. Anderson, M. Kerr Muir, V. Mehra, A.G. Salmon, *Brit. J. Ind. Med.,* vol. 45, pp. 469-475, 1988.

[16] Letter by Kelley Drye and Warren to Judge Keenan, U.S. District Court, New York, May 8, 1985.

[17] "1,021 died in Bhopal survey," *The Times of India,* February 15, 1985. p. 5.

The moment came when serious estimators were trying to arrive at the figures of the dead by guessing the amount of wood that was used in the fires that the Hindus used as funeral pyres. (The State Government later announced...that its Forest Department had provided 20,000 quintals of wood, two million pounds, for the crematory holocaust.) Nobody knows how many bodies were cast into the waters. One small boy pulled himself from the waters into which he had been tossed as dead.[18]

Given this unfortunate reality, the exact number of dead and injured will probably never be known.

With the toxic gas primarily affecting the victims' eyes and lungs, the local hospitals were in immediate need of equipment and supplies for ophthalmic and pulmonary medicine. Many countries and organizations contributed a variety of hospital equipment, medicines, and other medical assistance to help the exposed and injured. The Royal Commonwealth Society for the Blind launched an emergency appeal for a "catastrophe, the likes of which the organization had not seen in its thirty-four years of developing eye care programs throughout the Commonwealth." It also sent a team of experts to assess possible long-term disability among the survivors. The limited study from a sampling of eight clusters in the affected area, indicated that the effect on the eyes was not as severe as the damage caused to the lungs. Follow-up studies of 490 people conducted two months after the disaster indicated that there were no cases of total blindness but only a few cases of corneal injury and excessive watering of the eyes.[19]

Further investigation also revealed that while all those exposed to the toxic fumes mentioned coughing and burning feelings in their eyes and throat, residents of different neighborhoods suffered additional symptoms. In those survey clusters which were closest to the plant, vomiting was cited as a common symptom, while clusters farthest from the plant showed more signs of choking and shortness of breath.

In one cluster, the second in distance from the factory, collapse and unconsciousness was a notable feature not reported in the other clusters. Those who had fallen unconscious reported few or no eye symptoms upon recovery and revealed few eye signs. Also in this cluster, signs

---

[18] Alfred de Grazia, *A Cloud over Bhopal,* Kalos Foundation, 1985, p. 35.
[19] N. Anderson, et al. *The Lancet,* March 30, 1985, pp. 761-762. See also *Br. J. Ind. Med.* 42, 1985, pp. 795-798.

of respiratory distress were most marked, affecting about 20% of the community. Many of these were too disabled by breathlessness to move more than a few steps or even to talk. In this cluster, over one half of the community demonstrated eye signs which could be attributed to the exposure.[20]

Based on this diverse pattern of symptoms, questions were raised about the possibility that the constituent components of the gas cloud may have actually changed during its movement across the town.

The August 1985 survey by the Gandhi Medical College in collaboration with the Indian Council of Medical Research (ICMR) covering a wider area had reported about 7,000 as having eye problems, without specifying the nature or the severity of the injuries.[21]

While much initial research focused on these immediate symptoms, there was also great concern regarding the potential for unforeseen, long-term complications, such as birth defects for children whose mother or father had been exposed to the gas. In follow-up studies, the ICMR also monitored 1,500 cases of pregnant women who lived near the plant. In June 1985, the ICMR reported that of 500 births, five were still births and three had congenital defects, "an incidence considered to be statistically no higher than in a normal population. Most babies were underweight (2 kg), but this too was considered to be not uncommon in India." In December 1985, at the three-day national seminar on reducing the incidence of low birth weight babies in India, Dr. V. Ramalingaswami, the director-general of ICMR, said that, "30% of infants born in the country have low birth weight. This situation has been persistent for the last two or three decades…and about 80 lakh (eight million) infants failed to achieve a weight of 2.5 kilograms (5.5 pounds) during intrauterine life."[22] The number of 17 abortions for 100 pregnancies was above the national average but according to Ramalingaswami, "this was not unexpected and that abortions increase by as much as four times during famine or epidemics, and the Bhopal tragedy was [a] comparable situation…. In women yet to be delivered, ultrasonic scanning has shown fetal retardation in 15 percent of the

---

20 Neil Anderson, Malcolm Kerr Muir, Vijay Mehra, *The Lancet,* December 22/29, 1984, p. 1481.

21 Paul Srivastava, *Bhopal: Anatomy of a Crisis,* Ballinger Publishing Co. 1987, pp. 68-69.

22 "High incidence of underweight babies," *The Times of India,* December 18, 1985, p. 4.

cases, not unusual in India."[23] The official estimates of the infant mortality rates for the state of Madhya Pradesh for the years 1970 to 1980 have ranged from 137 to 151 per 1,000 births, among the highest of the states in India. The mortality figures for rural areas are generally slightly higher.[24,25] There are no precise figures for the population in the lowest socioeconomic sector. Comparative studies to statistics of similar groups elsewhere might have given a better indication of the effect of exposure.

Ten years later, a cross-sectional, randomly sampled survey of 454 adult survivors of the disaster indicated that breathing problems had persisted. The study concluded that the symptoms reported and the differences in lung function detected, are compatible with chronic airflow limitation and particularly with disease of the small airways.[26]

A hotly debated medical controversy was whether or not the gas cloud contained the highly toxic chemical hydrogen cyanide. This possibility was raised by Dr. Heeresh Chandra, head of the Department of Forensic Medicine and Toxicology at Bhopal's Gandhi Medical College, Bhopal, who reviewed the results of many postmortem examinations. The bright red coloration observed in some organs was interpreted as due to cyanide poisoning. Since doctors were not quite sure how to treat some of the most severely affected survivors, Dr. Chandra recommended the use of sodium thiosulfate as an antidote. While other doctors disagreed with this treatment, there was little scientific evidence at the time to support either position. This issue will be discussed in greater detail in Chapter 3.

Further details of the medical research conducted by ICMR in the early part of 1985 are recorded in the minutes of the ICMR review meetings – *Researches on Health Effects of Exposure to Toxic Gas at Bhopal,* held

---

[23] K. S. Jayaraman, "Birth defect fears allayed." *Nature,* Vol. 316, July 23, 1985, p. 288.

[24] Frank B. Hobbs, *Demographic Estimates, Projections and Selected Social Characteristics of the Population of India,* Center for International Research, U.S. Bureau of Census, Washington: 1986, p. 84.

[25] P. N. Mari Bhat, Samuel Preston, Tim Dyson, *Committee on Population and Demography, Vital Rates in India, 1961-1981,* National Academy Press, 1984, p. 41.

[26] P. Cullinan, S. Acquilla, V. Ramana, "Respiratory morbidity 10 years after the Union Carbide gas leak at Bhopal: a cross sectional survey," *Br. Med. J.* 314, 1997, pp. 338-342.

on May 3-4, 1985.[27] Other studies and surveys by the various agencies include:

1. Survey of blood samples taken from people in and around Bhopal by King Edward Memorial Hospital.
2. Survey (unspecified) conducted by Drs. R.N. Bhalerao and Subash R. Naik, and others with aid from Bhopal Relief Trust of Bombay and the New Delhi-based Voluntary Health Association of India.
3. Survey of affected vegetation by the Indian Council of Agricultural Research.
4. Gynecological study conducted by Drs. Rani Bang and Mira Sadgopal
5. Survey by the Health Secretary and Relief Commissioner of the State of Madhya Pradesh, under the auspices of Dr. Ishwar Dass's office.
6. Survey by ICMR relating to eye and gastric conditions.
7. Study of pulmonary function and blood gas analysis conducted by Dr P.S. Narayanan.[28]
8. CSIR Studies. Two years after the tragedy (1986) CSIR disclosed their detailed findings in a 310-page report, entitled "CSIR's Contribution to Understanding the Chemical Phenomena Leading to the Tragic Toxic Gas Leakage at the Union Carbide Pesticide Plant, Bhopal and Aftermath, Volume II" (marked restricted). It also included the findings of a follow-up study by the Indian Toxicology Research Institute.

This book does not follow up on the results of these studies as they are outside its scope. Comprehensive reviews on the various health aspects of

---

[27]   *The Bhopal Tragedy – One Year Later, an APPEN Report,* Sahabat Alam Malaysia Friends of the Earth, Malaysia: 1985.
[28]   Response by the plaintiff to Interrogatory No. 49, (1985), pp.18-20 – U. S. District Court, MDL No. 626, Misc. No. 21-38 (JFK).

the medical research carried out and the long-term effects of exposure to the toxic gases have been published elsewhere.[29,30,31]

On April 9, 1985, Minister Veerendra Patil reported to the Indian parliament that the state government had spent over 10 crores of rupees ($8 million) in providing *ex gratia* relief to the victims in cash and kind. The central government had given 5 crores of rupees ($4 million) to the state government. Patil further stated that "so far as relief is concerned, sufficient relief has been provided and it is still being continued." A sum of 67.94 lakhs ($543,520) in cash was distributed immediately to 14,227 affected people as follows: Seriously injured were paid 2000 rupees ($160) each, with 1000 rupees ($80) given to those who sustained minor injuries. In addition, 26.7 lakhs ($213,000) was distributed among 267 families of the dead. Each family of the deceased was paid Rs. 10,000 rupees (($800). The relief in kind, which totaled 100 lakhs ($802,320), consisted of wheat, rice, sugar, edible oils and milk.[32] UCC, UCIL and many Indian states are also reported to have contributed in cash and kind.[33]

---

[29]   Pushpa S. Mehta, Anant S. Mehta, Sunder J. Mehta, Arjun B. Makhijani, "Bhopal Tragedy's Health Effects. A Review of Methyl Isocyanate Toxicity," *J. Am. Med. Assoc.,* vol. 64, 1990, pp. 2781-2787.

[30]   Daya R. Varma, Ian Guest, "The Bhopal Accident and Methyl Isocyanate Toxicity," *Toxicol. Environ. Health,* vol. 40, 1993, pp. 513-529.

[31]   John R. Bucher, Methyl Isocyante: "A Review of Health Effects Research Since Bhopal," *Fundam. Appl. Toxicol.* vol. 9, 1987, pp. 367-379.

[32]   Letter by William A. Krohley to Judge J.F. Keenan of May 8, 1985.

[33]   UCIL offered 10 million rupees ($840,000) to the State of Madhya Pradesh for emergency relief and additional 122,000 rupees ($10,000) for medical supplies and medicines. It also offered their buildings and facilities to be used as an orphanage in Bhopal and a separate medical center for treatment of victims, but the state government rejected these offers.

UCC offered $1 million to the Prime Minister's Relief Fund, which was initially rejected but later accepted, and spent an additional $1 million for medical supplies and health services support. On April 18, 1985, at the urging of the U.S. District Judge, UCC gave the Indian Red Cross in Bhopal $5 million in humanitarian aid. This aid was initially offered to the Indian government, which declined. It was later given to the International Red Cross, which acted as an intermediary. A $2.2 million grant was given to Arizona State University to establish a vocational-technical center in Bhopal and offered to fund a hospital for the victims.

Chapter Two

THE MAKING OF A CATASTROPHE

India's Economic and Political Development in the Twentieth Century

While it is often easy to identify direct causes for any given problem, it is also important to focus on the underlying factors that contribute indirectly to that problem. Thus, any analysis of the Bhopal disaster and Union Carbide's role in it must be done within the larger context of India's recent history, particularly, the perception by India's future political leaders of how colonial policies had affected the country's traditional economy, and how the new laws enacted by the government would steer its future growth.

In the seventeenth century, when the British East India Company began trading operations in India, the company was primarily engaged in buying Indian-produced goods, cotton textiles, dyes, and spices. With the onset of the Industrial Revolution in the eighteenth century, Britain increasingly looked to India not only as a main supplier of raw materials, but also as a vast potential market for the goods manufactured by British industry. In the classic mercantilist sense, the British Parliament passed legislation to ensure that the British market became closed to Indian products, while simultaneously opening the Indian market to British manufacturing. Not surprisingly, the East India Company found itself in control of a valuable monopoly. As a result of these actions, the Indian textile industry soon collapsed, and with it, the livelihoods of hundreds of thousands of weavers and artisans.[1]

In the nineteenth century, these restrictive measures expanded into other industrial sectors, thus causing the breakup of India's shipbuilding, metalworking, glass, paper, and other small industries. The millions of artisans and craftsmen whose skills were no longer required had nowhere to go but back to their villages. Railroads were built primarily to facilitate exports of agricultural raw materials and crops to the seaports, and for the distribution of imported manufactured goods. This export-oriented mar-

---

[1]   Jawaharlal Nehru, *The Discovery of India,* Oxford University Press, New Delhi: 1997, pp. 298-299.

ket to a large extent determined the regional growth pattern of cash crops within the country.

From 1891-1921, India's annual population growth averaged less than one-sixth of 1 percent due in large part to severe famines from 1891-1901 and the great influenza epidemic of 1918-1919.[2] After World War I, the economy was crippled and agriculture became stagnant. In fact, during the second quarter of the twentieth century, total food production actually declined and there was a serious food shortage.[3]

During World War II, India provided considerable support to the Allied war effort, in terms of raw materials and equipment that came from Indian mines, plantations, and factories. India produced three-fourths of the forty thousand articles needed by the British India army. Auto assembly plants were set up to manufacture vehicle chassis, and the manufacture of soda ash, chlorine, and caustic soda was increased. Steel production, shipbuilding and ship repair industries were also expanded.[4] With the tremendous growth in war-related businesses "the Indian manufacturing and trading classes made enormous profits from war contracts...[but] the life of the masses was seriously disturbed by the economic dislocations of war. There was a grave shortage of goods, prices in some cases increased 300 percent, and food supplies especially were insufficient.... A tragic reflection of this economic disequilibrium occurred in Bengal, a province with a population of sixty million, where thousands died of famine."[5] Excluding the factories geared up during the war and dismantled afterwards, the war years had not "enabled India materially to expand her industries and industrial capacity."[6] These economic facts were uppermost in the minds of the political leaders in the Indian Congress Party, who fought for the independence of the country.

---

[2] Ansley J. Coale, Edgar M. Hoover, *Population Growth and Economic Development in Low-Income countries, A Case Study of India's Prospects*, Princeton University Press, 1972, p. 29.

[3] Susanta K. Ray, Ralph W. Cummings, Jr. Robert W. Herdt, *Policy Planning for Agricultural Development, The Indian Example*, Westview Press, Boulder, Colorado: 1979, pp. 19, 20.

[4] Walter T. Wallbank, *A Short History of India and Pakistan*, The New American Library, New York: 1958, pp. 208-209.

[5] Ibid, p. 212.

[6] Speech by J.R.D. Tata in London on May 30, 1945, cited by Jawaharlal Nehru, *The Discovery of India*, Oxford University Press, Delhi: 1997, p. 503.

After World War II, Britain finally granted independence to the sub-continent, and in the process partitioned its colony into two entities – India and Pakistan, the latter comprised of an eastern half (now Bangladesh) and a western half. Given the role religion played in determining the boundaries of these new countries, massive population migrations sparked communal riots and bloodshed, compounding the economic problems. Jute producing fields in East Pakistan were separated from their processing mills in Calcutta, while main cotton- and wheat-producing districts in the Punjab, which became part of West Pakistan, were forced to find new markets to the west. These partitions caused considerable disruption to long-established trading patterns and the livelihoods of millions of workers who depended on them.

After India attained independence in 1947, its leaders worked to establish a new federal system of government for its original fourteen states and six union territories. In 1950, India became a republic and adopted a new constitution, while choosing to remain within the British Commonwealth. Two years later, India's first complete Parliament was directly elected on the basis of adult universal suffrage. At the national level, the executive, legislative, and judicial branches were largely modeled after the British system. The president, whose role is mainly ceremonial, is elected indirectly by the national and state legislatures. The real power rests with the prime minister, who heads the Council of Ministers chosen from the elected members of Parliament. The bicameral Parliament comprises the *Lok Sabha* (House of the People or Lower House) and the *Rajya Sabha* (Council of States or the Upper House). At the next level, each state has its own legislature and cabinet of ministers, all of whom are elected members. The chief minister heads the state government, and the functions and powers of the state legislators closely parallel those of the central government. State governors are appointed by the president, and perform similar representational duties. They may also be empowered by the president to assume full executive powers in case of emergencies.

The Constitution of 1950 explicitly states that "the regulation of foreign and interstate commerce falls within the exclusive domain of the Parliament.... The executive power of the Union Government extends over matters that are within the competence of the Parliament of India and the executive power of the states."[7]

---

[7]   Douglas Bullis, *Doing Business in Today's India,* Quorum Books, Connecticut: 1998, p. 214.

Due largely to his leadership role in the Indian National Congress Party during the struggle for independence, Jawaharlal Nehru became India's first prime minister in August 1947. Later, as chairman of the National Planning Commission, with his perception of India's economic history, Nehru immediately charted a policy of mixed (public and private) economy to "establish a social order where justice and equality of opportunity shall be secured to all the people."[8] Soon after, the Indian Parliament enacted a series of laws to protect and promote domestic industrial growth.

In 1947, the Foreign Exchange Regulation Act (FERA) came into being as an interim measure that gave the central government wider powers to control the capital and speculation in foreign currency. FERA was drastically revised in 1973 (discussed in greater detail later in the chapter). The Industrial Policy Resolutions of 1948 and 1956 laid out the general guidelines for a socialistic pattern of economy, which earmarked important industries for the public sector and mandated that the industrial development of the country be closely managed by the central government. The Monopolies and Restrictive Trade Practices Act of 1969 was designed to curb and check the economic power in private companies. The socialistic policies had already been envisioned by the Congress party many years prior to independence and influenced by Gandhi's philosophy of *swadeshi* (use of indigenous or homegrown products) – a policy that encouraged the growth of Indian industry by promoting locally made products at the expense of foreign-made ones. These import substitution strategies had the added benefit of helping the federal government to conserve hard-to-come-by hard currency for strategic purchases in the area of defense and for the development of key national industries. As was the case in many newly liberated developing countries, import substitution was aimed at economically and psychologically reversing centuries of mercantilist colonial policies. In India's case, these new policies clearly jump-started national production in a number of industries in the short- and medium-terms. Over the years, however, such heavy political involvement in day-to-day affairs of industries led to widespread inefficiencies and quality control problems throughout the Indian economy.

India's Regulation of Foreign Investments

All technology, once imported into India, is Indian technology.

---

[8]   Government of India Resolution on Industrial Policy, April 6, 1948.

In 1948, the Government of India adopted a Resolution on Industrial Policy, which created a framework for dealing with foreign collaborators. It stated that:

> …while it should be recognised that participation of foreign capital and enterprise, particularly as regards industrial technique and knowledge, will be of value to the rapid industrialisation of the country, it is necessary that the conditions under which they may participate in Indian industry should be carefully regulated in the national interest. Suitable legislation will be introduced for this purpose. Such legislation will provide for the scrutiny and approval by the Central Government of every individual case of participation of foreign capital and management in industry. It will provide that, as a rule, the major interest in ownership and effective control should always be in Indian hands; but power will be taken to deal with exceptional cases in a manner calculated to serve national interest. In all cases, however, the training of suitable Indian personnel for the purpose of eventually replacing foreign experts will be insisted upon…. Import of technology is at the core of collaborations…. Where technology is available in India, it must be preferred to foreign technology. Where it is not available, it should be imported at the lowest cost. All technology, once imported into India, is Indian technology. It should not be paid for beyond a period of five years, and its use must be preferred to import of similar technology.[9]

This resolution legally formalized four important principles that would determine how foreign companies would conduct business in India for decades to come. First and foremost, it affirmed the primacy of the "national interest" and "the import of technology…at the core of collaboration" when considering any joint venture by foreign companies in India. Obviously, national interest would be determined by the central government, or more specifically the political parties and politicians that held important positions in that government. A second key point of the resolution emphasized that "Indian hands" should always have control over the decision-making processes, if not majority ownership, of these companies. While not specific on the issue of whose hands these would be, it is quite clear given the context of the first principle and the prevailing culture of Indian society at the time that they would essentially be manipulated by

---

9   Ashok V. Desai, *Foreign Technology and Investment – A Study of their Role in India's Industrialization,* National Council of Applied Economic Research, New Delhi:1971, pp. 53,76.

government officials at both the national and state levels. The third principle insisted on the eventual replacement of all expatriate personnel by Indian nationals regardless of the continued investment and involvement of foreign companies in a given joint venture. Finally, notice was given to foreign companies that they were essentially being courted for the sole purpose of securing imported technology and would lose all special business advantages after five years.

The enactment of the Industries Development and Regulations Act (IDRA), in 1951 further regulated private businesses. It was now mandatory for industries to obtain government license in:

1. establishing any new industry or for existing industries producing new products,

2. substantially expanding the capacity, carrying on the business of an existing industrial undertaking which was previously exempt from the license or changing the location of an existing plant.[10]

In addition, the Government of India, in consultation with the Central Advisory Council, reserved the right to "recommend targets for production, coordinate production programmes and review progress…assist in distribution of controlled materials and obtaining local supplies."[11]

The Industrial Policy Resolution of 1956 classified these industries into: (a) those under the exclusive responsibility of the state, (b) those in the private sector under the initiative of the state which would progressively become state owned, and (c) those that would be permitted to develop through private enterprise.[12]

In today's liberalized, free-market perspective of a globalized society, these conditions would certainly raise a red flag in any Wall Street boardroom. However, such policies were not uncommon in developing countries during the post-World War II years. As one of the first and largest nations to free itself from European colonial domination, India offered seemingly limitless potential for American companies eager to expand into new markets. By the 1950s, Union Carbide had already established itself as one of India's leading multinational corporations and had decided to try and

---

[10]   Bullis, p. 222.
[11]   *The Gazetteer of India,* (ed.) P.N. Chopra, Department of Culture, Ministry of Education and Social Welfare, Government of India, (1975), p. 494.
[12]   Bullis, p. 222.

adapt to these new conditions as the cost of doing business in the country. At the time, the company did not realize to what extent each of the above principles would contribute to its eventual demise.

The Origins of Union Carbide in India

Union Carbide Corporation (UCC), the multinational chemical company that first produced acetylene for commercial use and pioneered the U.S. petrochemical industry, grew through mergers of several smaller companies in related interdependent businesses.

The history of UCC dates back to 1886 when the National Carbon Company was formed to commercialize the electric arc for street lights and carbon electrodes for electric furnaces. This new technology gave birth to another company started by Thomas L. Wilson and James Turner Moorehead, called Union Carbide, which converted aluminum oxide to aluminum by using the electric arc furnace. In 1898, Union Carbide Company also started producing acetylene by the calcium carbide process. In 1917, these two companies merged to form Union Carbide and Carbon Corporation.

In as early as 1934 UC&CC expanded its market to British India. Its Indian subsidiary initially named the Ever-Ready Company (India) Limited was incorporated and registered as a public company under the Indian Companies Act of 1913. In 1941, the company merged with its distribution arm, United Battery Distributors, and was renamed National Carbon Company (India) Limited.

Prior to 1956, the Indian subsidiary was wholly-owned by the U.S.-based UC& CC, whose main business revolved around the sale of carbon products like dry cells, industrial carbon electrodes, cinema arc carbons, acetylene, and flashlights, which provided light to many of the 99 percent of Indian villages which did not have access to electricity at the time of independence. When the parent company sought approval for further expansion into plastics and other chemicals, the Government of India objected to it continuing to hold full equity in the subsidiary and insisted upon a financial restructuring in accordance with IDRA and FERA guidelines. Negotiations with the government ultimately led to the reduction of UC&CC's equity from 100 percent ownership to 60 percent of total capital. This was accomplished in 1956 by selling eight hundred thousand shares to the Indian public and government-owned institutions and registering as a public Indian company. Shares were traded on the Calcutta Stock Exchange. In

1959 the Indian subsidiary changed its name to Union Carbide India Limited (UCIL), keeping in line with the recent name change of its parent company to Union Carbide Corporation (UCC).[13]

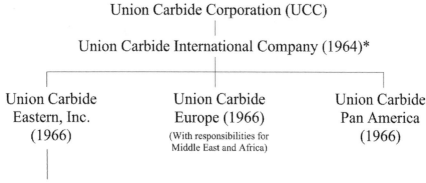

Union Carbide Corporation (UCC)
|
Union Carbide International Company (1964)*

| Union Carbide Eastern, Inc. (1966) | Union Carbide Europe (1966) (With responsibilities for Middle East and Africa) | Union Carbide Pan America (1966) |

Union Carbide India Limited (UCIL)
· Agricultural Products Division (Bhopal Pesticide Plant)
· Battery Products Division
· Carbon, Metals & Gases Division
· Chemicals and Plastics Division
· Marine Products Division

*The International Company was dissolved in 1966.
Ref. Robert D. Stief, A History of Union Carbide Corporation, 1998

Figure 2-1

Union Carbide International Company, a wholly owned division of UCC, was created in 1964 and was primarily responsible for marketing UCC products globally. In May of 1966, the International Company was dissolved and in its place three world area companies were formed – Union Carbide Europe, Union Carbide Eastern, and Union Carbide Pan America. Union Carbide Eastern (UCE, with its main offices in Hong Kong) was responsible for the eastern region and the Indian market, which included its interest in UCIL. All formal business contacts between UCC management in the U.S. and UCIL were thus channeled through the UCE Division. UCE was responsible for overseeing UCC's interests and equity in UCIL and some of its top executives served as members of the UCIL board of directors. It also provided guidance in strategic planning to UCIL manage-

---

[13] See Appendix C-1 for the History of UCIL: A Chronicle of Significant Developments.(n.d.)

ment. The lines of communication between UCIL and UCE are shown in Figure 2-1 and in greater detail in Appendix C-3.

The Role of Pesticides in India's "Green Revolution"

Historically, subsistence agriculture has been the predominant occupation across rural India. Pestilence and famines in the early part of the twentieth century and post-independence population migrations resulted in a precarious food situation, which was compounded by a history of large fallow landholdings by absentee landowners, high rents, cyclical indebtedness to moneylenders, and complex land tenure rights. Most subsistence farmers planted seeds saved from the previous harvest, relied on organic manure as fertilizer, and used human labor and animals to plow fields. In 1950-51, the country produced 52 million tons of food grains with the use of 55,000 tons of chemical fertilizers.[14] The use of improved seed varieties and chemical pesticides was almost non-existent. At the beginning of the Second 5-Year Plan in 1956-1957 (government's planning cycle), a mere 9,500 tons of formulated (diluted with inert ingredients) pesticides were used.[15]

To remedy the inefficiency inherent in these historical agricultural practices, further aggravated by droughts, and concerned about its adverse impact on programs for industrial development, the Government of India in the early 1960s launched a drive toward self-sufficiency by reducing import of food grains and promoting the "Green Revolution." This thrust was prompted by technical breakthroughs in the genetic breeding of new hybrid grain varieties. High-yielding dwarf varieties of wheat and paddy rice were developed in Mexico and the Philippines, while improved hybrid varieties of maize and sorghum were bred by Indian scientists, in collaboration with the Rockefeller Foundation at Indian Council of Agricultural Research (ICAR) stations. A particularly high-yielding variety of pearl millet was developed at the Punjab Agricultural University, Ludhiana, and released in 1965.

For his pioneering work in improving crop yields and helping agriculture in the developing world, American-born Dr. Norman E. Borlaug,

---

[14]   C. Steven LaRue, Fitzroy (Ed.) *The India Handbook,* Fitzroy Dearborn Publishers, Chicago: 1997, p. 5.

[15]   P.C. Bansil, *Agriculture Planning for 700 millions: A Perspective Study,* Lalvani Pub. House, Bombay: 1971, p. 341.

scientist and director of the International Center for Maize and Wheat Improvement (with the Spanish acronym CIMMYT)[16] based in Mexico, was awarded the Nobel Peace Prize in 1970. The *Atlantic Monthly*, in a feature article, described Borlaug as "an eighty-two-year-old plant breeder who for most of the past five decades has lived in developing nations, teaching the techniques of high-yield agriculture. He received the Nobel in 1970, primarily for his work in reversing the food shortages that haunted India and Pakistan in the 1960s."[17] It was the culmination of a ten-year program jointly supported by the Ford and Rockefeller Foundations. During this period hundreds of research awards were made in developing countries for improving the acute food shortage faced by these countries. In 1960, also jointly with the Rockefeller Foundation and the government of the Philippines, the Ford Foundation helped establish the International Rice Research Institute (IRRI) at Los Banos in the Philippines. The Ford Foundation gave $6.0 million to IRRI and $10.5 million for projects to increase food production in India.[18] The dwarf wheat varieties developed in Mexico helped increase yields in some areas from 750 kilograms per hectare (kg/ha) to 9,000 kg/ha.[19]

For optimal yields from these new varieties, the farmers were also required to ensure a consistent supply of water, fertilizers, and pesticides. The subsequent priority given to the increased usage of fertilizers and pesticides by the government can be appreciated in the speech by C. Subramaniam, India's minister of food and agriculture, at the Rockefeller Symposium on Agriculture held in New York on April 1, 1968:

[An]...important element in our strategy was the massive emphasis on fertilizers and pesticides – what I have called elsewhere the chemicalisation of agriculture. In 1964-65, we were using 538,000 tonnes of nitrogen equivalent in Indian agriculture. While this was a considerable advance over a mere 58,000 tonnes used in 1950-51, our per acre usage was still at a considerably low level...even if we could use more fertil-

---

[16] Centro Internacional de Mejoramiento de Maiz y Trigo.

[17] George Easterbrook, "Norman Borlaug, the agronomist whose discoveries sparked the Green Revolution, has saved literally millions of lives, yet he is hardly a household name", *The Atlantic Monthly*, vol. 279, No.1, January 1997, pp. 75-82.

[18] *A Selected Chronology of the Ford Foundation [1936-1979]*, booklet, p. 7. (n.d.)

[19] Norman E. Borlaug, "The Green Revolution: Peace and Humanity, Acceptance Speech," Nobel Peace Prize, Oslo: December 11, 1970.

izers, foreign exchange was a bottleneck to import them in sufficient quantities.[20]

Subramaniam is credited for having played a leading role in launching the Green Revolution and in averting large-scale suffering and starvation during the two successive years of drought in 1966 and 1967.

Initially, India was not able to meet its own insecticide requirements and was thus forced to import from abroad. However, much progress towards self-sufficiency was made in the following decade and domestic production increased from a total of 14,000 metric tons (MT) in 1966 to over 50,000 MT by 1979. It was estimated that a total of 65,000 MT of pesticides was used in 1979.[21] This increased level of consumption – around 330 grams/ha, however, was still low when compared to the 1,500 g/ha used in the United States and 11,000 g/ha in Japan.[22] A considerable amount of this tonnage was imported from international companies and foreign governments, including Union Carbide Corporation, which exported 1,400 MT of its patented insecticide, Carbaryl, known better by its brand name, SEVIN™. In 1963, the Government of India also accepted an additional 850 MT of SEVIN formulated as fine dust, a gift from the Red Cross and paid for by U.S. Agency for International Development (USAID), as part of the U.S. government PL 480 (Public Law 480) and Food for Peace program.

SEVIN had received wide publicity when the Egyptian cotton crop – that country's main export – was saved from total destruction in 1961 after it was discovered that the cotton worm was totally resistant to DDT and other chlorinated insecticides. The massive airlift of 1,000 MT of 85 S (sprayable formulation) SEVIN, transported to Egypt by more than 150 aircraft, averted what could have been an economic disaster.

The impetus to use insecticides in India gained momentum by the studies conducted by All India Rice Improvement Project of ICAR. In 1969, ICAR scientists demonstrated that, with the use of insecticides, the average yield of the hybrid rice varieties IR 8 and TN 1 increased by 108 percent and 194 percent respectively. Based on these promising results,

---

[20] C. Subramaniam, *India of My Dreams,* Orient Longman Limited, New Delhi: 1972, p. 115.

[21] *HEXAGON,* a UCIL Quarterly Publication, January-March 1980.

[22] Ibid.

the Government of India projected that by the end of their 5-Year Plan, domestic consumption of pesticides would grow to 100,000 MT.[23]

Within a year of its commercial introduction to the U.S. market in 1958, SEVIN was registered for use on fifteen crops, including cotton, apples, peaches, and grapes. By 1970, the U.S. government had extended the approved uses of SEVIN to 160 different insects affecting over 90 different types of commercial crops. In the Indian context, farmers used SEVIN to control major cotton pests and rice pests such as stem borers, gall midge, brown plant-hamper, and green-leafhoppers.

Carbaryl is the first member of a class of insecticides called carbamates to be invented and commercialized for wide agricultural use. Unlike DDT and other chlorinated hydrocarbons, it acts by a different mechanism on the nervous system and it is not persistent in the environment. In addition to its acceptable safety margin, many farmers preferred SEVIN as an alternative to DDT since a number of pests had developed resistance to the latter chemical due to its prolonged and incomplete usage. This success was also demonstrated in Guatemala, where SEVIN received widespread publicity after having been successfully used against DDT-resistant pests. Carbaryl was also considered to be much safer to mammals.[24]

Given the promising results of its field tests, the Government of India projected domestic demand for Carbaryl to increase from 1,400 MT in the early 1960s to 5,900 MT by 1974. Based on these projections, Union Carbide India Limited saw an opportunity to expand its business in India's vast agricultural market and decided to formulate Carbaryl in India. In response to a UCIL application filed in December 1960, the Government of India issued the company a license to import technical grade Carbaryl, produced at the UCC plant in Institute, West Virginia. Upon this material's arrival in India, it was formulated for commercial use by diluting with local inert ingredients, packaged, and sold as SEVIN® insecticide. The commercial products contained anywhere from 1 to 20 percent of the technical grade Carbaryl, depending on its intended usage by crop.

---

[23] *Madhya Pradesh Chronicle,* Bhopal, (Special Supplement). "Ambitious Joint Endeavour of Union Carbide Corporation, USA & Union Carbide India Limited," February 9, 1982.

[24] *The Pesticide Manual, A World Compendium,* Charles R. Worthing (ed.), British Crop Protection Council, 7th ed. 1983, pp. 88, 159. With values for rat acute (oral) or LD_{50} of 850 mg/kg and acute percutaneous (through skin) greater than 4000 mg/Kg versus 113-118 and 2500 mg/kg respectively for DDT. For definitions of the LD_{50} values see the Glossary.

In order to import this technical grade Carbaryl, UCIL was required to pay UCC in hard currency, i.e., U.S. dollars. To do this, UCIL needed to generate at least an equivalent amount of hard currency through export of its other products. With the Indian economy focused inward on import substitution policies, such a task was not easy. For its own part, the Government of India did not look favorably on UCIL's dependence on imported technical grade Carbaryl and pressured the company to produce it locally. In 1966, after a series of discussions between UCC, UCIL, and the Government of India, UCIL agreed to submit an application to manufacture Carbaryl in India.

On April 7, 1966, UCIL submitted the first proposal to the Ministry of Petroleum and Chemicals for an industrial license to manufacture technical grade Carbaryl in India. Following several meetings between the two parties, a second application was submitted on May 27, 1966, which focused on the manufacturing process, raw material requirements, equipment requirements, investment, foreign exchange savings, and foreign technical collaboration issues. The application submitted by the managing director of UCIL stated:

> Government estimates place the demand for SEVIN insecticide at approximately 5,900 tonnes per annum by the end of the Fourth [5-year] Plan.... In line with the anticipated demand, Union Carbide India Limited proposes to manufacture 5,000 tonnes of SEVIN, Technical.... The annual foreign exchange outlay on the importation of SEVIN would be in excess of Rs. 52.8 million [$11 million]. Besides this direct foreign exchange saving, a very substantial indirect saving will result from the reduced level of importation of commodities such as cotton whose output the application of SEVIN will materially augment...

> Union Carbide India Limited is in a particularly advantageous position to implement this project as a result of its close association with Union Carbide Corporation, U.S.A. which holds Indian Patent 59443 covering the manufacture, sale and use of SEVIN insecticide in India. Union Carbide Corporation has agreed to license Union Carbide India Limited the use of its patents on this product, as well as use of all trademarks within the context of a suitable license contract. Union Carbide International Company, a division of Union Carbide Corporation, will engineer the plant, supervise construction, train Indian personnel and provide start-up manpower.... We shall be glad if a Letter of Intent is issued to us at an

early date for the manufacture of 5,000 tonnes of SEVIN, Technical per annum.[25]

During the early years of production, UCC manufactured Carbaryl by first reacting alpha-naphthol with phosgene to form a chemical intermediate – naphthylchloroformate – which was then reacted with methylamine to produce Carbaryl. The two-step chloroformate route was labor-intensive and not suitable for continuous operation and automation. In the mid-1960s UCC changed the manufacturing process and began to produce Carbaryl at its Institute plant in West Virginia using a new and more economical single step, by reacting alpha-naphthol with methyl isocyanate (MIC). In the initial discussions with UCIL, UCC engineers had recommended that the Carbaryl plant in Bhopal use the chloroformate route for the Indian facility since it was already a proven process. The Government of India and UCIL management, however, insisted on adopting the newer MIC route since it was the latest technology used by UCC, and was less expensive.[26] (See the letter in Appendix A-4).

In reply to UCIL's application, the Ministry of Petroleum and Chemicals issued a Letter of Intent on December 6, 1966, which allowed UCIL to proceed with the plans to manufacture 5,000 MT of Carbaryl. However, it also stipulated that the terms of foreign collaboration, including import of equipment, should be settled to the satisfaction of the government; that 50 percent of the actual production of the technical grade material should be reserved for other formulators in the country.[27]

By these terms, in accordance with The Monopolies and Restrictive Trade Practices Act of 1969, the government restricted UCIL's total control in the formulation and sales of the pesticide, so as to promote the businesses of smaller domestic pesticide formulators. As negotiations to build the plant continued, additional restrictive laws were enacted to limit foreign investments.

---

[25] Letter from Jack W. L. Russell, Managing Director UCIL to the Secretary, Ministry of Petroleum and Chemicals, dated 27 May 1966.

[26] Ernest R. Marshall, Richard C. Back and Warren J. Woomer, *Union Carbide Agricultural Products - 1925 through 1986-1996,* p. 54.

[27] Letter from the Under Secretary, P.S.V. Raghavan, Ministry of Petroleum and Chemicals to UCIL No. A & I - 32(14)/66, Serial No. 621, dated 6th December 1966. (Court Exhibit 2).

Increased Assertion of India's National Interest

On January 1, 1974, Parliament revised its original 1947 Foreign Exchange Regulation Act with FERA (1973) to "...consolidate and amend the law regulating...currency for the conservation of the foreign exchange resources of the country and the proper utilization thereof in the interest of the economic development of the country." More importantly, it regulated and curtailed foreign investors and their equity in Indian affiliates. This landmark legislation was specifically designed to promote indigenous industrial development and "Indianization" of businesses so as to free them further from foreign decision-making influences.

Section 28 of the revised FERA legislation restricted and controlled the employment of nonresidents and foreign nationals in India. Employment of foreign consultants and technical advisors by a domestic company required prior approval from the Reserve Bank of India, the principal government agency empowered to regulate and enforce these policies. Thus, no foreign national could work in India without prior approval of the central government.

Section 29 specifically dealt with restrictions on the establishment of place of business in India by foreign companies. Only those foreign companies that provided sophisticated technology and contributed significantly to exports were allowed to own more than 40 percent of any domestic company's shares. In no case, however, could this ownership in Indian companies exceed 74 percent.

According to this law all non-banking subsidiaries with foreign equity exceeding 40 percent required the permission of the Reserve Bank of India to carry on business in India or purchase shares in existing companies. In 1976, a third level of 51 percent of foreign equity was introduced in order to provide more flexibility, provided the company had a turnover of 60 percent in the core sector activities and exported at least 10 percent of their production.[28]

Such increasingly strict regulatory policies stipulating how Indian companies should collaborate with foreign entities, and the additional pressure on some companies to disclose their trade secrets, triggered the exodus of companies like IBM, Coca-Cola, and others in 1977. Following the introduction of FERA, the number of branches of foreign corporations in India

---

[28] John Martinussen, *Transnational Corporations in a Developing Country, The Indian Experience,* Sage Publications, New Delhi: 1988, pp. 45-46.

decreased from 540 in 1973 to 315 in 1980, with the number of foreign subsidiaries experiencing a corresponding reduction from 188 to 118 over the same period.[29] Consequently, the level of new foreign investment fell to an all-time low.[30] By the end of 1987 foreign direct investment in India amounted to only $1.6 billion of the estimated $983 billion of the world stock of direct foreign investment. "Not only was India's share insignificant as a percentage of the world's total but was also low in comparison to that in the other Asian countries," such as Indonesia, Malaysia, Singapore, and Thailand.[31] According to Sanjaya Lall of Oxford University's Institute of Economics and Statistics, India had one of the most regulated economies of all the industrially advanced developing countries and had:

> ...persisted the longest in a relatively inefficient policy of 'import substitution at any cost, and has combined with this a battery of controls to promote the public sector and hold back large private business.... The gradual tightening of controls on foreign investment has led to a situation where during the eleven years 1969-79, the new foreign equity capital approved amounted to only $70 million and the net inflow (after deducting dividends and repatriation) was negative.[32]

Nevertheless, a number of companies opted to comply with these new policies and continued doing business in India. Union Carbide, which had a well-established marketing and distribution network to sell batteries in the country, was one of them.

In 1977-1978, to raise funds for newer industrial development, a special rights offer (option to buy shares at a discount) was made by UCIL to the existing Indian shareholders. UCC was excluded from this offer, as a necessary condition for UCIL to obtain the Government of India's approval to build the proposed pesticide plant in Bhopal. The sale of these additional UCIL shares to the Indian public resulted in UCC's equity in UCIL to decrease from 60 percent to 50.9 percent. Much of the remaining

---

[29]   Ibid, p. 158.

[30]   Dennis J. Encarnation, *Dislodging Multinationals. India's Strategy in Comparative Perspective,* Cornell University Press, Ithaca: 1989, p. 73

[31]   The Associated Chambers of Commerce and Industry, *Assessment of Foreign Direct Investment and Technology Transfer in India, Foreign Direct Investment and Technology Transfer in India,* United Nations Centre on Transnational Corporations, United Nations, New York: 1992, p. 64.

[32]   Sanjaya Lall, *Multinationals, Technology and Exports,* St. Martin's Press, New York: 1985, pp. 82-83.

shares were owned by large government-controlled institutions, including the Unit Trust of India, the Industrial Development Bank of India, the Life Insurance Corporation of India, the Industrial Finance Corporation of India, and the Industrial Credit Investment Corporation of India.

UCC was one of the few foreign companies that was allowed to retain more than 40 percent equity because it used sophisticated technology not available domestically and had met the export quota as per the criteria of FERA (1973). These conditions are elaborated in greater detail in a letter from the joint controller of the Reserve Bank of India to UCIL, dated July 4, 1977.

> We note that the company has undertaken a diversification programme envisaging manufacture of items covered by Appendix I to the Industrial Licensing Policy, 1973 and expansion of the levels of exports out of its own production. If, therefore, during the period of two years allowed for dilution of non-resident interest to 40%, the turnover from the items covered by the said Appendix I and exports from the company's own production falling outside Appendix I reaches a level of at least 60 (sixty) per cent of the annual turnover from all activities and the ex-factory cost of the company's exports out of its own production is not less than 10 (ten) per cent of the ex-factory cost of its total annual production, we would be prepared to consider your case at the appropriate stage for retaining non-resident interest at a level higher than 40 (forty) per cent, as permissible under the guidelines prescribed by the Government of India for administering Section 29(2) of the Foreign Exchange Regulation Act 1973, with reference to the changed character of the company.[33]

This special privilege was again reviewed in 1980, and since it was determined that UCIL had met the export performance for the full year ending December 31, 1979, the Reserve Bank of India granted permission to carry on UCIL's manufacturing activities unchanged.[34] UCC's share of the equity in the Indian Company was thus determined by the Reserve Bank of India, after periodic evaluation of UCIL's export performance.

With funds assured from the sale of additional shares and loans from government financial institutions, UCIL proceeded with plans to build the pesticide plant in Bhopal. The next few pages will deal with how UCIL

---

[33]   Letter from the Reserve Bank of India to UCIL, Ref. No: EC. CO. FCS. 76/366 (Activity)-77, dated 4th July 1977.

[34]   Letter from the Reserve Bank of India to UCIL, Ref. No: EC. CO. FCS 82/366(Activity)-80/81, dated 5th July 1980.

acquired the site in Bhopal, obtained MIC technology from UCC, constructed the facility (with emphasis on MIC storage tanks), and trained their key managers and engineers to operate the plant.

UCIL Acquires Plant Site in Bhopal

Bhopal is the capital city of the Indian State of Madhya Pradesh. Located near the geographic center of India, Bhopal has a major railway hub that offered good access to rail transportation for obtaining raw materials and distribution of finished products to markets across the country. In addition to its natural beauty with parks, scenic lakes, and mosques in the middle of the city, Bhopal has a long and distinguished history. It was built on the site of the eleventh century town of Bhojpal (or Bhojapal), founded by Raja Bhoj of Dhar (1010-55). Plans for the present city were laid out in 1722 by Dost Mohammad Khan (1672-1728), an Afghan "soldier of fortune" who fled his native Tirah after he killed his cousin in an act of passion in a triangular love affair.[35] In India this Pathan nobleman distinguished himself with the sword and rose in the army ranks to become a distinguished officer of Mogul Emperor Aurangzeb (1659-1707). In the confusion following the death of the Mogul Emperor, Dost carved out a small principality and ruled as nawab of the State of Bhopal. Later, along with the 600 princely states of India, this state became a protectorate of the British Crown, with Bhopal City as its capital city. After the partitioning of British India and independence for the two new countries in 1947, most of the princely states became part of either India or Pakistan. In 1949, the State of Bhopal was merged into the Indian Union and six years later became the capital of the new State of Madhya Pradesh.

The 1981 census of India ranked Madhya Pradesh as the sixth most populous state in India with a population of 52,178,844. Over 51 percent of the rural and 40 percent of the urban population lived in chronic poverty, with income considerably below the national per capita GNP of $260 (1983).[36] Infant mortality rate for the State of Madhya Pradesh in 1980

---

[35] For more details about the life of Dost see Shaharyar M. Khan, *The Begums of Bhopal, A Dynasty of Women Rulers in Raj India,* I.B. Tauris Publishers, London: 2000, pp. 1-29.

[36] George Thomas Kurian, *Encyclopedia of the Third World – INDIA,* 3rd Edition, vol. II, 1987. p. 884.

was estimated at 142 per 1,000 births as compared to the national average of 114.[37]

Bhopal district covers an area of 2,772 km^2 and maximum temperatures during the summer months of April through June regularly exceed 40°C (over 100°F). The 1981 census recorded a population of 671,018 for Bhopal district, which includes the capital city. In 1984, this figure was estimated to have surpassed 700,000. Adult literacy rates in Bhopal – 55 percent for males and 38 percent for females – were higher than the state's average. Muslims accounted for approximately 28 percent of the city's population, having doubled their numbers since 1961.[38]

The majestic old mosques and palaces – Taj-ul-Masajid, Jama Masjid, Moti Masjid, Shaukat Mahal, Sadar Manzil, and the historic Ahmedabad Palace (now Safia College) located to the north of Upper Lake and in the older section of the city, stand as silent testimonials to the achievements of the former rulers. Among them were four powerful *begums* (female rulers), who ruled from 1819 to 1926. The old city also hosts a crowded marketplace and is predominantly Muslim. With the help of British engineers, Sultan Jehan Begum is credited to have built the first railway line connecting Itarsi to Bhopal, completed in 1864. She was also responsible for the first steam factory in nearby Shahjahanabad, for sawing timber, grinding grains, and for cleaning and baling cotton brought from all parts of the state for export to Bombay and abroad.[39]

In the 1970s, five major hospitals with eighteen hundred beds and several clinics provided primary health care to the residents of Bhopal. The Upper Lake is the city's main source of water but the city "provided water to residential taps for only a few hours a day.... Open sewage dumps were common in many parts of the city, and city sewage was indiscriminately dumped into the two local lakes."[40]

Since the entire State of Madhya Pradesh was classified as an underdeveloped region of India (due to high unemployment rates and low

---

[37] Frank B. Hobbs, *Demographic Estimates, Projections and Selected Social Characteristics of the Population of India,* Center for International Research U. S. Bureau of Census, Washington: 1986, p. 85.

[38] Chandralekha Lehri, *Socio-Demographic Profile of Muslim, Study of Bhopal City,* Rawat Publications, New Delhi: 1997, pp. 49-55

[39] Sultan Jehan Begam, *An Account of My Life*, John Murray, London: 1910, p. 82.

[40] Paul Shrivastava, *Bhopal:Anatomy of a Crisis*, Ballinger Publishing Company, Cambridge, Massachusetts: 1987, p. 60.

socioeconomic indicators) in the 1960s, both the federal and state governments offered a number of tax breaks and other incentives to attract major industries. The attractiveness of the central location in the nation and convenient rail transport facilities induced UCIL to consider Bhopal as the site for its new insecticide plant. In addition, the Madhya Pradesh government offered a long-term, low-cost lease for the proposed industrial site, located about 3 km north of the Hamidia Hospital and about 1.5 km northwest from the Bhopal Railway Station and close to the railroad track (see Figure A).

Several letters of correspondence between the government ministries and UCIL, UCC's written statements, and sworn affidavits cited in this section are from U.S. court archives, provided by the plaintiff and the defendant during the litigation in the New York and Bhopal courts. These documents present an interesting window into the extent of the bureaucracy and the close supervision by the central government in controlling and monitoring the activities of the Indian company, and in their dealings with the foreign business partner.

In early 1968, UCIL obtained from the Director of Industries of the State of Madhya Pradesh the registration to set up a pesticide formulation facility in Bhopal, and on June 28, 1968 a lease for five acres of land. This site was "in an area which had been designated for industrial use according to the interim master plan adopted in 1962 by the Bhopal Town Master Plan and Improvement Committee."[41] In September 1970, UCIL applied to the Ministry of Industrial Development, for a COB (carrying on business) license for a pesticides plant in Bhopal. In this letter, UCIL informed the ministry that, with a Letter of Intent granted earlier by the Government of India, a pilot plant was installed in 1967 on a temporary permit at Trombay near Bombay (now Mumbai) for the development of formulated products. Subsequently, the plant was shifted to Bhopal in 1969 since the government of Maharashtra objected to a permanent setup.[42]

On October 10, 1972, the governor of Madhya Pradesh, acting through the Director of Industries, granted to UCIL a Deed of Lease for an addi-

---

[41] Affidavit of Dr. Ishwar Dass, Additional Chief Secretary for the Government of Madhya Pradesh, India, in Re: UCC gas leak Disaster at Bhopal, U.S. District Court Southern District of New York, MDL Docket No. 626 Misc. No.21-38 (JFK) 85 Civ. 2696 (JFK).

[42] The plant was registered with the Director of Industries, Madhya Pradesh and regulated by the Ministry of Petroleum, Chemicals, Mines and Metals. See letter in Appendix A-I.

tional 49.25 acres, situated in the Kali Parade Industrial Area of the Tehsil Huzur, of the Sehore District, for a term of ninety-nine years. It was specifically "for the purpose of construction and establishing thereon a factory for the manufacture of Methyl Isocyanate-based Pesticides and purposes ancillary thereto." As described in the Deed of Lease, the property was bounded in the north by the Western Railway line, to the south by a proposed eighty-foot wide road (now called Kali Parade), to the east by Chola Road, and to the west by the existing unit of M/s Shama Forge Company (see Figures A and B). According to the terms of the lease, UCIL agreed to pay 19,700 rupees (approximately $2,500) within thirty days and thereafter an annual ground rent of 1,970 rupees for the next thirty years. In turn, UCIL agreed "to construct and establish on the said land a factory for the manufacture of Methyl Isocyanate based Pesticides and allied products" within a period of three years.[43]

An additional 5.75 acres of land were leased on April 19, 1973 for the MIC Project. For the effluent disposal pond and a railway siding, another 25.23 acres were leased on April 30, 1976, and finally, another 2.39 acres of Khasra No. 10 at Chola Village on November 19, 1977. All these tracts were adjacent to the previously allotted sites and "had been designated industrial pursuant to both an interim master plan adopted in 1962 by the Bhopal Town Master Plan and Improvement Committee."[44]

When the necessary land was being leased for the construction of the plant facilities, a sizable tract of land in the vicinity was unoccupied and undeveloped. This was indicated in a letter dated 16 September 1976, by UCIL's Works Manager C.S. Ram to the Director of Industries, Madhya Pradesh.

...this piece of land is such that, by itself, it will not be of much use to anyone else since it is a corner of Khasra No. 10, of which a major portion has been allotted to us, it touches the boundary of Khasra No. 9 which we are hopeful of being allotted in due course and on the remain-

---

[43] Deed of Lease dated 10th. Oct. 1972. Appendix A-2.

[44] Sworn statement by Dr. Ishwar Dass, Additional Chief Secretary for the Government of Madhya Pradesh. Submitted to U.S. District Court. MDL Docket No. 626, Misc. No. 21-38 (JFK) 85 Civ.2696 (JFK) ALL CASES, 21/11/1985. Doc. No. 251.

ing sides, it is surrounded by other agricultural fields. There appears to be, therefore, no access to this patch of land, except by ourselves.[45]

UCIL's insecticide plant in Bhopal was built in three phases. The SEVIN formulation facility commenced production in 1969 and construction of alpha-naphthol and SEVIN carbamoylation units from 1975 to 1977. The methyl isocyanate facility was built last, having started in mid-1978 and completed in February 1980. The last phase also entailed the construction of manufacturing facilities for carbon monoxide and phosgene, both intermediates for manufacturing MIC, based on the process technology design package acquired from UCC.

While UCIL had received the go-ahead from the Ministry of Petroleum and Chemicals through its 1966 Letter of Intent by 1970, this approval had lapsed since UCIL did not meet the stipulated conditions within the prescribed time. So in 1970, Edward A. Munoz,[46] general manager of the Agricultural Products Division of UCIL, wrote a proposal to the Industrial Development Internal Trade & Company Affairs for permission "to erect facilities to manufacture up to 2,000 tons of methyl isocyanate and 5,000 tons a year of methyl isocyanate-based pesticides." Less than 20 percent of the equipment would be imported and all engineering and construction would be fabricated domestically.

The total investment in equipment is estimated at Rs. 41,250.000, Rs. 33,900,000 of which will be indigenously fabricated and Rs. 7,350,000 imported. Practically all of the engineering will be done in India. Foreign exchange requirements for overseas engineering is not expected to exceed 4% of the total investment.

A foreign collaboration agreement will be entered into with Union Carbide Corporation.

---

[45] See letter from C. S. Ram, Works Manager UCIL to The Director of Industries, Madhya Pradesh, Bhopal, letter of 16th September, 1976, – Appendix A-3.

[46] The Argentinean native, whose name in Spanish is Eduardo Alejandro Munoz, joined UCC in 1959 as a technical representative of UCC International Division. In 1966 he joined Union Carbide India, Limited where he rose to the position of General Manager of UCIL's Agricultural Products Division and later as Managing Director and as Regional Director.

On a first phase, Union Carbide India Limited proposes to erect MIC, carbamilation, recovery and formulation facilities to react [with] purchased alcohols. The MIC unit will be a <u>fully integrated plant</u> operating with coke, chlorine and monomethyl amine as basic intermediates under Union Carbide Corporation process, modified to reduce incidence of exotic materials of construction and imported equipment. It will have a total capacity of 2,000 tons high purity MIC a year, <u>based on continuous operation</u>.[47] [Emphasis added].

Coke was to be used to manufacture carbon monoxide, chlorine to produce phosgene, which was then reacted with methylamine for conversion to MIC (Figure 2-4). The proposal was for the fabrication of a fully integrated plant in a closed system and continuous operation, using mostly indigenous and fewer "exotic materials of construction and imported equipment." In such a system, the hazardous liquid chemicals are moved through the system during production and storage along the connecting pipelines, applying pressure using nitrogen gas. This method involves little or no manual handling and minimal exposure of plant operators to toxic gases and chemicals.

In addition to presenting the economics and other characteristics of the MIC unit, Munoz also presented to the central government a broader view of UCIL's long-term strategic plan with emphasis on research and development, discovery of new products in India, and the export potential of these products in the region.

In response to this proposal made in January 1970, the government agency requested and received additional information from UCIL. These included: 1) names, quantities, and sources of various raw materials necessary for the production of MIC; 2) names of MIC based pesticides with available technical literature on each; 3) import data, e.g., present landed cost and expected cost of production in India.[48]

Two years later the Ministry of Petroleum and Chemicals issued a Letter of Intent to manufacture 5,000 MT of MIC-based pesticides annu-

---

[47] Letter from E.A. Munoz, General Manager, Agricultural Products Division, UCIL to The Licensing & Progress Section, Industrial Development Internal Trade & Company Affairs, New Delhi: January 1, 1970. See Appendix A-4.

[48] Cited by UCC in the Written Statement to the Court of the District Judge, Bhopal: December 10, 1986. In N. R. Madhava Menon (ed). *Documents and Court Opinions on Bhopal Gas Leak Disaster Case*, National Law School of India University, Bangalore: 1991. p. 94.

ally, with the stipulation that "the letter of intent would be converted into a license, after the [earlier] specified conditions were fulfilled." The license was also contingent on UCIL starting the manufacture of alpha-naphthol in India and reducing the equity of its foreign collaborator (UCC) to comply with FERA regulations. UCIL had fulfilled this latter condition by issuing additional shares of up to 25 percent of the total cost of this project. Other stipulations detailed in the Annex of the letter included:

(i) Government would consider favourably proposals of foreign collaboration in which a suitable favoured licensed clause is incorporated in the draft agreement to obtain a process license, know-how, royalty, and research and design assistance.

(ii) Approved/Registered Indian Engineering Design and Consultancy Organizations must be the prime consultants and Government will consider permitting the purchase of only such design and consultancy services from abroad as are not available within the country.

(iii) Proposals for the purchase of overseas technology (process license fees, know-how, royalty, R&D etc) must be accompanied by proposals regarding the programme of further development and improvement of technology in this field (as distinct from analytical or quality control) in the country.

(iv) It is desirable that approved/registered Indian Engineering design and consultancy organizations should be associated right from the start in any evaluation, selection and negotiation conducted for the purchase of overseas technology.

(v) It is desirable that inquiries to overseas parties should be made on the basis of obtaining separate quotations for technology (license fees, know-how, royalty, R&D assistance, etc.) and design and consultancy services not available in the country.

Copies of this letter were also forwarded to ten other agencies of the central government and to the Director of Industries for Madhya Pradesh.[49] These guidelines were designed to promote and develop indigenous industries without "unwholesome dependence on foreign agencies";

---

[49]   See Appendix A-5 for the complete text of the letter.

the objectives set out in the Government of India's fourth five-year plan (1969-1974).

Under clause (iii) of the annex, the government specifically instructed UCIL to limit the purchase to foreign technology not available in the country and to exclude the technology for "analytical or quality control." This ancillary technology of developing analytical procedures and analyzing all the raw materials, intermediates and products, and maintaining the high standards in quality control was considered unnecessary since it could be developed locally by Indian scientists and engineers.

On November 22, 1972, as a follow-up to the Letter of Intent from the Ministry of Petroleum and Chemicals, a chief government scientist at the National Chemical Laboratory in Poona (now Pune) requested additional technical details for the envisaged MIC process. These included chemical names, specifications and quantities of all raw materials to be imported per year, services, fees, and royalties payable to the foreign collaborator.[50] On matters of industrial licensing and other technical problems, the Ministry of Petroleum and Chemicals and other government agencies are normally advised by scientists at the National Chemical Laboratory, the Government of India's premier chemical research laboratory under the umbrella of the Council of Scientific and Industrial Research (CSIR).

In a letter dated August 25, 1973, the Ministry of Petroleum and Chemicals indicated that it was prepared to approve the application for the construction of the MIC plant and the manufacture of carbamate-based insecticides, provided additional terms and conditions were met. These were elaborated in the annex to the letter and thus served as guidelines for UCIL to acquire the technology from UCC and build the MIC plant. It specifically stated that:

1. The Indian company should be free to sub-license the technical know-how/product design/engineering design under the agreement to another Indian party, should it become necessary. The terms of such sub-licensing will, however, be as mutually agreed to by all the parties concerned including the foreign collaborators and will be subject to the approval of Government

---

[50]   Letter Ref. 456 20/DTS/72, to UCIL from A. M. Lele, Scientist i/c, Div. of Tech. Services, National Chemical Laboratory, Poona: dated November 22, 1972. – Court Doc. 10151823

2. The deputation of foreign technicians either way shall be governed by specific approval to be granted by the Government on application in terms of numbers, period of assistance and training, rate of allowance to be paid travelling charges and other items of expenses etc.

3. Import of capital equipment and raw materials would be allowed as per import policy, prevailing from time to time.

4. Foreign brand names will not ordinarily be allowed for use on the products for internal sale although there is not objection to their use on products to be exported.

Export shall be permitted to all countries except where foreign collaborator has existing licensing arrangements for manufacture.

The duration of the agreement shall be for a period of five years from the date of agreement or five years from the date of commencement of production provided production is not delayed beyond three years of signing agreement (i.e., a maximum period of eight years from the date of signing of the agreement). Within this period the Indian company should develop and set up their own design and research plant so that continued dependence upon foreign collaborator beyond this period will not be necessary.

In case any consultancy is required to execute the project, this should be obtained from an Indian Consultancy Engineering firm. If foreign consultancy is considered unavoidable, an Indian consultancy firm should nevertheless be the prime consultants.

The Indian Company should send three copies of a return about the progress of the undertaking as in the form enclosed showing the position as on 31st December each year. The annual returns should be sent 31st January of the following year. The annual returns should be sent till the date of the expiry of the foreign collaboration agreement....[51]

Prior to signing the Design Transfer Agreement with UCC, UCIL applied to the Ministry of Petroleum and Chemicals for permission to send seven selected engineers to the U.S. to "help the Design Group in the

---

[51] N. R. Madhava Menon (ed), (Cited by UCC in the Written Statement of 10th December 1986 to the Court of District Judge, Bhopal.) p. 95.

U.S. in the Indianization" of the MIC project. UCIL wanted the Indian engineers to be "associated from the very beginning of the design and engineering work of the project to maximize indigenous capability in the interest of our country."[52]

While the Ministry initially rejected this request as premature, on the grounds that "there was no contract yet with the foreign collaborator," it later relented and approved. The Indian engineers, along with UCC design engineers at South Charleston and Institute, West Virginia, worked for three to six months before the technology package was completed to their satisfaction. Engineers A.S. Ajagaonkar and S. Bandopadhyaya, along with the UCC engineer Gordon E. Rutzen, were primarily involved in the design of the MIC unit. P.G. Shrotri (deceased) was responsible for the instrumentation. He was specifically required "to evaluate minimum requirements of instrumentation suiting Indian conditions" and to dispense with "sophisticated instrumentation" used in the U.S. Not opting for the electronic instrumentation used at the Institute plant, the Indian engineers preferred to use pneumatic instrumentation due to unavailability of the necessary electronic parts in India.[53]

The Design Transfer Agreement between UCC and UCIL

During the first ten years of the UCIL pesticide project, Carbaryl was produced locally using imported MIC from UCC's Institute plant that was shipped to Bhopal in specially designed 55-gallon (400 pounds) stainless steel drums, in accordance with the U.S. Department of Transportation specifications. For a period of time, alpha-naphthol was also imported from the U.S. to be reacted with MIC to produce Carbaryl and then formulated with local inert ingredients to the final marketable products. The lack of technology to manufacture MIC was the major obstacle that prevented UCIL from being able to fully integrate the manufacture of Carbaryl in India. This situation was resolved when the necessary technology was acquired from UCC following the guidelines and conditions delineated in the letters from the Ministry of Petroleum and Chemicals and other ministries of the government.

---

[52] For names of individuals, see Appendix A-6 - Letter dated November 24, 1972. Court Document Nos. 10151615 -10151616.

[53] Woomer, Affidavit to U. S. District Court, NY, MDL No. Docket No. 626, dated December 27, 1985.

On November 13, 1973, UCIL and UCC signed two separate agreements – the Design Transfer Agreement and the Technical Services Agreement – by which the latter agreed to sell UCIL the technology package, needed to manufacture MIC in India. The design package comprised of the basic plan of the MIC factory, which consisted of (1) a unit for manufacturing MIC by a continuous process, (2) a phosgene manufacturing facility, (3) a carbon monoxide generation plant, and (4) the technology to produce Carbaryl. (Phosgene is an intermediate for MIC, produced from carbon monoxide and chlorine). The technology package was sold to UCIL for Rs. 1,237,500 (approximately $160,000 at the time). The package did not include the technology to manufacture alpha-naphthol, as UCIL opted to develop the technology in India.

Article IV of the Design Transfer Agreement states that it was the "best manufacturing information available" at the time and that the drawings and design instructions included were "sufficiently detailed and complete as to enable competent technical personnel to detail design, erect and commission the facilities." It also included a disclaimer that UCC "shall have no responsibility with respect to the use made thereof by UCIL and shall not, in any way, be liable for any loss, damage, personal injury or death resulting from or arising out of the use by UCIL of the Design Packages."[54] The agreements were duly signed by representatives of UCIL and UCC and recorded by the Ministry of Petroleum and Chemicals, as indicated in the letter from the Ministry, No. A&I /26(7)/72 dated February 6, 1975, cited in the letter by UCIL.[55] The legality of this agreement and the disclaimer was not determined as the lawsuit was settled out of court.

Raymond Vernon, citing a UN study, wrote that this arrangement of payments for technology transfer was one of the methods preferred by developing countries at that time to rapidly promote their industrial development. "Countries like India have strongly preferred arm's-length licensing

---

[54] For other relevant Articles of the Design Transfer and Technical Services Agreements, (Appendix A-7.)

[55] Letter by P. L. Joseph, Union Carbide India Limited, to the Secretary, Ministry of Petroleum and Chemicals, dated February 27, 1975. (Court Document Exhibit 7.)

arrangements between Indian firms and foreigners and have resisted the establishment of foreign owned subsidiaries."[56, 57]

The MIC technology sold to UCIL included the process improvements made over the first MIC plant at Institute, West Virginia, built in 1965-1966. The present MIC plant at Institute built in 1978, is more streamlined and a fully automated facility. While the basic plant design and manufacturing process of this third generation plant are similar to that of Bhopal, the two plants are not identical. The MIC design for the Bhopal plant was not automated but more labor intensive and geared to create employment. It was also specifically modified to meet Indian specifications, including local climatic and soil conditions and the use of locally available materials and instrumentation.

As indicated earlier, the original process used by UCC to manufacture Carbaryl in the 1950s was a two-step, non-MIC-based process. By the older process, alpha-naphthol was first reacted with phosgene, then with methylamine to produce the final product, Carbaryl. This technology produced hydrochloric acid as a side product that needed to be neutralized. The neutralization process produced a large quantity of salt as a waste product. The difficulty and the cost involved in recovering the Carbaryl, as well as the problems associated with disposing of the waste products, meant that this older process was neither cost effective nor environmentally friendly.

In the 1960s, with innovative engineering design, UCC developed a commercially viable manufacturing process to produce MIC that was more cost-effective. UCC used this technology to build the first plant of its kind at Institute, West Virginia in 1966. Munoz, in his letter of January 1970, informed the central government ministry the cost advantage of the newer technology, in seeking the necessary construction permits. It

---

[56]   Cited by Raymond Vernon, from UNCTAD, Proceedings, 3d Sess., New York: 1973, TD/180,111: 113-116); in *Foreign Technology and Investment – A Study of their Role in India's Industrialization, Storm over Multinationals – the Real Issues,* Harvard University Press, Cambridge, Massachusetts: 1977, p. 10.

[57]   See also Ashok V. Desai, *Foreign Technology and Investment – A Study of their Role in India's Industrialization,* National Council of Applied Economic Research, New Delhi: 1971. (cited earlier.)

was this plant design and the technology developed for the manufacture of MIC that was sold to UCIL in 1973.[58]

After the disaster, UCC was criticized that it used older MIC technology in India when other companies used newer and safer technology without having to store large quantities. In the late 1970s and 1980s, after the Bhopal plant was built, Farbenfabriken Bayer AG[59] and E.I. Du Pont de Nemours & Co.,[60] two UCC competitors in the agricultural-chemicals sector, had patented alternative novel processes to manufacture MIC. These newer processes offered the added flexibility of producing and using MIC on demand. The patents gave these companies exclusive rights to use these technologies for the life of the patents (seventeen years in the U.S.), thus restricting their use by other companies.

Financing and Construction of the Bhopal Plant

Having secured the Letter of Intent from the Ministry of Petroleum and Chemicals, the lease on the eighty-plus acre site in Bhopal from the State of Madhya Pradesh, and the necessary technology from UCC, UCIL moved forward with plans for the construction of the pesticide plant. It was financed with the capital raised through the sale of additional shares and loans. According to a senior UCC spokesman, "UCIL obtained local financing by borrowing solely on its own credit. At no time did UCC participate in the financing of the Bhopal plant nor did it directly or indirectly guarantee any loans extended to UCIL. The financial plans for the construction and development of the Bhopal Plant were presented to and approved by the Indian Government before any work was actually commenced. Moreover, some of the funding for the Bhopal plant was provided by Indian Government-controlled financial institutions."[61] The MIC project was estimated to cost "approximately $26,500,000.... The Industrial

---

[58] UCC had previously recommended the naphthylchloroformate route as most suitable to the India Carbaryl process but UCIL preferred to obtain the more efficient and cost effective route of using the MIC technology.

[59] German Application No. DE 2756928. (1979): U.S. Patent No. 4,195,031 (1980).

[60] U.S. Patent Nos. 4,469,640 (1984); 4,698,438 (1987)

[61] Sworn Affidavit by John Macdonald, Assistant Secretary for UCC, in support of Union Carbide's motion to dismiss on grounds of *Forum Non Conveniens*, Southern District Court of New York: July 26, 1985.

Development Bank of India and the Industrial Credit Investment Corporation of India (ICICI) were the lead financial institutions."[62]

On February 27, 1975, P.L. Joseph of UCIL informed the Ministry of Petroleum and Chemicals that the proposal for dilution of UCC's equity was "submitted to the Reserve Bank of India, Bombay and the Ministry of Finance, Department of Economic Affairs, New Delhi. Having fulfilled all the conditions of the Letter of Intent, we request that the Letter of Intent be converted to an Industrial License."[63] The Controller of Issues sanctioned the allotment of 3,294,500 new equity shares to Indian residents that raised Rs. 527.12 lakhs, approximately 22.3 percent of capital financing, bringing down UCC's equity to 50.9 percent.[64]

Following the guidelines set forth by the Ministry of Petroleum and Chemicals, UCIL contracted Humphreys and Glasgow Consultants Pvt. Ltd. – an Indian subsidiary of the British consulting firm based in Bombay – as contractors and consultants in building the MIC plant in Bhopal. The finalizing of the plant's design and construction, including the MIC storage tanks and its associated pipelines, were carried out by UCIL engineers and several other Indian contractors.

In November 1972, UCIL informed the Ministry on the status of the contracts signed with Messrs. Tata Consulting Engineers and other Indian construction companies.[65] The activities of the contracting firms were supervised by about fifteen UCIL engineers from Bombay, who were involved in the plant's design. Larsen and Toubro fabricated the MIC storage tanks, while the plant's instrumentation aspects were contracted to Taylor of India, Limited. These consultants and contractors were established Indian companies at the time with good reputations in engineering and in-

---

[62]   Affidavit of K. Subramanian, Joint Secretary in the Ministry of Law and Justice, MDL Docket No. 626, Misc. No. 21-38 (JFK), Nov. 22, 1985, p. 14.

[63]   Letter by P.L. Joseph, dated February 27, 1975, to N. Srinivasan, Ministry of Petroleum and Chemicals. (Exhibit 7, presented to the District Court, N.Y., cited earlier in this chapter.)

[64]   Letter by S. Kumaraswami of UCIL to the Under Secretary, Ministry of Petroleum, Chemicals and Fertilizers, March 23, 1973. (Court Document 10151526.)

[65]   Letter by C.L. Dhawan from UCIL to the Ministry of Petroleum and Chemicals, dated November (?), 1972. Court doc. Nos. 10151617-10151619. (Appendix A-18.)

strumentation. At no point were UCC engineers involved in this process, nor was UCC informed of any alterations made to the plant's design.[66]

As part of the "Indianization" process, the Government of India restricted the amount of foreign materials and foreign consultants' time, and insisted on the use of Indian materials and experts whenever possible. To minimize foreign exchange losses through imports, the government also insisted on approving purchase orders for equipment to be procured from abroad, through the mechanism of a capital goods license.[67]

This close monitoring of the construction of the Bhopal plant by the government, and the urgency in completing the project, is also reflected in the following letter from the Ministry of Chemicals and Fertilizers to UCIL:

> As pointed out during the discussions held in this Ministry on February 27, 1976, it is of utmost importance that your MIC Project should be implemented without delay. You are, therefore, requested to take effective steps to ensure expeditious implementation of this project within the schedule already indicated by you. In this connection this Ministry would like to receive from you quarterly reports indicating the progress achieved during the quarter, impediments, if any encountered in maintaining the requisite progress and the steps taken/being taken to overcome them and completion of the project as per schedule.[68]

This was in accordance with the centrally controlled economic policies, mandated by FERA (1973). These documents demonstrate that UCIL had the primary responsibility for all aspects of the Bhopal plant construction, from planning, financing, and design modifications, to safety of the plant and its employees. UCIL was required to report progress and any impediments faced directly to the government. By reducing UCCs foreign equity and Indianization of UCIL management, the government effectively stopped all foreign control in managing the business on a daily basis. UCC through its appointees (drawn from UCE management) on the

---

[66] Dutta Affidavit, at.16, 19-24, Cited by Judge John F. Keenan, Opinion and Order (Judgment) of the U.S. District Court, dismissing Union of India's Case on grounds of Forum Non Conveniens, May 12, 1986.

[67] Dutta Affidavit, at 35, 48-50; Brown Affidavit, at 6, cited in Judge Keenan's Opinion and Order.

[68] See text of the letter to UCIL, Ref. No. L-36016/2/75 from the Ministry of Chemicals and Fertilizers, of 19th May 1976, (Appendix A-8.)

UCIL board of directors, used its influence only in strategic planning and overseeing the financial health of all the UCIL divisions.

MIC Storage Tanks – "The Black Boxes"

While Humphreys and Glasgow was the general contractor responsible for constructing the Bhopal plant, specific technical work was subcontracted to other Indian companies who specialized in these areas: Sub-contractors Larsen and Toubro fabricated the three MIC storage tanks, and Taylor of India, Ltd., the necessary monitoring instrumentation for the tanks.

The MIC storage tanks were each forty feet long and eight feet in diameter with a holding capacity of fifteen thousand gallons. Constructed on site at Bhopal using type 304 stainless steel, the tanks were designed to hold full vacuum and pressures of up to 40 psi at 121°C, according to the specifications provided by UCC in the technology package. Since the tanks were located outside and buried partly below ground level, they were also coated with coal tar enamel with fiberglass reinforcing and cathodic protection. The three tanks coated in black, designated E-610, E-611, and E-619, were placed parallel to each other four feet below ground level. After being surrounded by a one-foot layer of sand underneath and a two-foot layer of ground fill on top, they were completely enclosed inside a concrete shell, except for the openings of the tanks at the top. These precautionary measures were taken because of the soil condition and the high water table. (Details of the design of various pipe connections and specifications are shown in Figure 2-2 and in Appendix A-9 respectively.)

These storage tanks were similar in design and materials to the MIC tanks used by UCC at the Institute (West Virginia) plant, which were located above ground from 1966 through1978. (In 1978, Institute upgraded to newer 30,000-gallon MIC storage tanks which had a different design and were placed underground.)

MIC STORAGE TANK

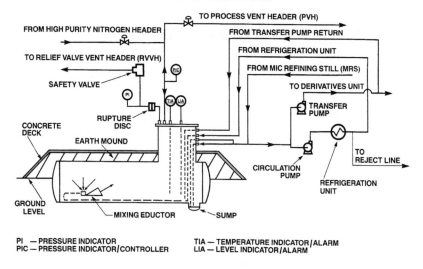

PI — PRESSURE INDICATOR
PIC — PRESSURE INDICATOR/CONTROLLER

TIA — TEMPERATURE INDICATOR/ALARM
LIA — LEVEL INDICATOR/ALARM

Figure 2-2. Description of MIC storage tank E-610 with the associated piping-connections with valves and gauges

Source: UCC Bhopal MIC Incident Report, March, 1985.

The refined MIC produced at the Bhopal plant was to be stored in tanks E-610 and E-611. The third tank, E-619, was provided for temporary storage of off-specification (impure) material or in case of an emergency. The forty-page safety manual – *Methyl Isocyante (F-41443A-7/76)* – lists detailed instructions about the various fittings and the proper use and maintenance of the storage tanks, clean-up procedures and other emergencies. This manual, originally developed by UCC for the first MIC plant at the Institute was later adapted by UCIL engineers for the Bhopal plant. Some of the relevant instructions listed in the safety manual are indicated below:

1. For safety reasons, size the tanks twice the volume required for storage. Use the added volume, in an emergency, for space to add inert diluent as a heat sink; addition of a diluent will not stop a reaction but will provide more time to control the problem. As an alternative, keep an empty tank available at all times. If the methyl isocyanate tank becomes contaminated or fails, transfer part or all the contents to the empty standby tank [E-619]...

2. Maintain an atmosphere of dry nitrogen, under slight pressure, in the vapor space of the storage tank...

3. Maintain tank's temperature below 15°C (59°F) and preferably at about 0°C (32°F). Equip a storage tank with dual temperature indicators that will sound an alarm and flash warning lights if the temperature of the stored material rises abnormally. Inspect the vent valve and safety valve on a regular schedule. Clean them if they are clogged with solids that could prevent proper operation of the vent system and emergency pressure relief system...

4. Use stainless steel for piping and valves. Seal threaded joints with fluorocarbon resin tape. Use spiral-wound gaskets made of fluorocarbon resin and stainless steel. Install relief valves on lines that can be valve closed at both ends...

5. Use fluorocarbon resin-lined (e.g. "Teflon" or "Kel-F") or flexible stainless steel hoses.

6. Do not use polyethylene or any plastic or plastic-lined hose, other than those based on fluorocarbon resin. Do not use quick disconnect fittings...

7. Keep the storage system and transfer lines free of contaminants. Handle only methyl isocyanate or dry nitrogen in the equipment. Install check valves or other devices to prevent back-flow of other materials into the methyl isocyanate system.

The Bhopal plant had met all the standards set by the Indian Standards Institution, the Factories Act of 1948 of the State of Madhya Pradesh, and Madhya Pradesh Factories Rules. It also complied with the Electrical Standard Guide of the National Electrical Code, the Fire Protection Manual of the Bombay Regional Councils, Indian Explosives Act, and the Environmental Protection and Pollution Abatement regulations.[69]

---

[69] Response by the defendant to Interrogatory No.17 by the plaintiff. U.S. District Court.

Personnel Training in USA and Start-up of MIC Plant

Along with the Design Transfer Agreement, another complementary document – the Technical Services Agreement – was also purchased by UCIL from UCC. Among the conditions stipulated in the second document, UCC was to provide training to UCIL scientists and engineers in the technologies associated with the construction and management of the MIC plant. The Government of India approved the foreign collaboration agreement for a period of five years, starting from the date of the signing or from the date of commencement of commercial production of MIC, provided it commenced within three years of the signing.[70] The two companies agreed that this training period would last from October 1977 to September 1982.[71] During 1978-1979, with the approval of the central government, over forty employees selected by UCIL, all Indian nationals, were sent to the U.S to receive training from UCC engineers and scientists at the Institute Plant and at the UCC Technical Center in South Charleston, West Virginia. The training was conducted under the general supervision of Warren J. Woomer, production manager, UCC Agricultural Products Division at Institute, and was deemed necessary so that UCIL personnel would be able to effectively operate the new MIC plant in Bhopal. These operations included routine plant maintenance, safety measures, industrial

---

[70] Affidavit of K. Subramanian, Joint Secretary, Ministry of Law and Justice, Union of India, deposited in the U.S. District Court, November 22, 1985, p. 12.

[71] Letter dated September 30, 1982, by S. Kumaraswami of UCIL to Secretariat for Industrial Approvals, Foreign Collaboration Section, Department of Industrial Development.

hygiene, fire and rescue operations, and other aspects necessary to run a sophisticated chemical plant.[72]

During their training period in the United States, the trainees were allowed to freely peruse UCC's internal memos, reports, operation and safety manuals, and review the relevant literature on MIC. They made copies of the safety manuals, operating and maintenance procedures, and chemical literature on properties and hazards of chemicals to be handled and produced at the Bhopal plant. Selected trainees also visited the vendors of materials and supplies to become more familiar with their use and maintenance. Others worked closely with UCC's technicians in fabrication, welding, and maintenance. On returning to Bhopal they used these resources and rewrote their own manuals and operating procedures.[73] C.R. Iyer, P.M. Pai, S. Khanna, V.K. Behl, and V.N. Agarwal wrote the MIC Job Safety Analysis Manual, which analyzed various segments of the MIC unit for potential hazards and risks with suggestions for preventive measures. K.D. Ballal reviewed the manual. Together, these individuals comprised

---

[72] Among those who initially received training at the UCC facilities in U.S.A. in various operational programs were: K.D. Ballal, Production Manager; C.R. Iyer, Plant Superintendent; and Satish Khanna, Engineer, in Production, Safety, and Maintenance of the MIC/Phosgene Unit; B.S. Rajpurohit, Safety Director; and P.M. Pai, in Safety, Medical, Industrial Hygiene, Fire and Rescue Equipment Test Inspection; K.S. Sivasankaran, Production Manager, in General Overview of Production and Formulations; D.N. Chakravarty, Works Manager, in General Overview of Operations, Formulations, Safety and R&D; G.M. Pillai, Assistant Works Manager, in Maintenance Operations; M. Kadirvelu, Instruments Engineer, in Instrument Selection and Maintenance; N.T. Parakh, Production Manager; T. Dutta, V. K. Behl, and N.C. Agnihortri, Production Assistants, in Operation Maintenance, Safety and Laboratory; S.P. Kochar, S.C. Bhandula, and R.G. Balchandani, Maintenance Engineers, in Maintenance Systems and Methods; S.P. Choudhary and Mr. A. Venugopal, Production Assistants, in Operations and Maintenance, Safety and Laboratory; Dr. K.R. Rajanarayaran, in Medical Planning, Safety and Health Toxicology, and Rescue Squad. Medical Planning, Safety and Health Toxicology, and Rescue Squad.

[73] Deposition by W.J. Woomer and K. Kamdar, at the U.S. District Court, in response to Interrogatories Nos. 11-13, by the Plaintiff attorneys representing the Union of India. R. Kapoor and J. Banerjee wrote the UCIL Agricultural Products Division (APD) General Operating Manual for the Bhopal Facility. V.K. Behl, S.P. Choudhary, V.N. Agarwal and S. Khanna wrote the MIC operating procedures Manual in 1979.

the nucleus of expertise at UCIL's Bhopal facility and were expected to train and pass this knowledge and experience on to others at the plant.

With the help of these individuals and hundreds of other UCIL plant employees, as well as assistance from UCC's consulting team of eight engineers, UCIL successfully commissioned the MIC plant on February 5, 1980. This yearlong commissioning process entailed a thorough check-up to ensure the integrity and fittings for each piece of equipment, including instrumentation, reactors, and valves, and to confirm that the carbon monoxide, phosgene, and MIC manufacturing units worked as expected. This confirmation was done by carrying out a wet-run (also called "shake-down") using suitable and innocuous liquid material to ensure that the manufacturing unit was ready for production. V.K. Behl and S. Khanna, who had earlier received training at the Institute plant, wrote the MIC/ Phosgene Commissioning Manual used for the commissioning process. During the commissioning, Stauffer Chemical Corporation also provided a consultant for a period of five months to assist in the final testing of the carbon monoxide (CO) unit, due to the fact that the CO technology was acquired from them. The UCC startup team of consultants returned to the United States once the plant was up and running.[74]

The MIC Plant Becomes Operational

On February 5, 1980, UCIL started full production of MIC at the Bhopal facility, the only other plant outside the United States to produce MIC utilizing UCC technology. The occasion was celebrated with visiting Union Carbide dignitaries from across its international corporate structure. These included Richard J. Hughes, senior vice-president, UCC; Robert Olford, president, Agricultural Products Company (UCAPCO), a wholly owned

---

[74] UCC's response to Plaintiff's First Combined Set of Interrogatories and Requests for Admissions, MDL Docket No. 626, Misc. No. 21-38 (JFK) All Cases, Interrogatory No. 15, dated 8-22-1985, p. 44. . The team included Larry A. Mulder, MIC Lead Engineer (July 1979 – July 1980); William McVeagh, Process Design Engineer and MIC Production Engineer (November 1979 – May 1980); Richard Faber, Instrument Engineer (Oct. 1979 – Jan. 1980); Jack Turner, Maintenance Specialist (Oct. 1979 – Mar. 1980); T. Jack Bishop, MIC Production Specialist (Sept. 1979 – March 1980); Tom Bonham, MIC Production Specialist (Sept. 1979 – March 1980) and Warren Linkenhoker, MIC Production Specialist (Sept. 1979 – March 1980). Warren J. Woomer was the U.S. Startup Team Leader and visited Bhopal in July 16, 1979 to July 27, 1979 and again from Jan.13, 1980 to Feb. 9, 1980.

division of UCC; and James B. Law, chairman of Union Carbide Eastern (UCE), accompanied by Dr. William R. Correa, managing director, UCIL and R. Natarajan, vice president of UCE.[75]

The plant complex on the eighty-plus acre site was built at a cost of $30 million and consisted of seven functional units and supporting departments. The functional units included: (1) Carbon Monoxide Unit, (2) Phosgene/MIC Unit, (3) Alpha-naphthol Unit, (4) Carbamoylation Unit, (5) Aldicarb Unit, (6) Formulations Unit, and (7) Utilities. (See figure B for the layout of the plant complex.) A number of these units were interconnected with many miles of intricate piping, reactors, pressure vessels, heat exchangers, and other equipment. Several service departments such as Quality Control, Industrial Relations, Maintenance, Purchasing and Stores, and Work Office were also established to support these units. During its peak years from 1980-82, the plant's total work force exceeded one thousand employees. Of this total, 63 worked in the Carbon Monoxide and Phosgene/MIC units, while another 171 worked in Maintenance. Quality Control was responsible for developing and providing all the special analyses to ensure the integrity of the chemical intermediates and products. With the commissioning of the MIC plant in 1980, UCIL was finally in a position to produce Carbaryl in India without having to import any raw materials or intermediates.

Because of his extensive experience as UCC's principal engineer and production manager for MIC production at the Institute plant and in training UCIL personnel, Warren J. Woomer was appointed as the works manager of the Bhopal MIC plant and was officially on the UCIL payroll as of May 2, 1980.

As required by FERA (1973) regulations, Woomer's appointment required approval from the Indian government. As the first works manager of the MIC plant, the job description was basically drawn up by him based on his experience at the Institute MIC plant, tailored for the Bhopal plant, and it was to serve as a model for succeeding managers. The job description required the works manager to:

---

[75]   R. Olford, formerly with UCC Linde Division, succeeded E.A Munoz as President of UCAPCO; W.R. Correa, Ph.D. Chem. Eng., Appointed as the first Indian Managing Director of UCIL in 1977. He joined UCIL in 1952; R. Natarajan, Vice-President of UCE, responsible for overseeing UCC's interest in UCIL and providing advice and assistance to UCIL.

1. Safely operate the carbon monoxide, phosgene and MIC facilities and to produce the required amounts of SEVIN insecticide in a timely fashion.
2. Maintain a suitably trained workforce for safe, efficient and cost-effective operation of the facility consistent with UCIL's safety standards and requirements.
3. Ensure adequate raw materials contracts and suppliers and utility supplies; minimize the use of imported materials and supplies, consistent with safe standards and government of India policies.[76]

The works manager reported to the general works manager, who had the overall responsibility for the Bhopal facility and approximately one thousand employees working at the seven operating units and various supporting departments. The departmental managers in charge of accounts, personnel, industrial engineering, training and safety, and industrial relations also reported directly to the general works manager, who in turn reported to the vice president, general manager, Agricultural Products Division based in Bombay. Besides overseeing the operations of the manufacturing units at the plant, the UCIL Bhopal general works manager also prepared the UCIL Bhopal plant budget which was then reviewed by the vice president and general manager of UCIL's Agricultural Products Division.[77]

---

[76] Personal communication with W. Woomer.
[77] UCC's response to plaintiff's first combined set of interrogatories and requests for admissions. (Interrogatory No. 7.)

Figure 2-3. Organizational Chart of UCIL Agricultural Products Division

Woomer soon realized that, despite his familiarity with MIC production, he was in a totally different work environment. Because of past management practices at the alpha-naphthol and other earlier built units, workers had developed defensive tactics when reprimanded, and did not report minor incidents, or would alter plant records to conceal the cause of an incident. The plant managers then introduced a policy that required the plant operators to record all readings and logs in triplicate carbon copies. The copies were stored in separate locked boxes at different locations. Working closely with the staff, Woomer also tried to instill a greater sense of safety consciousness at the workplace based on knowledge and personal responsibility without fear of reprisals. First-time minor safety infractions and lost-work hours were dealt with fairly but firmly and all safety-related incidents were properly documented and action plans developed to minimize similar incidents in the future.[78]

On completing the initial two-year contract (May 1980 to July 1982), and a six-month contract extension, Woomer returned to the United States in December 1982 to resume his previous post at Institute, West Virginia. UCIL's request to the Government of India for an extension by another year was denied.

Jagannathan (Jay) Mukund was then appointed the new works manager. An Indian national and an engineer educated at Cambridge Univer

---

[78] Woomer personal communication.

sity and Massachusetts Institute of Technology, he had previously been the works manager at CHEMCO (Chemical and Plastics Division of UCIL), located in Trombay, near Mumbai. Later, for personal reasons,[79] he sought employment with UCC and was based at Institute, West Virginia from 1979 to 1982. During his stay in the United States, Mukund also visited the various UCC manufacturing facilities to get familiar with every aspect of the MIC, phosgene and related plants so as to be able to assume his new responsibilities at Bhopal.[80] While in the U.S., Mukund also visited UCC's plant at Woodbine, Georgia, where he familiarized himself with the Carbaryl formulation and other production units. He also spent time at UCC's Technical Research Center in South Charleston, West Virginia, and visited several UCC contractors and vendors. Given this background, Mukund entered his new job as works manager of the Bhopal plant with the appropriate technical qualifications and experience. He held this position until the plant was closed in 1985.

Plant Construction Spawns Shantytowns

The tracts of land leased from the state government for the Bhopal plant, just outside the city limits, were undeveloped agricultural fields in an area zoned for industrial use with limited access by road. The inhabitants were mostly illiterate daily laborers who came from the poorer classes. A large percentage of the men were employed as construction workers, casual workers in stone quarries, sweepers, porters, rickshaw drivers, and cobblers, while some of the women worked as maids or in other menial jobs. By the late 1970s, about a dozen shantytowns had mushroomed in the vicinity of the plant. What started out as a temporary living space for the laborers during the construction of the plant turned into *de facto* permanent residential areas. According to one estimate, by the end of 1984, the slum dwellers numbered as many two hundred thousand in the old section of Bhopal. Many were out of work or recovering from a fifteen-day curfew imposed on Bhopal following the assassination of Indira Gandhi, the prime minister of India, on October 31, 1984.[81] These new residents were also entitled to vote, and any attempt by elected officials or politi-

---

[79] UCIL had made a special request of UCC to employ Jay Mukund in USA because of his need to be closer to a family member with a serious medical condition requiring treatment at an U.S. hospital. Woomer Affidavit, p. 31

[80] See deposition by W. Woomer, U.S. District Court, p. 73.

[81] "Gas-struck hit by joblessness," *The Statesman,* February 6, 1985, p. 6.

cians to displace the now entrenched migrants would have been political suicide. And yet, with such large populations living in an industrial zone, the city and UCIL authorities were faced with a challenging dilemma for which there was no easy solution. With 1984 being an election year, the state government actually exacerbated the problem by granting official land leases to all shantytown residents for the patches of land on which they lived. Additionally, they were promised piped water and electricity in the near future. Instead of looking to remedy this potential safety hazard, the government decided to support and legalize the shantytowns for valuable votes.

As early as 1970, realizing the potential danger of the expanding slums, UCIL made an offer of Rs. 25,000 to the Bhopal Municipal Corporation to develop a "green belt" park around the plant, but the authorities took no action.[82] This issue was also raised in the state legislature, with no results. Two years before the tragedy, during a Question and Answer Session in the State Assembly, a member of the Legislative Assembly specifically raised the issue of safety at the plant. Responding to a demand to move the factory the then Labor Minister Tarasingh Viyogi said; "There is no danger from the poisonous gases used in the plant. Safety arrangements are foolproof...It is a Rs. 25 crore investment. It is not a small stone which can be picked from one place and put at another."[83]

In his analysis of the Bhopal gas leak, Trevor Kletz has aptly concluded:

> The death toll at Bhopal would have been much smaller if a shanty town had not been allowed to grow up near the plant. In many countries' planning, controls prevent such developments, but not apparently in India...it is much more difficult to prevent the growth of shantytowns than of permanent dwellings.[84]

The fact that the MIC plant was built outside the city limits and on the site designated by the state government, attracting thousands to the vicinity for jobs, is also supported by other reports:

---

[82] "A Gas Tragedy in Bhopal," *Asian Recorder,* January 15-21, 1985, p. 18129.

[83] Ibid. See also *India Today,* December 31, 1984, p. 11.

[84] Trevor, Kletz, *Learning from Accidents,* Butterworth-Heinemann, Oxford: 1994, pp. 96-98.

There is certain inevitability to such creeping urbanisation. Factories provide jobs, and workers prefer to live near their source of work. It was only in May this year that a large number of the unauthorised tenements were regularised by the Arjun Singh Government.

The real failure of urban policy in Bhopal is reflected in the Bhopal Development Plan, better known as the Master Plan for 1975-1991. The plan lists "obnoxious industries" insecticides among them and says that all such industries must be located on the northeastern side of the city. Union Carbide was, indeed, in the correct part of the city but the plan assigned all the areas around it to commercial premises and residential accommodation.[85]

The showpiece UCIL factory and other industries that set up shop in Bhopal surely contributed to the staggering rise in population from 350,000 in 1969 to 700,000 in 1981 to over 800,000 in 1984.[86]

UCIL's Pesticide Business Begins to Falter

By 1984, UCIL's business had expanded to five divisions – Agricultural Products Division, Battery Products Division, Carbon, Metals and Gases Division, Chemicals and Plastics Division and Marine Products Division – with a combined total of fourteen plants, fifty warehouses, and nineteen sales offices spread across India. With a work force of over nine thousand Indian employees, the company produced a diverse array of products, including dry cell batteries, flashlights, industrial carbon electrodes, cinema arc carbons, electrolytic manganese dioxide, photo engraving plates, chemicals, and polyethylene plastics. Union Carbide's strength in India still focused on its dry cell Eveready® batteries, which accounted for approximately 50 percent of total sales of Rs. 185,42.14 lakhs ($185.5 million) in 1981. While total company sales of pesticides that same year was much smaller at Rs. 22.13.59 lakhs ($22 million), this figure nevertheless represented a 78 percent increase over the previous year. Shrimp exports from the Marine Products Division also greatly helped the company to maintain a favorable foreign exchange balance in 1981.[87]

---

[85]   *India Today,* December 31, 1984, p. 23.

[86]   B. Bowonder, Jeanne X. Kasperson, and Roger E. Kasperson, "Avoiding Future Bhopals," *Environment,* vol. 27, No. 7, 1985, p. 7.

[87]   See Appendix C-2 for a listing of UCIL's Operating Divisions and Products.

In addition to its pesticide manufacturing plant, in 1975 UCIL also built a modern Research and Development Technical Center at Shamla Hills[88] overlooking Bhopal's Upper Lake, on the site of the original Jehan Numa Palace.[89] The once beautiful palace, built by General Obaidullah Khan in the early part of the twentieth century, was bought by UCIL and razed to erect the modern concrete and glass building. The "Baradari" – an ornate pavilion (see the photograph and glossary) – is the only remaining relic of the former palace grounds. This research facility, fully-equipped with a research-oriented library and state-of-the-art instrumentation, was considered as "a base for Carbide research for the entire South East Asia Region."[90] Over fifty chemists and biologists, headed by Dr. B.P. Srivastava, were engaged in the chemical synthesis and biological screening of novel molecules. Biological testing facilities also located at the eleven-acre site consisted of three greenhouses, five insect-rearing laboratories, and an experimental farm. These unique facilities were considered to be the most sophisticated of their kind in India. Novel techniques were developed in these laboratories for rearing insects for testing purposes. UCIL scientists also served on several government pesticides committees and were associated with many agricultural universities and research institutions throughout the country.[91] The management had grand plans for discovering and registering new pesticides for rice and other crops of economic importance in India and for export to other countries in the region. Following the plant's disaster, these promising plans were abruptly discontinued and the last UCIL research conducted at the technical center turned out to be the preliminary chemical analyses of the tank residues from the plant's "black box." The building was subsequently taken over by government authorities and all UCIL research programs disbanded.

In spite of this impressive network of manufacturing and research infrastructure, several unforeseen technical and marketing problems began

---

[88] The Technical Center which cost Rs. 2 crore (about $3 million) was inaugurated on January 24, 1976.

[89] The palace and the surrounding land was sold for about Rs. 5 lakhs ($100,000). The nearby 12-room office-cum-stables "DAS NUMBER," facility, which also belonged to General Obaidullah, the second son of Sultan Jehan Begum and brother of Nawab Hamidullah Khan, was later expanded and re-named Jehan Numa Palace Hotel. (Information provided by Sonia Jamal, a family member of the nawab's descendants).

[90] *HEXAGON*, a UCIL publication, January-March 1980.

[91] Ibid.

the decline of UCIL's agricultural chemical enterprise. A major technical problem revolved around the efficient production of alpha-naphthol, the intermediate required to produce Carbaryl.

As early as 1970, UCIL management had realized that the Indian government's projected domestic tonnage requirements for Carbaryl (5,900 MT annually by 1974) was overly optimistic and notified the central government that it wanted to change the nature and the scope of the project. In a letter to the Ministry of Petroleum Chemicals, Mines and Metals dated July 2, 1970, UCIL informed the government that "production of high-grade alpha-naphthol at a reasonable cost" was very complicated and would require expensive equipment, particularly in the recovery and purification steps. The long-term concern was that:

> ...within the present state of the art and in view of the uncertain long-term usefulness of this intermediate, erection of the alpha-naphthol facilities in India would amount to wasting of foreign exchange resources of the Country and the capital of the Company. Again, our feeling is that the best interests of the Country and the Company will be served by accelerating the replacement of Sevin by newer, non-naphthol based pesticides through our internal research and development efforts.[92]

The Ministry did not heed UCIL's concern, however, as they considered the company's proposal in the context of India's primary need to increase food production, growing import requirements for the industrial sector, and the unfavorable foreign exchange situation. This imbalance in foreign currency was further aggravated,

> ...when the oil prices quadrupled, from $2.69 in the middle of 1973 to $11.65 a barrel in early 1974. Its direct impact was a massive escalation in the foreign exchange expenditure on oil imports which, in turn, imposed severe pressure on the balance of payments. The import bill on account of fertilizers and other oil-based chemicals also rose by substantial amounts.... Successive shortfalls in agricultural production during the early 1970s – a fundamental factor underlying the current economic crisis in India – meant that large quantities of food grains, constituted mostly of wheat, had to be imported.[93]

---

[92] Letter by E.A. Munoz of UCIL to the Ministry of Petroleum, Chemicals, Mines and Metals, July 2, 1970. (See Appendix A-10.)

[93] Deepak Nayyer, *India's Exports and Export Policies in the 1960's,* Cambridge University Press, 1976, pp. 371-372.

Given this context, improving India's foreign exchange reserves and the increase of food production weighed heavily in the federal government's plan. As a result, UCIL's proposal to modify the nature of the project was rejected, and the Ministry insisted on the local manufacturing of alpha-naphthol to the extent that this condition was included in the company's industrial license for the Bhopal plant. This example not only confirms the level of involvement the government had in UCIL's operations, but reinforces the concept that its rigid interpretation of India's national interests directly impeded UCIL's efforts to base its strategic plans on realistic assumptions. Even though UCIL reiterated these concerns in 1982 to the government ministry after they had begun experiencing production problems with their alpha-naphthol plant, it was too late to do anything about it – capital had already been invested in the plant.

The manufacturing process technology for alpha-naphthol was not included in the 1973 Design Transfer Agreement as UCIL had opted to develop a more economical process indigenously. While the initial small-scale experiments carried out at Trombay appeared promising, UCIL never succeeded in making this process commercially viable in the scaled-up plant. This strategic miscalculation was only realized after the company had constructed the alpha-naphthol plant at the Bhopal site.

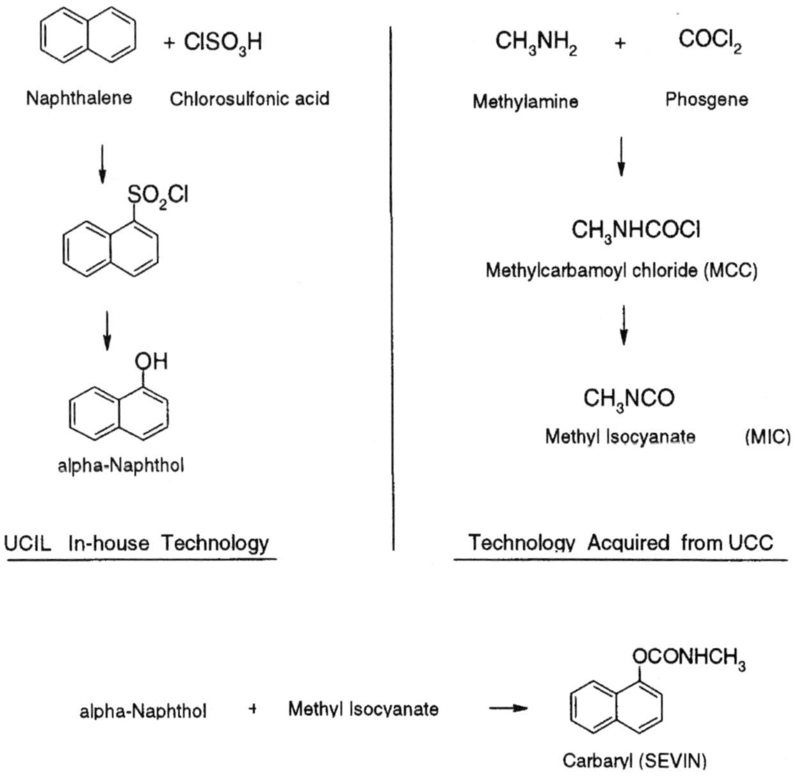

Figure 2-4. The manufacturing process for alpha-naphthol,
MIC, and Carbaryl used by UCIL

There are two known processes for the manufacture of alpha-naphthol from naphthalene. The older, well-known sulfonation method adopted by UCIL (Figure 2-4) is a two-step process that also produces an undesirable and toxic side-product beta-naphthol (wherein the OH group is attached on the adjacent carbon of naphthalene). To maximize the yield of the desired product requires a very delicate balance of the reaction conditions. A newer, three-step tetralone process, developed by UCC in the 1960s produced a purer grade of alpha-naphthol, but at a much higher cost. UCC specifically developed the tetralone process to minimize the formation of the undesirable beta-naphthol and thus be in compliance with U.S. government regulations.

In the early 1970s UCIL scientists had successfully demonstrated the feasibility of producing high grade alpha-naphthol by the sulfonation route at their pilot plant in Trombay and were confident that it could be utilized as a manufacturing process. This initial success prompted the UCIL management to opt against the costlier tetralone process as being uneconomical for the projected markets in India and the Asian region.

Unfortunately, it was only after completing the construction of its alpha-naphthol plant at Bhopal in 1978 that UCIL realized the difficulty of replicating the promising results of the pilot plant on a larger scale. From the very start, three main problems arose. First, UCIL engineers were unable to control the ratio of alpha-naphthol/beta-naphthol formation in favor of the desired alpha type. Second, they were unable to purify this mixture in an efficient manner and isolate the desired product. Finally, they were unable to control metal corrosion in the reactor due to the use of strong caustic solutions at high temperatures. (These problems are normally manageable when carried out on a smaller scale.)

Despite the best efforts of top researchers at UCIL's Shamla Hills Technical Center, as well as technical assistance provided by UCC scientists and engineers, these problems persisted. After spending almost Rs. 37 million ($2.5 million) attempting to resolve these problems, UCIL finally suspended operations at the alpha-naphthol plant in mid-1982, and was forced to explain these problems in a detailed report to the Ministry of Petroleum and Chemicals.[94] The closure of the trouble-stricken alpha-naphthol plant forced UCIL to begin reducing its work force through layoffs, incentives with severance pay, and transfers to other units within the plant complex and other divisions. The consequences of these actions were lowered staff morale and an increasing loss of experienced and qualified workers.

Failure to develop an in-house commercial process to produce this key intermediate compound was a major setback to UCIL's effort to produce Carbaryl. As a result, UCIL was left with little choice but to resume imports of alpha-naphthol from UCC. While the Government of India reluctantly reapproved such imports, the hard currency required to purchase it would contribute to a worsening of UCIL's financial position. The foreign exchange required for the import of alpha-naphthol was in part paid from the earnings from UCIL's Marine Products Division. This export-oriented division, which was formed in 1971, relied on a fleet of shrimp trawlers to harvest, freeze, and transport shrimp from the Bay of Bengal. From 1971

---

[94] Letter from S. Kumaraswami of UCIL to Aghoramurthy, Adviser, Dept. of Chemicals & Fertilizers, Government of India, December 10, 1982. (see Appendix A-17.)

to 1979, the reported earnings from this division increased from Rs.8 lakhs ($107,000) to Rs.451 lakhs ($5.5 million).

The centrality of the alpha-naphthol dilemma to UCIL's financial problems is best summarized by Shyamal Ghosh, a high-ranking official in the Ministry of Industry of the central government:

> UCIL was unable to establish manufacture of pesticide within the allotted two-year period.... Accordingly, UCIL sought and obtained extensions of industrial license agreement through October 31, 1978, through June 30, 1980, through March 31, 1981.
>
> The principal difficulty which UCIL reported which required continued requests for extension of the license was the inability to indigenously manufacture alpha-naphthol of the required specifications. Accordingly, during this entire period, while the production of pesticides was in progress, UCIL had been importing alpha-naphthol.
>
> The original foreign collaboration agreements were by their terms, to expire in September 1982. On September 30, 1982, UCIL submitted an application for renewal of the foreign collaboration agreement with UCC, for a period of seven years...
>
> The extension of the foreign collaboration agreement was approved by the Government of India to be valid for a period up to January 1, 1985, with minor modifications of the proposal.[95]

In essence, the government gave UCIL a strict time limitation for its partnership with UCC, despite the many delays and problems associated with the manufacture of alpha-naphthol. As described later in this chapter, UCIL was unable to accomplish its business objectives by January 1, 1985, at which point UCC's involvement was mandated to end by the government. The MIC gas leak occurred less than one month prior to this deadline. Although there were several minor accidents and two worker deaths reported during the previous years, there had never been a leak from the MIC storage tanks.

---

[95] Sworn Affidavit of Shyamal Ghosh – Joint Secretary, Department of Chemicals and Fertilizers, Ministry of Industry, Government of India, Filed in U.S. District Court, S. D. of N.Y., Dec. 6, 1985.

The History of Accidents at the Bhopal Plant

Documents since submitted to the District Court in New York record a total of six safety incidents prior to the December 1984 disaster. This number is in agreement with Chief Minister Arjun Singh's comments after the Bhopal disaster that six accidents were reported since 1978 in the Union Carbide factory in Bhopal.[96]

In 1978, fire caused extensive property damage in the storage area. There was one fatal accident in 1981, and four accidents in 1982. All the accidents were reported to the state government. UCIL management and the government officials investigated all cases reported, and recommendations to prevent similar accidents were duly recorded. There was also one fatality not included in the court documents, which occurred in 1975, before the MIC plant was built.

On November 24, 1978, during a welding operation, naphthalene, a raw material used to produce alpha-naphthol stored in the Coal Storage adjacent to the Carbon Monoxide Unit (see Figure B), caught fire from a flying spark. The welder apparently carried out the operation while standing on the top of the naphthalene bags. This was a serious safety violation by the supervisor, who did not notify the welder of the presence of flammable material in the bags. City firefighters along with those from the airport and BHEL (Bharat Heavy Electrical Ltd.) assisted in extinguishing the raging fire. No one was injured, but the property damage was estimated to be 6.2 million rupees ($730,000). The state government inspectors reviewed the incident and, in a letter of December 13, 1978, instructed UCIL to eliminate all ignition sources from the vicinity of the raw material.[97]

The first serious accident resulting in a fatality occurred three years later, on December 24, 1981. This incident received wide publicity and raised serious concerns in the community about the safety of the plant. The official notification about the accident, handwritten that same day by UCIL's manager of industrial relations to Bhopal's deputy director of industrial health and safety, gave the following description:

> We wish to inform you about an accident which occurred today (24/12/81) at about 6:30 am in our MIC unit. Three persons were involved in the accident, i.e.

---

[96] *Asian Recorder,* January 15-21, 1985, p. 18128.

[97] Court Document No. 10115259.

1. Mr. Kalyan Roy - Supervisor.

2. Mr. Ashraf Mohd. Khan - T. No. 4029

3..Mr. R.P. Bajpai - T. No. 4024

The incident occurred when the above crew was working on the phosgene line. While removing one of the flanges, all of a sudden liquid phosgene spurted and splashed all over. The above-mentioned persons were immediately given First Aid in our Dispensary. Soon after they were rushed to Hamidia Hospital for further medical treatment. One of the persons (Mr. Ashraf Mohd. Khan) is said to be in serious situation and is admitted in the Intensive Care Unit. Phosgene is a toxic gas and is used as a raw material in the manufacture of MIC.[98]

Woomer was the works manager at Bhopal at the time and the case was thoroughly investigated and documented.[99,100] According to Woomer's sworn testimony, two maintenance pipe fitters were asked to take out slip blinds (no-leak metal insertions in the pipeline) in the MIC/phosgene unit, in order to put the equipment back in service. Because residual phosgene vapors are usually present in the piping system, the workers were instructed to take the appropriate precautionary measures. According to *The New York Times* report, Ashraf was illiterate.[101] In the early hours of the morning, the two workers protected with gloves, hard hats, and air-masks connected to a fresh air-supply source worked on different jobs just a few feet apart. Upon opening the flanges of the pipes, a small amount of liquid phosgene spurted out of the pipe and fell on Ashraf Khan. In a panic he removed his mask and was overcome by the toxic phosgene vapors. He was soon carried to the safety shower and then to the dispensary at the plant premises. Later he was transferred to the nearby Hamidia Hospital, where he died the following evening as a result of phosgene exposure.

The factory inspector of the State of Madhya Pradesh visited the plant on December 28, 30, and 31, 1981 to investigate the cause of the accident. To reduce further risk, he instructed that each pipe worker "first remove

---

[98] Court Document No. 10115352.

[99] Woomer, Court deposition, pp. 364-365.

[100] Accident Report by F.O. Sullivan to Dr. W.R. Correa, dated January 18, 1982. See also Court Documents Nos. 10101168–10101170.

[101] Robert Reinhold, "Disaster in Bhopal: Where Does Blame Lie?" *New York Times,* January 25, 1985.

the bolt away from him and only then the bolts on his side" and that each worker be properly instructed in the use of breathing equipment. He ordered a formal inquiry to follow his initial review. The Central Labor Institute in Bombay, operated by the central government, also sent an investigator. According to the director of the institute, their official concluded that "the plant's safety equipment was of international standards and that the plant posed no significant problem."[102] At the request of Khan's brother, an inquiry was also undertaken by the state Agriculture Department, which reached a similar conclusion.[103] The victim's family received a compensation of 70,000 rupees (then approx. $8,640). The employee was also covered by the Employees State Insurance Corporation pension plan.[104]

Before the agitation surrounding Khan's death had abated, another incident also involving phosgene occurred on February 10, 1982. In the course of operating the unit between 2:00-3:00 a.m., a leak developed in a rotating seal of the pump used to transfer phosgene through the pipe. The workers donned protective gear and sprayed the area by turning on the water sprinkler. The toxic vapors were contained within the plant premises. About twenty-five employees were exposed and suffered respiratory distress and excessive tearing. While some employees were able to receive treatment at the UCIL dispensary on site, sixteen others were admitted to Hamidia hospital. All were released at varying times over the next five days. The state factory inspector visited the plant on the day of the accident, and the chief inspector of factories came five days later. The accident was also thoroughly investigated by the plant management. The cause was attributed to the maintenance workers using a ceramic seal in place of the recommended metal seal. It was also recommended that the seals be tested and maintained regularly.[105]

On the same day of the second incident, the state government appointed Dr. S. Siddique, professor of chemistry at Motilal Vigyan Mahavidyalaya College, Bhopal, to investigate Ashraf's death, the February 10 incident, as well as the safety practices and lapses at the factory. He submitted his report two years later and concluded that "the worker died from his own mistake but also there was poor coordination between the production and the maintenance staff, which allowed him to open a pipe

---

[102] Ibid
[103] Ibid.
[104] From Court Document No. 10115260.
[105] From Court Document No. 10115261.

that was not cleared of deadly poison."[106] The report was not made public and nothing further was heard about this investigation until after the 1984 tragedy when the press reported that:

> Siddique submitted his report on March 5, 1984, but nobody acted on it. Two officials have been suspended for not forwarding the Siddique report for a full seven months.

> The then deputy secretary V.K. Pachor, and under-secretary R.S. Tholia, found guilty of the same crime, are facing departmental inquiry. The services of Pachor, employed after his retirement by the Madhya Pradesh Agricultural Board, has been terminated.

> Labour Secretary Arun Kumar and Special Secretary H. Mishra have been asked to go on leave pending a decision. Both men came to know of the Siddique report in October 1984 but took no follow-up action. The axe also fell on C.P. Tyagi, chief inspector of factories, who was accused of having renewed the Carbide factory license annually without considering earlier safety lapses.[107]

On April 22, 1982, three electricians sustained minor burn injuries due to a short circuit in the electrical panel when a screwdriver fell from the hands of a worker. The factory inspector visited the plant the same day and after investigation along with the management, recommended that all electrical connections in the control panel be better insulated and that electricians should be more vigilant in the future.[108]

On October 6, 1982 a mixture of chloroform, MIC, and hydrochloric acid leaked from a loose-fitting valve when this mixture was being piped to the pyrolyzer – a unit that converts the precursor intermediate to MIC. Three employees, Agrawal (supervisor), Wandekar (operator) and Salim (helper) suffered burn injuries; and fifteen others suffered temporary eye irritation and returned to work after rinsing their eyes with water. The three more seriously affected employees were treated at the plant's dispensary and released after four hours. After discovering several breaches in normal operating procedures, the factory inspector recommended that information

---

[106] Robert Reinhold, *New York Times*, 1985

[107] Ramindar Singh, "The Evacuation –Tragic Farce," *India Today*, January 15, 1985. p. 103.

[108] From Court Document No. 10115262.

from the master cards (a tags with information after servicing) also be recorded in a permanent plant register. Additionally, the management should ensure that red tags are tied to the machines not to be operated, and that no unauthorized person should be permitted to work in the MIC plant.[109]

Eight days later, on October 14, 1982 there was yet another incident involving a plant worker. Sabu Khan injured his hand while attempting to manually remove wet coal from a moving conveyor belt, instead of using the iron rod provided for this purpose. The inspector visited on the following day and suggested closing the openings between the supporting structures of the conveyor belt. This was implemented immediately.[110]

These widely publicized, avoidable, and unrelated accidents were attributed to either human error or improper maintenance and poor communications. Ashraf Khan's sudden death from exposure to phosgene created great fear and panic among the plant workers and nearby residents, and for the first time there was an awareness of the potential dangers at the plant. The workers' cause was taken up by the Labor Unions, which began campaigning for safer working conditions, with rallies and public meetings in the vicinity of the plant.

As early as 1979, UCIL plant operators had organized themselves into two unions. The majority of Hindu workers joined Bharatiya Mazdoor Sang (BMS), affiliated with the national political party Bharatiya Janata Party (BJP), under the leadership of Madanlal Ranjha and R.K. Yadav. The others aligned themselves with the Indian National Trade Union Congress (INTUC), under the leadership of Hatim Jariwala, an activist in the Indian Congress (I) – Indira Gandhi's Congress Party. The two groups competed aggressively for support from the workers, each trying to outdo the other in representing the workers' grievances.

The workers blamed the management for the malfunctioning valve and for not providing Ashraf with protective PVC (polyvinylchloride) overalls. Shanker Lal Malviya, a plant worker and a member of the Indian National Trade Union Congress (INTUC), went on a fifteen-day hunger strike when a memorandum issued by the labor union to UCIL management and the state government about safety lapses at the plant failed to have any impact. The then labor secretary was said to have assured Malviya that workers would be given a "sympathetic hearing in the due course"

---

[109]   From Court Document No. 10115263.
[110]   From Court Document No. 101115264.

by the government. Instead, "the union activists were given the stick."[111] The management's response to the February 1982 union protest for a safer work environment led to termination of three workers, Sharad Shandilye, Basheerullah, and Malviya, all active union leaders, effectively silencing the voices of the workers.[112]

The accidents at the Bhopal plant were also fully aired and discussed in the state legislative assembly. During the February-April 1982 Session of the Madhya Pradesh *Vidhan Sabha*, the legislators discussed the accidents that occurred at the UCIL plant in December 1981 and February 1982. The death of Ashraf M. Khan in December 1981 was first discussed at the February 25, 1982 session of the state legislature and continued on March 3.[113]

Question: By Dr. Gaurishankar Shejwar

Is it true that one worker, Ashraf Mohd Khan died on 24/12/81 at the Union Carbide Factory at Bhopal?

Answer: By the labour minister, Shri Tarasingh Viyogi.

Yes. Accident happened on 24/12/81 and the workman died on 25/12/81.

Q: If yes, whether Ashraf died because of being exposed to phosgene?

A: Yes, as per the information received, Ashraf Khan died because of phosgene gas exposure.

Q: Total number of employees died in the factory since its inception till 31/12/81, their names and causes of death.

---

[111] Radhika Ramasheshan, "Profits against Safety," *Economic and Political Weekly,* Dec. 22-29, 1984. reproduced in *Bhopal: Industrial Genocide,* Arena Press, Hong Kong: 1985.

[112] Ibid.

[113] Madhya Pradesh Vidhan Sabha [Legislative Assembly], "Question and Answer List." At the February 25, 1982 and March 3, 1982 Sessions. (Reproduced *verbatim* except that the grouped questions and answers are separated for clearer presentation.)

A: In Union Carbide India Ltd., there had been two deaths since its inception till 31/12/81. Information on these death accidents is given below:

(i) Shaturghan Shah on 28/12/75 because of electric current,

(ii) Ashraf died on 25/12/81 due [to] phosgene exposure.

At the March 3, 1982 session, the Labor Minister Viyogi was questioned again:

Q: Shri Babulal Gaur:

Would the Labour Minister kindly tell us that (a) In Union Carbide Bhopal, between 1980 & 1981 how many workers fell sick and how many died due to the effect of polluted air and smelly insecticide powder? This should be given year-wise.

A: Not a single workman was affected in the year 1980. During 1981, we received information of eight workmen being affected. One worker died on December 25, 1981.

Q: What was the amount paid as compensation to the families of the affected workmen?

A: Payment of compensation to the heir-at-law is being processed through State Employees Insurance Corp. Carbide management has announced payment of Rs. 50,000/- to the dependents of the deceased....

Q: In Union Carbide, one worker died in 1979 [?], one in 1981 and there was a major phosgene gas leak in the factory on February 1982. What action has Government taken on this? Such plant in Indonesia was closed down due to its hazardous nature...

A: Labour minister, Tarasingh Viyogi.

I have personally visited Union Carbide factory for about two hours and found adequate safety measures in the factory....

Q: Has Ashraf's family received the Rs. 50,000/-?

A: No. Only Ashraf's wife is entitled to receive the above amount and she has refused to sign papers in this connection. There is some dispute going on in Ashraf's family in this regard....

Q: How much amount will Ashraf's family get from the Company in addition to Rs. 50,000/- ?

A: Approx. 22,000 Rupees, against Gratuity, Pension, PF [Provident Fund], Insurance.

Q: Who conducted enquiry in Ashraf's case? Whether he is competent enough?

A: Professor Siddiqui from MVM [Motilal Vigyan Mahavidyalaya] College is conducting the enquiry. He is assisted by Mr. Lambore. [sp.?] They are competent enough to handle this enquiry. However, if required, a specialist could be deputed for this purpose

Q: Does your office receive report of each and every accident?

A: Yes. Information of each and every incident reaches us within 48 hours....

Q: Do they [UCIL] have any measure to control water/air pollution?

A: Yes. They have adequate measures to control water/air pollution.

Under Indian law, the Ministry of Industry of the central government issues industrial licenses, but state governments are responsible to enforce the Factories Act with respect to workers safety and environmental affairs. The Factories Act of India's Labor Laws ensures minimum standards of safety, health and welfare conditions of factory workers. Throughout the State of Madhya Pradesh, fifteen factory inspectors monitored over eight thousand plants. The Bhopal office of the Labor Department, which had jurisdiction over the area and UCIL plant, had just two inspectors – "both mechanical engineers with little knowledge of chemical hazards."[114]

---

[114] Robert Reinhold, "Disaster in Bhopal: Where Does Blame Lie?" *The New York Times*, January 25, 1985.

Operation Safety Survey – 1982

In addition to the Dr. Siddique's ongoing investigation, UCIL also requested UCC to send inspectors for a safety audit of the Bhopal plant. This audit, the third inspection performed by UCC since the commissioning of the MIC unit in 1980, went by the code name Operation Safety Survey, which was carried out in May 1982. The audit team was comprised of three engineers: team leader John Poulson, Steve Tyson and Leonard Kail. The team's final report, entitled *Operational Safety Survey CO/MIC/SE-VIN Units (OSS)*, was issued within a month.

The deficiencies and recommendations cited in the OSS were based on interviews with the operating, maintenance, and supervisory personnel in all three units – carbon monoxide, MIC, and SEVIN – of the Bhopal plant as well as plant personnel responsible for fire protection, safety, and training. In addition, the team conducted a detailed physical inspection of the facilities, including unit storage and raw material receiving areas. At the request of the Bhopal plant management, "The focus of the survey was heavily directed towards possibilities for exposure of both maintenance and operating personnel to the wide variety of toxic materials handled or processed."

The audit report cited a number of deficiencies and potential problems with the release of toxic chemicals. A number of these were connected with the carbon monoxide, phosgene, and Carbaryl manufacturing units, particularly the possibility of over pressuring the SEVIN MIC feed tank under item 6 (see footnote).[115]

While the auditors did not consider these findings to be imminently dangerous, they did make a number of recommendations to correct the de-

---

[115] Specific deficiencies cited in the Report. 1. Lack of reliable automatic backup for cooling water on the CO [carbon monoxide] converter shells; 2. Possibilities for air entry into the flare header at the CO unit; 3. Potentials for release of toxic materials in the phosgene/MIC unit and storage areas, either due to equipment failure, operating problems, or maintenance problems; 4. Lack of fixed water spray protection in several areas of the plant; 5. Possibilities for dust explosions in the SEVIN area; 6. Potentials for contamination, overpressure, or overfilling of the SEVIN (or MIC) feed tank [a holding tank between the MIC storage tanks and the reaction vessel to produce Carbaryl, which is located inside the building]; 7. Deficiencies in the safety valve and instrument maintenance programs; 8. Deficiencies in Master Tag/Lockout procedure applications; 9. Possibilities of nitrogen header contamination; 10. Problems created by high personnel turnover at the plant, particularly in operations.

ficiencies. In particular, four specific recommendations addressed concern #6, in connection with the SEVIN (or MIC) feed tank:

1. A positive nitrogen purge from the tank to the vent scrubber, with alarm on loss of purge, should be provided.
2. Water spray protection should be provided for the MIC feed tank, and consideration to either removing the walls of the room or locating the tank outside.
3. The adequacy of the relief valve on the tank should be checked, and a larger valve be provided if necessary.
4. An automatic high level shutoff or other means of limiting tank level should be provided.[116]

The other deficiencies were of a more general nature related to preventive maintenance of instruments and alarm systems, proper record-keeping, and more rigorous training programs for operators and maintenance personnel.

The team critiqued the safety valve testing program and the effectiveness of the Master Tag and Hazardous Work Permit procedures among other minor safety lapses.

The safety valves on the phosgene and quench filters had three different color codes on their bonnets, indicating three different test years, and the procedure and timing for rupture disc replacement was not clearly spelled out. An electrician had to work on three electric motors with only one Master Tag. Maintenance people had to sign permits they could not read.

The team was unable to determine the effectiveness of the instrument preventative maintenance programs since there was a heavy reliance on manual control and checking of liquid levels. It was also observed that the alarms and instruments were checked at shutdowns and no records were maintained.

While UCC auditors provided a service to UCIL through Operation Safety Survey, at no time did UCC have control over UCIL to ensure that the report's recommendations were acted upon promptly. As delineated in the Technology Transfer Agreement and by FERA regulations, UCC's role was limited to consulting and advising.

---

[116] L.A. Kail, J.M. Poulson, C S. Tyson, *Operational Safety Survey CO/MIC/Sevin Units, Union Carbide India Ltd., Bhopal Plant,* May, 1982.

A year later, in a nineteen-page report entitled "Action Plan – Operational Safety Survey, May 1982," dated April 25, 1983, UCIL indicated that a number of the issues listed in the report were either corrected or were in the process of being corrected.[117] Regarding the adequacy of the relief valve on the MIC feed tank, it stated that "the existing relief valve was found to be adequate." The June 26, 1984, report from Works Manager Mukund about correcting the deficiencies was addressed to George Merryman of UCC's Agricultural Products Company in North Carolina. It stated that "as of June 23, 1984, the only unfinished item from the OSS Action Plan for the Bhopal plant is the one relating to the MIC feed tank at SEVIN [same as SEVIN feed tank] (OSS comment No. 4.2(c) & (d)). From the attached action plan it will be seen that even this is almost complete and is only awaiting delivery of a control valve expected next month. It is therefore proposed to discontinue this progress report and this will be the last issue."

After the tragedy, Tyson, one of the inspectors who conducted the Operation Safety Survey, said that a normal part of the training process of technicians was preparation for "what if" situations, to be able to react to emergencies. This was a major shortcoming of the Bhopal facility. "It is an entirely different setup…the demand is on the human [labor] out there… that Indian designers had provide[d] manual systems to create more jobs." He further added that "maintenance people [were] signing permits they cannot read" and that "personnel were being released for independent operation without having sufficient understanding of safe operating procedures."[118] Warren Woomer later noted that all instructions and permits were read to those operators who could not read English.

Judge John F. Keenan, United States District Court, Southern District of New York, in his Opinion and Order document of May 12, 1986, (in footnote 14), also alluded to the OSS Report and the issue of accountability:

Mr. Woomer asserts, and plaintiffs do not refute, that this survey was intended to 'serve a policing function', but was performed at the specific

---

[117] With respect to method of installation of blind flanges only 60% of the valves were procured by 25th February 1983, and 40+% of the valves were installed. Only 40% of the pumps were provided with double seals and scheduled for completion by 25 June 1983.

[118] "Inspector Calls Indian Plant Below U.S. Standard," *The New York Times,* December 12, 1984. pp. 1, 6. See also *Legal Aftermath,* pp. 90-91.

request of UCIL. In addition, 'follow-up' rested exclusively with UCIL plant management. (Woomer Aff. at 37-38). Moreover, Union Carbide [UCIL] states that the Union of India, itself, conducted similar safety audits and made recommendations. (Dutta Aff. at 58-64).

When the OSS report of May 1982 was made available to the press after the tragedy, UCC management was widely criticized for not taking a stronger position in correcting the deficiencies that may have appeared to contribute, in part, towards the MIC gas leak. Specifically, the critics blamed the deficiencies of the SEVIN/MIC feed tank cited under item (6) in the OSS Report. There was much confusion about the difference between the MIC feed tank and the MIC storage tank. The feed-tank was a much smaller tank and was located inside the building. It was used for temporarily holding one-ton quantities of MIC drawn from the larger MIC storage tanks, before it was introduced into the carbamoylating reaction vessel for conversion to Carbaryl, by reacting with weighed amounts of solid alpha-naphthol. The feed tank gave an exact measurement of the amount of MIC required for the conversion.

When interviewed by a *New York Times* reporter soon after the disaster, V.P. Gokhale, UCIL managing director, said, "The Bhopal plant was responsible for its own safety, with little scrutiny from an outside source... the many problems cited in the 1982 report had been corrected...[and] we had no reason to believe there were grounds for such an accident."[119]

After the last batch of MIC was produced in October 1984, the only major activity at the plant was the final conversion of MIC to Carbaryl and formulation to marketable products.

The Final Days of the Bhopal Plant

The UCIL Board has been quite vocal in their criticism of the Bhopal operations and the directors are averse to any further investment in Bhopal.... The Board would like to see this 'bleeding' stop.

According to the company's original strategic plan, which reflected the projected tonnage and the priorities of the Government of India, UCIL was expected to produce 5,900 MT of Carbaryl. The Bhopal plant was scaled to produce the necessary tonnage of the required intermediates – alpha-

---

[119] Stuart Diamond, "The Bhopal Disaster: How It Happened," *The New York Times*, January 28, 1985. p. 6.

naphthol and MIC. UCIL's failure to successfully develop the technology to produce alpha-naphthol using indigenous technology or to successfully market other types of carbamate pesticides produced in minor quantities (like Temik, BPMC, Propoxur, or combinations of SEVIN-BHC),[120] marked the beginning of the downward spiral of the entire Bhopal project. With the introduction of newer, more effective pesticides by UCIL's competitors in India, the company's share of the projected SEVIN market was not being realized. Although precise total tonnage of Carbaryl produced is not available, it can be estimated from the consumption of the intermediate alpha-naphthol for the years 1979-1981. Alpha-naphthol used during these three years was 1,144 MT, 1,074 MT, and 1,990 MT respectively, as compared to the annual licensed and installed capacity for MIC-based pesticides of 5,900 MT.[121] These figures suggest that the Bhopal plant never exceeded a third of its capacity. The sales of pesticides were also adversely affected when:

> A drought in 1977 forced many farmers to take out government loans, many of which began to fall due in 1980. The farmers exchanged the expensive UCIL pesticides for others less costly and less effective. Meanwhile, the Indian government was providing incentives for small-scale manufacturers to produce pesticides that they could afford to sell at half the price of Union Carbide products. In addition, inexpensive, non-toxic synthetic pyrethroids made their debut and sales of traditional insecticides began to drop. The Bhopal operation, never very profitable, broke even in 1981 but after began to lose money. By 1984 the plant produced less than 1,000 tons of the projected 5,000 tons and lost close to $4 million. Many of the skilled workers left for securer pastures. Things were not going well.[122]

Court documents indicate that as early as 1970, UCIL had realized that the proposed Bhopal plant was oversized, given the Government of India's overly optimistic forecast for the future market for carbamate pesticides. (See Appendix A-10).

By June 1981, UCC and UCIL decided that its Bhopal operations needed to be significantly restructured if it was ever to become profitable. Earlier, Robert Olford, president of UCAPCO, informed Ramasami

---

[120] For more on these carbamate insecticides see the Glossary.
[121] Taken from *UCIL's Annual Reports* for the years 1980, 1981 and 1982.
[122] Bowonder et al., *Environment,* vol.27, No.7, 1985, p.7.

Natarajan, director of agricultural products for UCE in Hong Kong, of the need to convene a special Bhopal Task Force to review the future of UCC's investment in UCIL. Specifically, they needed to assess the Bhopal plant's capability, marketing and market development programs in the context of India's market trends, and to come up with specific recommendations for improving the Bhopal operations.[123]

Natarajan delineated his views for UCIL's strategic plan in a three-page telex dated June 11, 1981 addressed to William R. Correa, managing director of UCIL. The proposal included the possibility of even "walking away from the investment." However, he also cautioned against taking such a drastic action, fearing "the upheaval any walking away could cause to UCIL as a whole."[124] Because of time constraints and the cost of traveling to Bhopal, the meeting was held at UCC's headquarters in Danbury, Connecticut in June 1981 to discuss the UCIL-APD (Agricultural Products Division) strategic plan. Richard Hughes, UCC's executive vice president, summarized the key points which emerged as a result:

> Sales estimates for SEVIN and TEMIK [another UCC proprietary carbamate insecticide] are overly optimistic in view of the registration difficulties with TEMIK and the advent of the pyrethroids as competitors for SEVIN in cotton.

> Sales growth for formulated SEVIN has been essentially static for a number of years and forecasted growth is for technical grade material which is hardest to sell and poorest return.

> Variable costs for naphthol via the Indian process are 4 times higher than UCC costs at Institute. SEVIN variables costs are 3-1/2 times Institute's costs.

> Indian selling prices are not significantly different than world prices and hence do not reflect indigenous raw material costs...

---

[123] Telex from Natarajan, dated 4/29/81. Court Document No. 0001758.

[124] Telex from Natarajan to W.R. Correa, (EHK 1002 06/11/81). Court Document Nos. 0001819-0001822.

Preliminary conclusions: Indefinitely delay the startup of alpha-naph-thol and import from Institute at $1.00 per pound FAS [free alongside ship].[125]

The fact that it was four times more expensive to produce alpha-naphthol and Carbaryl in India than to import it from the U.S. indicated that SEVIN produced in India could not compete in either the Indian or the world market. This is not surprising since the alpha-naphthol plant was plagued with problems and was utilizing imported alpha-naphthol, and the plant was operating at less than 50 percent of capacity.

Additional topics on the agenda were the possibility of manufacturing other types of carbamate insecticides and herbicides, such as Carbofuran, BPMC, and Tribunil at the Bhopal facility, and to also develop with the Government of India a marketing program for other imported pesticides. Salvaging the mothballed alpha-naphthol plant by modifying it to produce the precursor phenol of Carbofuran was also seriously considered but rejected. (Carbofuran, a competitor's product and also a carbamate pesticide based on MIC, was found to be very effective to control rice pests). Regarding the proposed UCIL-Carbofuran Project, Natarajan wrote:

UCIL/UCE believe that there is a reasonable chance of obtaining a Government of India industrial license to manufacture Carbofuran, but our 'friends' add that the real answer will be known only when an application is submitted.... The UCIL Board has been quite vocal in their criticism of the Bhopal operations and the directors are averse to any further investment in Bhopal.... The Board would like to see this 'bleeding' stop.[126]

Since the market analysis by UCIL and UCE managers for developing Carbofuran profitably was not encouraging, the idea was shelved.

In response to the concerns expressed by the UCIL board of directors on the long-term viability of the Agricultural Products Division business, Natarajan wrote a five-page report with attachments to James B. Law, Chairman, UCE, on February 24, 1984. He reviewed in detail UCIL's Ag

---

[125] Memo by R.J. Hughes to J.M. Rehfield, UCIL – APD Strategic Plans, dated July 29, 1981. Court Document No. 0001761.

[126] Letter from R. Natarajan to R. Olford, dated January 26, 1984. (Court Document No. 0001707-1709.)

Products business for the past year, with future estimates in the context of the competitive market environment, and raised some concerns:

> UCIL invested approximately $30 million on the pesticide project in Bhopal. As of the end of 1983, the net fixed investment amounted to $18.1M. Tax savings totaled $9.8M and negative earnings $7.5M during 1978-83. In support of this investment, during the period 1977-83, UCC sold UCIL $33.1 million of SEVIN and intermediates. Alpha-naphthol and Temik oxime continue to be imported costing $3.5 million a year.... UCIL Board is less than enthusiastic as to any further investment in Ag Chem.

> The future of the existing business does not look any brighter than the poor financial results obtained to date. Inexpensive chlorinated hydrocarbons continue to dominate the market; a local competitor with $2 million investment has carved out a 10% share of the carbaryl market and, as feared earlier, pyrethroids entered India in the '83 season and [were] well received in the cotton market, the major crop for SEVIN accounting for about 70% of its sales. UCIL's major market diversification efforts during 1981-83 did not yield satisfactory results.... A major OIP [optimization and improvement] effort (including reduction of 335 employees) resulted in a $1.25M (annual) cost savings in 1983 but future savings of such magnitude will not be easy.

Accordingly, UCIL/UCE offered the following proposal:

> ...to reduce the UCIL AG Chem business to that of a MIC manufacturer/ seller only as a means of minimizing NIAT (net income after tax) and Cash Flow losses and protecting MIC technology. In this case, UCIL will write off its unproven alpha-naphthol facility ($3.5 million as of the end of '83 and it will be impossible to sell this plant), and search for a buyer...for the carbamoylation and formulation facilities...

> With APC's [UCC's Agricultural Products Company] concurrence, UCIL could probably increase a buyer's interest level further by offering to sell technology for other MIC based insecticides. UCIL will fence off the MIC plant and run the utilities for its own as well as the buyer's needs...

We seek your endorsement of this change in strategic direction which will enable us to look for an interested party...[127]

Since UCC had a major equity in UCIL, any major strategic decisions proposed jointly by UCIL and UCE also required the consent and approval of UCC executive management. For UCIL to pursue a more independent course in planning and future investments, UCC's equity in UCIL would have to be further reduced. In response to the proposal of May 23, 1984 by UCE,[128] the management committee of UCC authorized UCIL to "proceed with UCC equity reduction from 50.9% to 40%...lease or sell all or part of Bhopal assets...investigate and implement a phased assets write down with the Indian tax authorities or even donating the alpha-naphthol plant to the Government of India."[129] According to the terms of the design transfer agreement (article VIII), any sale or export of MIC technology to a third party also required the agreement of UCC. Most of these recommendations were approved by Warren M. Anderson, chairman of the board and chief executive officer, UCC,[130] and the management committee.

The proposal to reduce UCC's equity was not immediately carried out since it was contingent on the sale of UCIL's CHEMCO (Chemical and Plastics) Division. A transcript of the telephone conversation between James B. Law (UCE) and Keshub Mahindra, chairman of UCIL board of directors – dated May 31, 1984 – gives further details.

KM [K. Mahindra]...stated that since the government's approval of Chemco sale (through the RBI) [Reserve Bank of India] stipulated that we could conform to their letter of July 4, 1977 granting permission under FERA to remain at 50.9% by complying with the core sector and export requirement, this pressure will be cancelled if the Chemo sale is not consummated. Therefore, he concurs that we should delay the equity

---

[127] Letter by Mr. Natarajan to J.B. Law, Chairman, UCE, entitled "A Review of U.C. India Ltd's Ag Product Business," dated February 24, 1984. (Court Documents Nos. 0001807-0001811).

[128] Court Document Nos. 0001785-86. UCIL-AG Products, dated May 23, 1984.

[129] Court Document No. 0001787. UCIL-AG Products, dated May 31, 1984.

[130] Born in Brooklyn, New York of working-class immigrant parents, he received B.A. in Chemistry from Colgate University and in 1956 the degree of LL.B from Western Reserve University. Joined UCC in 1945 as a salesman and steadily rose up the management ranks. He became President in 1977 and elected chairman of the board and CEO in 1982.

reduction assuming UCC is willing to accept higher financial loss and reduced cash flow from the sale.[131]

The preliminary discussions concerning the financial drain from problems at the Bhopal plant not only involved the top UCIL executives but also a few others, including Jay Mukund, works manager of the Bhopal plant, and key UCC managers.[132]

A sense of urgency prevailed to determine the fate of the Bhopal plant before the foreign collaboration agreement expired on January 1, 1985. The possibility of dismantling the plant and shipping it overseas was now being seriously considered. To this effect, in a letter dated October 26, 1984, Natarajan asked K.S. Kamdar, vice president and general manager of UCIL's Agricultural Products Division in Bombay, to look into the feasibility and cost of shipping the MIC plant to Brazil, and the carbamoylation unit to Indonesia. Also to be explored was the possibility of eliminating the sales and marketing organization in Agricultural Products Division and letting a third party sell UCIL agricultural products.[133] In mid-November, Kamdar responded that Umesh Nanda was given one month to report the estimated cost of dismantling and shipping the MIC and carbamoylation facilities.[134] Only a few days before the tragedy, two additional telexes were exchanged.

Natarajan also requested Phil Nelson, Vice President International, of Union Carbide's Agricultural Products Company, to make additional inquiries:

I have asked UCIL [K.S. Kamdar] to make a preliminary study and hope to have the information second-half of December 1984. In the meantime, I understand that shipping of used equipment or even new equipment into Brazil is nearly impossible because of some government regulation. Would you kindly let me know whether this is true and if so, whether I

---

[131] Transcript of the telephone conversation between J.B.Law and Keshub Mahindra, dated May 31, 1984. (Court Document No. 0001788/16001780.)

[132] Response by UCC to plaintiffs' Interrogatory No. 10, pp. 13-14.

[133] For a complete text of the letter by Natarajan, dated October 26,1984, (Appendix A-11. Court Document 10114506f/g.)

[134] For complete text of telex of November 13, 1984, from K.S. Kamdar to Natarajan, (Appendix A-12. Court Document 10114506b/c/d.)

should confine the study to carbamoylation plant only which is related to Indonesia.[135]

Due to the tragedy just a few days later, K.S. Kamdar's response to Natarajan, dated November 29, 1984, was not delivered since CBI seized all UCIL's documents. The aborted telex (which ended up in the court) gives the cost estimates developed by UCIL for dismantling and shipping of CO/MIC units from Bombay to Surabaya Port, Indonesia.[136]

Given the sophisticated technology and high profile of the Bhopal facility, UCIL had initially been able to recruit highly qualified people to operate the plant. Many of these staff benefited from training and visits to the United States and saw a bright future ahead for the company. The closure of the alpha-naphthol plant in 1982 and the cost-cutting measures introduced in 1983 came as a shock to many of the experienced, highly trained personnel, causing some of them to leave the company. Kamal K. Pareek, a former senior project engineer who began working at the Bhopal plant in 1971, resigned in December 1983 because the plant was losing money and didn't seem to have a future. With resignations and lay-offs, UCIL's Bhopal work force was reduced from about 1,350 in 1980 to 950[137] by the end of 1984. In 1983, UCIL decided to reduce its plant operators by half, from twelve to six per shift.[138] In some cases staff were transferred from other units, with no previous experience in the MIC plant to replace the experienced employees who had quit. Towards the end of 1984 much of the necessary maintenance and repairs had been neglected or discontinued, since the eventual demise of the plant was under serious consideration. Employee grievances were not addressed in a timely and professional manner and employee morale was at its lowest.

In anticipation of the closing and dismantling of the Carbaryl plant in Bhopal, UCIL produced the last batch of MIC in late October 1984. All of the MIC produced was distilled to the last drop and stored in tanks E-610 and E-611. The very last batch of MIC, distilled at a higher temperature (which also distilled a considerable quantity of the solvent chloroform)

---

[135]   Telex from Natarajan to P.A. Nelson, entitled Dismantling and Shipment of MIC & Carbamoylation facilities in Bhopal, dated November 21, 1984.

[136]   For details of the contents of the telex dated November 29,1984, (Appendix A-13. Court Document 10114566i.)

[137]   The permanent workforce was about 600 and the rest were seasonal temporary hires.

[138]   Stuart Diamond, *The New York Times*, January 28, 1985.

was stored in tank E-610. The MIC production unit was then closed and isolated from the rest of the operations. The termination of production of MIC freed the operators for duties elsewhere. The stored MIC was then gradually reacted with alpha-naphthol – one-ton at a time – to produce Carbaryl, which was then formulated into the final pesticide product, SEVIN™. These were the only manufacturing operations going on at the plant prior to the night of the disaster. The riots and the curfew in Bhopal, after the October 31 assassination of the prime minister Indira Gandhi, temporarily halted the activities at the plant during the month of November.

To further reduce the operating costs, UCIL management neglected to carry out the necessary maintenance and repairs of ancillary equipment before all the stored MIC was used up and manufacturing operations ceased. Even though the MIC storage tanks contained large quantities of MIC, the refrigeration unit for cooling the tanks was shut off and the coolant removed. A four-foot piece of corroded tubing leading to the flare tower that would burn any escaping gases was not replaced; the caustic scrubber used to neutralize the fugitive MIC and other acidic gases liberated was not operational.[139,140]

As detailed in this chapter, the MIC plant was designed, constructed, and operated within the broader context of the Government of India's policies regulating foreign investments in India. The several letters exchanged between UCIL and the government ministries indicate the extent of the government's involvement from the very inception of the UCIL Bhopal plant. The government determined the tonnage of SEVIN pesticide that would be required and insisted that UCIL manufacture the product domestically rather than be dependent on imported materials, which required payment with hard-to-come-by foreign currency. Following government guidelines, UCIL purchased the technology to manufacture MIC from UCC, the foreign collaborator. A necessary precondition to signing the agreement was that "registered Indian Engineering design and Consultancy Organizations must be the prime consultants and Government will consider permitting the purchase of only such design and consultancy services from abroad as are not available within the country." Even before the Technology Transfer Agreement was signed, Indian engineers who

---

[139] Praful Bidwai, "Two colossal safety lapses at plant," *The Times of India,* December 10, 1984, p. 1.

[140] Stewart Diamond, "The Bhopal Disaster: How It Happened," *The New York Times,* January 28, 1985, p. 103.

would be involved in the plant design visited the UCC Technical Center in Charleston, West Virginia, to learn about the U.S. plant specifications and adapt them to Indian conditions. UCIL later provided the government with every detail of the plant design along with the properties and quantities of the raw materials to be manufactured.

The inability of UCIL scientists and engineers to locally develop a viable manufacturing process for alpha-naphthol was a major factor that contributed to the failure of UCIL's pesticide business. Furthermore, the government ignored UCIL's earlier concern about the long-term viability of SEVIN insecticide when it sought, unsuccessfully, for a mid-course change of project in favor of other newly discovered pesticidal compounds. Because the Carbaryl plant did not operate at full capacity and was dependent on imported material, the agricultural products business of UCIL began to falter and was no longer profitable, and the future of the Bhopal pesticide facility was questioned by UCIL board of directors and UCC management. The options under serious consideration were to either modify the alpha-naphthol unit for other uses or to close and dismantle the plant. During the later half of 1984 there was a sense of urgency to arrive at a decision, as the foreign collaboration agreement was to expire on January 1, 1985.

Before the year ended, just after midnight on December 3, a massive cloud of toxic gases billowed out of the factory stack and engulfed the city, killing and injuring thousands of nearby residents. There was no explosion or fire and no damage to the equipment or casualty among the plant workers. Even before the real cause of the tragedy was fully investigated, Union Carbide was widely criticized for defective plant design, poor maintenance and unsafe working conditions at the plant. Critics cited the history of prior accidents and concluded that a major tragedy was inevitable. What really happened?

Chapter Three

INVESTIGATING THE GAS LEAK

Initial Response of Plant Managers

Bhopal's Superintendent of Police Swaraj Puri was awakened around 1:00 a.m. by a telephone call from a town inspector to inform him of a gas leak at the UCIL plant and that residents of the nearby Chola neighborhood were fleeing the area. When he arrived at the Police Control room, he found the place in chaos with everyone coughing violently and rubbing their eyes. His staff had tried to contact the plant authorities several times between 1:25 and 2:10 a.m. to inquire if there was a problem at the factory. Twice they were told that "everything was OK" and once, "we don't know what happened, sir," before the connection was terminated at the other end.

When the additional district magistrate contacted UCIL's works manager Jay Mukund at his residence, his initial response was disbelief: "The gas leak just can't be from my plant. The plant [MIC production] is shut down. Our technology just can't go wrong, we just can't have such leaks." He then drove to the plant.

UCIL night-shift supervisors did not sound the emergency siren until after 2:00 a.m. (2:15 a.m. according to police accounts.) Ramlal, a day laborer who lived just behind the plant, also supports this timeframe:

> The saabs [bosses] of Union Carbide never sounded the siren. If they had done so before or just after the gas leaked out, we would have known what to do. We'd at least have had a chance to run.... I lost my wife and two sons only because they didn't warn us.[1]

When interviewed by a reporter several years later, S.R. Deshmukh the timekeeper at the plant, recalled the timing of the plant's siren and the confusion and panic which ensued inside the plant complex soon after the event.

---

[1]   Praful Bidwai, "The Poisoned City – Diary From Bhopal," *Sunday Review, The Times of India,* December 16, 1984, pp. I and IV.

I heard a muted siren and...came to know that there was heavy leakage from the MIC plant. After some time, Utility Operator U.S. Teagle came to me to get a pass to go out to start the water pump.... When he returned to the factory, he said that the outside situation was terrible: that people were fleeing in panic and dying in the road. The whole of the old city was getting covered by the gas.

Around 1:30 a.m., the workers began to flee the factory premises to save their lives. After some time, Plant Superintendent K.V. Shetty came to me and asked how many workers had left the factory. I told him that I did not know because they did not stop for proper pass cards.... I heard the loud siren continuously at 2 a.m. only.[2]

The confusion during the early hours of the disaster can also be gleaned from the excerpts of the interview given by Mukund to an Indian reporter a few days after the incident.

Q: Would it be correct that you did not inform the public, the police and the civil administration in time...?

A: Nobody had any idea about the extent of the leak when I reached the plant on being informed that there had been a mishap. This was about 1.55 a.m. When I got here, I found that the (storage tank) pressure had dropped and that the air in the plant had become breathable. I could not contact the police on the telephone...lines were not working properly.... So I sent a man to the police control room to inform them that the gas had stopped leaking

Q: That was about 3 a.m. The police say that they made several attempts to get through to the plant on the phone and succeeded at least three times, but that they failed to get any confirmation...

A: I don't know.... There was much confusion...

Q: Are you aware that many of the control instrumentation systems are malfunctioning?

---

2   T.R. Chouhan and Others, Bhopal – *The Inside Story,* The Apex Press, New York: 1994, pp. 93-94.

A: Well in a large plant…we have maintenance people who set things right.

Q: …Is it true that you had disconnected the scrubber from the flare tower…?

A: Yes.[3]

Later in the evening, officers from the Central Bureau of Investigation (CBI) took control of the plant and two days later a scientific investigation team headed by the director of the Council of Scientific and Industrial Research began the investigation. UCC's investigation team arrived in Bhopal on December 6, and were granted permission to enter the plant a day later. Since there was still a large quantity of MIC stored on the premises, the investigation into the cause of the gas emission was deferred until the remaining stock of MIC was neutralized and the plant was made safe.

Operation Faith

When Dr. Srinivasan Varadarajan, the chief government scientist and director general of CSIR, arrived at the scene on December 5, he was informed by the plant managers that a large amount of MIC still remained on site, mostly stored in tank E-611 and some in tank E-619 and 55-gallon steel drums. Since the plant managers claimed ignorance of the cause of the uncontrolled gas emission from tank E-610, there was much concern that the contents in tank E-611 might react similarly. Thus, priority was given to neutralizing the remaining MIC.

This precautionary step took on greater urgency when chemical analysis of the SEVIN feed tank (the tank cited in the OSS Report) and the contents of the connecting piping showed a green coloration with higher than normal levels of chloroform, and some solid contaminants. Since the three MIC storage tanks were interconnected through common pipelines, the investigators were most concerned that all the tanks might be contaminated. Varadarajan informed the government authorities of this immediate issue and the plans being devised to neutralize the remaining MIC. Not content with the plant's remaining safety system, CSIR scientists insisted on stringing together a series of *ad hoc* precautionary measures. Once these

---

[3]   Praful Bidwai, "A deadly delay in Bhopal," *The Times of India*, December19, 1984, p.9.

plans were finalized, Arjun Singh, the chief minister of Madhya Pradesh, announced to the press through a prepared statement that:

> The scene is set for the operation to neutralize the poisonous gas in the Union Carbide plant. I visited the factory last night and saw the arrangements and precautions taken. Dr. S. Varadarajan was with me. Even though the actual handling is to be done by the Union Carbide people taking full responsibility, the 'go ahead' has to be given by us – that is, me...

> Even though faith springs eternal in the human heart, at this moment of time, it stands rudely shaken by the horrendous events of the last few days. That faith has to be restored. It shall be restored and none but God Himself will see to it. This operation shall, therefore, be called Operation Faith. Let us pray for its success.

Such responses from the government were not reassuring to the public and baffled reporters from the news media.[4]

On December 12, the government announced that the MIC neutralization process would start on the sixteenth and that all schools and colleges in the city would be closed until December 23. The State Road Transportation Department kept three hundred buses ready in case an emergency evacuation was necessary. Special trains and additional coaches were also brought in. All government employees, including those on leave, were called to duty. All of these preparations naturally confused Bhopal's inhabitants.

> Within a day more than 50,000 people left and the city was almost desolate within three days.... As an added precautionary measure, the critical part of the plant was covered with a sheet of tarpaulin and the boundary wall with makeshift jute. Throughout the five-day operation, fire tenders and helicopters sprayed water all over the plant and the surrounding roads.[5]

In connection with Operation Faith, the contents of the MIC storage tank E-611 were also analyzed. Though the contents of the feed tank and

---

4   Anees Chishti, *Dateline Bhopal: A newsman's diary of the gas disaster*, Concept Publishing Co., New Delhi: 1986, p. 61.
5   Lalit Shastri, *An Eye-witness Account,* Criterion Publications, New Delhi: 1985, pp. 67-70.

the connecting piping showed unexplained impurities, the MIC stored in E-611 (adjacent to tank E-610) was found to be of high purity and met product specifications. UCC/UCI engineers recommended that the remaining MIC be neutralized by the usual method, by reacting with alpha-naphthol to produce Carbaryl. This recommendation was initially challenged by Varadarajan but was finally adopted. All the other methods for neutralization suggested by the CSIR scientists but not utilized are described in the CSIR Report under Operation Faith.

Although the vent gas scrubber was put back in operation, the flare tower was not. As described, many of the visible safety measures adopted by the CSIR scientists were "designed more for a public demonstration of their intent than for an effective prevention or containment of a potential leak." CSIR scientists did not know "the nuts-and-bolts-level command of the whole operation; the job was left to the Union Carbide people. In Varadarajan's own words 'we really did not know the plant that well.'"[6]

Simultaneously, during the first two weeks following the disaster, other CSIR scientists with expertise in environmental protection and toxicology assessed the damage to the environment by examining the air, water, plants, and aquatic life. The results of "the tests carried out did not show any presence of MIC or related toxic materials in the environment…[However] the public were advised to wash all vegetables and food articles with water and clean floors, walls, and surfaces with water."

Initial Speculations

Experts were far more than sources of information about the causes and dimensions of the accident: "They were image makers, a source of credibility, and persons to talk to the persistent and ever-present press."[7]

Not unlike other major accidents, after the gas leak the public demanded answers from Union Carbide and the Government of India as to its cause and the nature of the gases emitted. Why were the safety and back-up systems not in use? Why was such a large quantity of MIC stored when the company knew of its extreme hazard? Why was UCC unable

---

6   Praful Bidwai, "Safety Measures not so Safe," *The Times of India,* December 16, 1984, pp. 1, 9.

7   Dorothy Nelkin, *The Role of the Expert at Three Mile Island, in Accident at Three Mile Island, The Human Dimensions,* David L. Sills, C.P. Wolf, and Vivien B. Shelanski (eds.), Westview Press, Boulder, Colorado: 1982, p.143

to provide more information on toxicity data of MIC and guidelines for appropriate treatment? Why was the public not informed sooner after the gas leak? There were no immediate answers from either UCIL and UCC management or the government investigators.

Within days, and before any formal investigation began, Varadarajan, the chief government spokesman, speculated on the probable causes of the gas leak. He first told the reporters that after discussions with the factory management, they estimated that about 1.5 to 2.5 MT (3000 to 5000 pounds) of water would be required to react with MIC in order to generate sufficient heat for about 40 percent of the material to evaporate. Later, he criticized the method used by the plant technicians to analyze MIC and he proposed an alternate hypothesis. Three weeks later, on January 4, 1985, speaking at the Science Congress in Lucknow, Varadarajan reiterated his hypothesis that "the small amount [of water] was enough to react with phosgene liberating hydrochloric acid which easily polymerizes the MIC.... [That] he could not figure out how one and a half tonnes of water got into the system unless there was a leak."[8]

Methyl isocyanate (MIC) is a liquid with a strong sharp odor; it is a lachrymator (provokes tearing of the eyes) and vaporizes at 39.1°C (102.4°F). On contact with water it reacts to produce carbon dioxide and methylamine – both gases – and much heat. Higher temperatures generally increase the rate of this reaction. The methylamine formed reacts immediately with remaining MIC to form dimethylurea (DMU). In the presence of an excess of MIC, the initially formed DMU can also react further to form trimethylbiuret (TMB), as indicated the by the equations in the footnote. Both of these materials, DMU and TMB, are stable white solids.[9]

In the presence of certain metals like iron (rust) and other materials, MIC can also react with itself to form another solid called MIC-trimer, a six-sided cyclic molecule, by condensation of three MIC molecules. This process, called trimerization, also generates heat to raise the temperature of the mixture. (For more information on physical properties and toxicity, see also Appendix D-1, MIC Fact Sheet). These three solid materials

---

8   L.K. Sharma, "Carbide safety system failed," *The Times of India,* Jan. 5, 1985, p. 5.

9   1. $CH_3N=C=O + H_2O \rightarrow CH_3NH_2 + CO_2$
       (MIC)   (water) (methylamine) (carbon dioxide)
    2. $CH_3NH_2 + CH_3N=C=O \rightarrow CH_3NHCONHCH_3$ (DMU)
    3. $CH_3NHCONHCH_3 + CH_3N=C=O \rightarrow CH_3NHCON(CH_3)CONHCH_3$
                              (TMB)

– DMU, TMB and the MIC trimer – when formed during the operation of the MIC plant are considered as nuisance impurities, which can clog the pipes. Normal operating procedures therefore required that the system be kept closed and dry at all times and that it not be exposed to iron or other corrosive materials.

MIC is the smallest and the most reactive member of a class of chemicals generically known as isocyanates. The higher related members or analogs are used extensively in the manufacture of polyurethane foams and plastics. The only commercial use of MIC is in the manufacture of a class of pesticides called carbamates. MIC is manufactured commercially from methylamine and phosgene, and in the process hydrochloric acid gas is liberated as a by-product.

To relieve any pressure buildup on standing, storage tanks are generally equipped with gas relief valves. With these safety precautions, experience in the agri-chemical industrial sector has demonstrated that MIC can be safely stored over long periods of time in appropriately designed containers and controlled environments.

Over 200 million pounds have been processed since UCC began production of MIC at the Institute plant in 1966. Prior to the Bhopal gas leak, MIC was shipped for several years to Brazil, France, and India in specially designed stainless steel drums, and across the United States in 8,000-gallon insulated, double-walled stainless steel tank cars, without a serious incident.

A few weeks after the disaster, reports on the cause of the disaster were published in two newspapers: *India Today* (12/31/84) and the *New York Times* (1/27/85). These unofficial reports, published independently by the papers' investigative reporters, also concluded that a small quantity of water most likely entered the tank during the washing of clogged filter pipes the previous evening, which was sufficient to trigger a reaction with MIC. These reports were based primarily on interviews with Varadarajan, and UCIL plant workers on duty the night of the incident.[10] This route of entry of water later came to be known as the "water-washing" hypothesis. It was speculated that while the plant operator was cleaning the clogged pipe the previous evening, without taking adequate precaution to seal the

---

[10] Since the description of the events in the two reports are similar, it is likely that both reporters spoke to the same group of plant operators. The NYT report also disclosed the names of the operators, who presumably understood English but preferred to speak in Hindi through an interpreter. It is not clear if they spoke to the reporters separately or a group.

section of the pipe from the rest of the system, water backed up in the pipe and entered the tank. Later, when only small amounts of DMU and TMB were detected in the tank residue, the chief Indian scientist speculated that the trace of phosgene, and metallic contaminants formed as a result, triggered a secondary reaction to further raise the temperature pressure inside the tank. This initial hypothesis, reinforced by media publicity, was readily accepted as the real cause of the disastrous gas leak.

Five major investigations were officially launched to determine the cause of the gas leak: Three by the Indian investigators – the Singh Commission, the CSIR, and CBI; two by U.S. investigators – UCC and Arthur D. Little (ADL). The CSIR report was presented to the Indian Parliament in December 1985 and has not been published. The one-man Singh Commission initiated by the State of Madhya Pradesh was disbanded within a year without issuing a formal report. CBI has yet to issue an official report of its findings. UCC disclosed the results of its investigation in a report entitled, *Bhopal Methyl Isocyanate Incident Investigation Team Report* in March 1985. ADL presented its findings in a paper entitled, *Investigation of Large-Magnitude Incidents: Bhopal as Case Study,* at the Institution of Chemical Engineers on Preventing Major Chemical Accidents, held in London in May 1988.

The UCC Investigation

When news of the disaster in Bhopal reached UCC headquarters in Danbury, Connecticut, in the early hours on Monday, December 3, it was already past noon in India (Indian Standard Time is 10 1/2 hours ahead of EST). Direct communication with Bhopal was slow or impossible as the city's two telephone trunk lines were overwhelmed. UCC executives, who held their first crisis management meeting at 6:00 a.m., received fragmentary information from telephone conversations with UCIL officials in Delhi and Bombay, who also taped and relayed BBC news reports. At 1:00 p.m., Jackson B. Browning, UCC's vice president for health, safety, and environmental programs, held a press conference at the Danbury Hilton hotel to announce that:

1. There was an accident at the UCIL plant in Bhopal and that UCC was preparing to send medical and technical experts to the aid of the people of Bhopal and to investigate the cause of the incident.

2. As a precautionary measure, UCC decided to halt the production of MIC at the Institute, West Virginia plant and convert any stored MIC into the final stable product, pending the outcome of the investigation. It also ordered the recall of MIC in trans-shipment to France and elsewhere.

3. A management task force was set up to deal with the crisis, headed by Warren Anderson, and President Alec Flamm would temporarily assume the responsibilities of running the company's business.[11]

Within twenty-four hours, a seven-member technical team was assembled to assist in the investigation. All were specialists who had previously worked at the MIC manufacturing plant at Institute or had first-hand knowledge of the Bhopal plant.[12] Ron Van Mynen, corporate director of occupational health, personnel safety and environmental affairs, led the team.

At the UCIL guesthouse on the grounds of the Technical Center at Shamla Hills, Woomer, the team spokesman, was confronted by a throng of reporters posing a barrage of questions: Were the two MIC plants – at Institute and Bhopal – of the same design? Were the instruments and controls different? How well were the people trained, and how competent were the people operating the plant?[13] Later that evening, Varadarajan visited the guesthouse and greeted the team members with the remark: "You killed thousands of innocent people."[14]

The UCC team was allowed to enter the plant at 3:30 p.m. the following day. The team members expressed frustration at being hampered in their investigation as they were not permitted to inspect the tank, personally examine plant records, or talk to plant operators, under threat of imprisonment. Zrij Shukla, a chief inspector for CBI, also informed Woomer to "tell the UCC folks that he could put them in jail any time he wanted to do it," if they violated the regulations. The only joint activity carried out by the UCC team was to assist during Operation Faith in planning and su-

---

[11] Jackson B. Browning, *Union Carbide: Disaster at Bhopal, in Crisis Response:Inside Stories on Managing Under Siege,* Jack A. Gottschalk (ed.) Visible Ink Press, Michigan: 1993.

[12] Dr. Srinivasan Sridhar, Gordon E. Rutzen and William J. McVeagh II, engineers; Charles D. Miller, Department Head – MIC, Synthetic Gas and Phosgene Units at Institute; Dr. David W. Peck, Senior Process Chemist, and Warren J. Woomer, now Assistant Plant Manager at Institute.

[13] Personal communication with Woomer.

[14] Personal communication with S. Sridhar.

pervising the neutralization of the remaining MIC stored in the other two tanks and small containers.[15]

Seventeen days after the incident and the completion of Operation Faith, the culprit tank E-610 was opened to withdraw a sample of the residue. This tank was found to be below atmospheric pressure, meaning a partial vacuum, an indication that the tank and the associated piping were intact and sealed. The only visible sign of any damage was a longitudinal crack along the concrete mound covering the tank.

A sharpened stainless steel pipe about fourteen feet long was introduced through the thermowell nozzle (a narrow inlet used to measure the temperature) and pushed to the bottom through the layer of residue. The material trapped inside the pipe – called the core sample – was then extruded using a close-fitting pusher rod. From the length of the core sample the engineers estimated that between ten to fifteen inches of residue was left at the bottom of tank E-610. Six core samples were taken at this time.

Two of the samples were delivered to UCIL's Shamla Hills Technical Center for analysis, with government scientists utilizing another three. The sixth sample was retained at the plant. When the tank was lifted and weighed in April 1985, the residue was estimated to weigh 12.5 MT. The tank residue was found to be 52 centimeters (20.5 inches) deep – more than the earlier estimate based on the length of the core sample.

Working jointly, UCC and UCIL research scientists immediately started preliminary analyses of this residue at UCIL's Technical Center. The core samples kept in custody of UCIL were later sub-sampled (about twenty grams total) by UCIL chemists and shipped to UCC Technical Center at Research Triangle Park, North Carolina.[16]

After staying for twenty-four days in India, fifteen of which were spent assisting in the neutralization of the remaining MIC, the UCC investigation team returned to the U.S. and closeted themselves at the secluded Arrowood Pepsico Conference Center, in Tarrytown, New York. To elude reporters, they worked under disguise as employees of Brooks International, a fictitious company. From this location they charted the plan of investigation and closely interacted by telephone with scientists at UCC's

---

[15]   Tank E-611 contained 20.5 MT (13,000 gals.), tank E-619 a little over a ton and about 1.5 tons in several drums).

[16]   The samples were received by Federal Express on January 7, 1985. These were immediately shipped to South Charleston Technical Center in West Virginia.

two research centers located in South Charleston, West Virginia and Research Triangle Park, North Carolina.

Chemical analyses of the residue were again carried out at the Central Research and Development Department at the UCC South Charleston Technical Center in West Virginia. These analyses indicated the presence of considerable amounts of MIC trimer, moderate amounts of two other cyclic materials, including one DIONE, which was surprising, and low concentrations of DMU and TMB, thus confirming the earlier preliminary findings at the UCIL Bhopal Technical Center.

Chemical Analyses of the Residue in Tank E- 610

The core sample of residue removed from the bottom of tank E-610 was found to be softer, less dense and darker in the upper region and firmer, more crystalline and lighter in color in the bottom region. Because of the heterogeneous nature of the sample, the material was divided into three sections to analyze the top, middle, and bottom layers separately. Using a combination of liquid-chromatography (LC), gas chromatography (GC), and ion-chromatography (IC), laboratory chemical analyses of these three subsections revealed the presence of about twenty different components in varying concentrations, some in trace quantities.

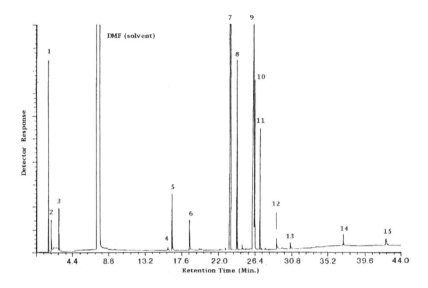

1. Trimethylamine; 2. methyl isocyanate; 3. chloroform; 4. 1,1-dimethylurea; 5. 1,1,3-trimethylurea; 6. 1,3-dimethylurea; 7. MIC trimer; 8. 1,1,3,5-tetramethylbiuret; 9. dimethyl isocyanurate (DMI);10. 1,3,5-trimethylbiuret; 11. Trimethyltriazenedione (DIONE); 12. methyl isocyanurate; 13-15. Not identified.

Figure 3-1. A typical gas chromatogram of the core residue.

For typical gas and liquid chromatograms (the chemical fingerprints) of the residue with the identities of the various peaks, see Figures 3-1 and 3-2 respectively. The chemical structures and their concentration ranges are depicted in Figure 3-3.

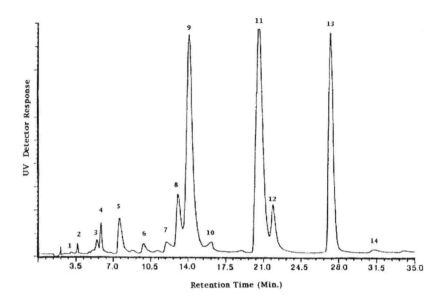

1. isocyanuric acid; 2. methylurea; 3. 1,3-dimethylurea; 4. methyl isocyanurate; 5. mol. wt. 156; 6. 1,3-dimethylbiuret; 7. 1,1,3-trimethylurea; 8. 1,5-dimethylbiuret; 9. dimethyl isocyanurate (DMI) and 1,1,3,5-tetramethylbiuret; 10. Dimethyl(methylamino)triazenedione; 11. 1,3,5-trimethylbiuret; 12. 1,7-dimethyltriuret; 13. MIC trimer; 14. mol. wt. 269, not identified.

Figure 3-2. A typical liquid chromatogram of the core residue

Individual compounds were separated and identified using state-of-the-art technology, including proton and carbon-13 nuclear magnetic resonance spectroscopy, infrared spectroscopy, and high-resolution GC-mass spectrometry. Further confirmation of the identities of the isolated materials was established by comparison with independently synthesized authentic samples. The metals found in the residue were analyzed by UCC Analytical Department and by independent commercial laboratories.

On April 5, 1985, in the presence of government officials and under the supervision of a team of scientists, the concrete shell covering the tank mound was removed and the tank weighed. Five holes were cut at different locations around the tank to inspect the inside and analyze the metal plates removed. Also present were Len Baker, director of technology, representing UCC; Dr. R. Sriram of Hindustan Chemicals, Bombay; and Dr. P.K.

Iyyer from Bhabha Atomic Research Center, Bombay.[17] At this time additional residue samples were also taken from other places within the tank to ensure that the residue previously analyzed was truly representative of the entire tank. An additional eighty grams collected from six of these core samplings were also made available to UCC chemists in the United States. Analyses of these samples helped confirm and refine the earlier analyses. However, a few additional compounds were detected in trace quantities, all of which are also chemically related to the earlier isolated materials and are the expected products from MIC reactions.[18] The three cyclic compounds – MIC trimer, DMI, and DIONE – comprised the bulk of the residue, amounting to 55-70 percent with higher concentrations in the bottom layer. Being white, crystalline, and heavier than the other components, these solids tended to settle and developed a gradient of increasing concentration of solids at the bottom. The upper layer contained higher concentrations of trimethylbiuret (TMB) and tetramethylbiuret (TRMB) and other less dense materials. TRMB is a liquid and breaks down at higher temperatures. Up to 1.5 percent of chloroform was also detected in the sample obtained in December from the "service-line end" (where all the pipes are connected) of the tank.

MIC Trimer - (40-50%)	DMI-(13-20%)	DIONE-(5-7%)

1,3,5-Trimethylbiuret	TMB	4-8%
1,1,3,5-Tetramethylbiuret	TRMB	3-6%
1,1,3-Trimethylurea	TMU	2-4%
1,3-Dimethylurea	DMU	1-2%
Chloroform	CCl3	0.4-1.5%
Methyl isocyanate	MIC	0.2-1%

Figure 3-3.
Chemical formulas of materials identified in the core sample of tank E-610

---

[17] "CBI experts cut open MIC tank," *Hindustan Times*, April 7, 1985, p. 1. See also *Legal Aftermath*, p. 673.

[18] These new chemicals are 1,3-dimethylbiuret, 1,5-dimethylbiuret, 1,7-dimethyltriuret, methylurea and methyl isocyanurate.

Laboratory Studies to Replicate the Tank Residue

Simultaneously, as the analytical results of the recovered residue were being confirmed, a second Team was assembled at the Technical Center at Research Triangle Park (RTP) in North Carolina and assigned the responsibility of replicating the composition of the tank residue in the laboratory. Not knowing the cause of the gas leak, this was deemed to be essential in determining the nature of the materials present in the tank just prior to the uncontrolled reaction which caused the gas leak. Given the number of products identified in the residue in varied concentrations, the chemists were faced with a challenging problem. This assignment also entailed surveying the chemical literature on MIC and all other products found in the tank residue, solvents used in the process of manufacturing it and other possible derivatives and products. Furthermore, all internally generated UCC project reports on MIC and related research were perused. Other smaller groups drawn from the Process, Analytical and Statistical Departments were assigned the task of setting up high-pressure experiments, analyzing the reaction products, and collecting and computerizing the massive experimental data generated. The research team at RTP was in constant contact with groups at the South Charleston Technical Center and the investigation team that had visited Bhopal, now working in seclusion in Tarrytown, New York.

The experimental results were critically analyzed and discussed at group meetings. Every possible scenario was considered and rigorously tested with additional experiments. In total, more than five hundred specially designed experiments were conducted at both the RTP and South Charleston laboratories between January and March 1985.

At the beginning, working without any clues as to what might have caused the leak or contaminated the tank, a number of experiments were designed by adding every feasible contaminant separately or in combination to MIC, and heating at different temperatures and over different time periods. The initial experiments included reactions of MIC with intermediates used in the process of its manufacture like phosgene, metal contaminants such as iron salts, and small amounts of water. These contributing contaminants were speculated on by the CSIR scientists and reported in the press. None of these experiments produced the entire array of compounds and in the right proportions found in the tank. As such, many of the speculations reported by the Indian and foreign media, when tested in the laboratory, were found to be baseless.

Round-the-clock laboratory experimentation and evaluation of the analytical results continued for more than two months. The RTP team met on a daily basis, including weekends, to monitor progress.[19] After carrying out hundreds of unsuccessful trials, the breakthrough came after four weeks, by the end of January 1985, when experiments that contained only MIC, chloroform, and water produced measurable amounts of the DMI, DIONE, and MIC trimer, in addition to the various expected ureas and biurets like, DMU, TMB and related compounds. This experiment gave the first indication that chloroform was absolutely necessary for the formation of DIONE. With further refinements it was determined that temperatures above 200°C (392°F) were necessary to produce the desired quantities of DMI. The composition of the residue found in tank E-610 was successfully replicated when a mixture consisting of 85 percent MIC, 12 percent chloroform and about 3 percent water was heated under pressure in a stainless steel reactor at about 225°C, for up to one hour.[20] Chloroform was used as solvent in the manufacture of MIC. The finding that a substantial quantity of chloroform had to be present in tank E-610 and that it participated in the reaction with MIC was extremely significant and its full implications will be discussed later.

Time-dependent experiments indicated that initially water reacted with MIC to form the expected initial products DMU and TMB. At higher temperatures, in the presence of chloroform, both of these materials decomposed and underwent further reactions to produce the cyclic products, MIC trimer, DMI and DIONE. DIONE was formed by the incorporation of elements of chloroform.[21] The product profile did not change significantly by the introduction of ferric chloride or low-grade steel (to simulate the presence of rust in tank E-610) to the MIC-chloroform-water mixture or

---

[19]   Hundreds of supporting experiments were also carried out simultaneously at the UCC Technical Center in South Charleston, WV.

[20]   In the course of the refinement of experimental conditions, it was also established that the amount of water in the mixture was also critical. By increasing the amount of water to more than 4%, the amounts of ureas and biurets increased and the concentrations of DMI and DIONE were reduced. Likewise, by reducing the amount of chloroform, the concentration of MIC trimer increased while that of DMI and DIONE decreased.

[21]   Chloroform was transformed to dichloromethane then incorporated into the DIONE molecule. The presence of dichloromethane was also detected in the residual material. It was subsequently demonstrated with C-13 enriched chloroform that it was incorporated into the DIONE.

even by carrying out the reactions in corrosion-resistant tantalum-lined reactors.

Based on knowledge of the precise amounts of water and chloroform required to replicate the residue and the earlier estimated bulk of the residue left in the tank, the UCC investigators estimated that between 120 and 240 gallons (1,000 to 2,000 pounds) of water entered tank E-610.[22] The analyses of the core samples and the results of the replication studies were made public by UCC in a report entitled *Bhopal Methyl Isocyanate Incident Investigation Team Report* on March 20, 1985.

The chemical information uncovered during these studies also gave an indication of the nature of the gases that may have escaped along with MIC. While a summary of this information is presented in the next section, more detailed studies of the chemical aspects of the investigation were published in peer-reviewed international chemical journals.[23]

Information Gleaned from the Chemical Analyses

The time-dependent analyses of the reaction of MIC-chloroform-water experiments have confirmed that when this mixture was heated, MIC was converted immediately into DMU and TMB. Within ten minutes, MIC trimer, DMI, and the DIONE (the cyclic products) were formed, with the concomitant decrease in the concentrations of DMU and TMB. The concentrations of the cyclic materials reached their maximum in about thirty minutes. Thereafter, DIONE started breaking down. Other specially designed experiments have further confirmed that the tank residue could also be replicated just by heating TMB and/or DMU and chloroform. These experiments have demonstrated unequivocally that the final products were formed by the decomposition of DMU and TMB. All of the designed experiments carried out to study the reaction pathway indicated that the reactions proceeded in a controlled manner and with high predictability and reproducibility.

---

[22] Since, the exact weight of the tank residue was determined to be 12.5 MT and 20.5 inches deep, the amount of water reacted should be closer to 2000 pounds or more.

[23] Themistocles D.J. D'Silva, Anibal Lopes, Russell L. Jones, Sureerat Singhawancha, and John K. Chan, "Studies of Methyl Isocyanate Chemistry in the Bhopal Incident," *Journal of Organic Chemistry*, vol. 51, 1986, pp. 3781-3788. Also in *J. Chem. Soc., Chemical Communications*, 1986, p. 795.

Chloroform participated in the reaction when the temperature reached 100°C. Only the elements of carbon and hydrogen from chloroform got incorporated into the DIONE molecule. The elements of chlorine were converted to hydrochloric acid that caused the metals from the inner surface of the stainless steel reactor to leach out slightly.

The analyses of the ratio of metals analyzed in the residue – iron, chromium and nickel – were consistent with their ratios in stainless steel type 304, used in the construction of the tanks. Metals analyses of the residue from the laboratory-simulated experiments also bore this out.

Direct measurements of temperatures inside the reactors indicated a brief surge in temperature, which did not exceed 275°C (527°F). The timing of the surge coincided with the appearance of the three cyclic products. The maximum temperature reached inside the tank was also estimated indirectly from the thermal stability of some of the materials in the residue. At higher temperatures, DMU, TMB and DIONE underwent decomposition. If the temperature inside the tank had exceeded 275°C, many of these heat-sensitive materials would have been destroyed and not detected. This was independently verified by heating the residue from the tank. This product stability data is extremely significant since it has given an indication of the upper limit of the temperature that may have been reached inside the tank E-610 at the peak of the reaction. The lower concentrations of DMU and TMB analyzed in the tank residue can now be explained; they decomposed at higher temperatures to form the cyclic products.

Nature of the Gases Released

Because of the prevailing circumstances soon after the incident, the nature and the chemical composition of the gaseous cloud were not determined. This uncertainty led to various speculations that other more toxic materials escaped along with MIC. The issue is still being debated. The detailed analysis of the residue and the replication of this residue in the laboratory helped determine the presence of a substantial quantity of chloroform in the MIC tank. Its participation in the reactions that took place in the tank was unexpected. The postulated mechanism of the chemical reactions, which occurred in the tank E-610, has helped investigators to consider the presence of several possible contaminants in the MIC cloud and reject the possibility of the presence of others.

It is well established in the literature that the initial products of MIC's reaction with water are methylamine and carbon dioxide – both gases at room temperature. Since carbon dioxide is not reactive, all of it would have escaped through the stack. Most of methylamine would have reacted immediately with available MIC to form dimethylurea (DMU). This product in turn would have further reacted with additional MIC to form trimethylbiuret (TMB). Under certain conditions, this process can continue to form triurets – by the addition of another molecule of MIC to TMB – until most of the DMU has reacted. The later formed substances, like triurets, being less stable at higher temperatures would revert back to TMB and DMU. It is possible that some unreacted methylamine was forced out through the stack along with the escaping carbon dioxide and MIC before it could react with MIC to form DMU, a solid.

The postulated mechanism for the formation of the cyclic compound requires the presence of ammonia and isocyanic acid as necessary intermediates. Dichloromethane was formed from the decomposition of chloroform. Ammonia, dimethylamine (DMA), and trimethylamine (TMA) were detected in the residue as hydrochloride salts.

It is highly unlikely that any phosgene or its addition product with methylamine, methylcarbamoyl chloride (MCC), was released into the atmosphere. Being very reactive, these molecules would have readily reacted with water or methylamine. More importantly, since the chloroform-containing MIC stored in tank E-610 was collected from the last batch of MIC distilled at elevated temperatures, it is unlikely that it would have contained phosgene, being lower boiling, it would have been removed in the earlier batches. If even traces of phosgene survived it would have reacted immediately with water to form hydrogen chloride and carbon dioxide.

The materials that could have escaped out of the stack along with MIC would therefore include carbon dioxide and varying amounts of ammonia, methylamine, dimethylamine, trimethylamine, chloroform, dichloromethane, and hydrogen chloride. All these materials, being heavier than air, would form a low-lying cloud in the vicinity of the plant and would probably not drift very far. The varied and unexplained medical conditions reported for the victims at different locations may be the result of exposure to any one or a combination of these materials.

There is no scientific evidence to indicate that hydrogen cyanide (HCN) gas was liberated into the atmosphere. This highly controversial issue will be discussed next in greater detail.

The Hydrogen Cyanide Controversy

BBC World News Service first announced that the gas leak in Bhopal, which killed nearly four hundred people, was cyanide based.[24] This general description of the gas was just one of the many such confusing reports on the nature of the toxic fumes. Some Indian newspapers have described the fumes as cyano gas, methyl isocyanide, methyl isocyanite, and even phosgene gas. Adding to the confusion, Professor Heeresh Chandra, head of forensic medicine at Bhopal's Gandhi Medical College, announced that, based on a number of postmortem examinations, there were indications of cyanide poisoning and recommended that the patients be treated with sodium thiosulfate – a known antidote for cyanide poisoning. Given the prestige of his position, Dr. Chandra's observations and recommendations were widely communicated. Others in the medical establishment rejected these findings. Professor N.P. Mishra disagreed with this decision and publicly rebuked Dr. Chandra as "a doctor of the dead and [someone who] has no business prescribing for the living" and advised against thiosulfate treatment.[25]

Within days, Dr. Max Daunderer, a German toxicologist, arrived in Bhopal with a consignment of about ten thousand ampoules of sodium thiosulfate to be used as an antidote for treatment of cyanide poisoning. The treatment was soon halted and Dr. Daunderer was sent back on December 13. By the end of January 1985, at the recommendation of the Indian Council of Medical Research (ICMR) – the equivalent of the National Institutes of Health in the United States – the order against the use of thiosulfate was rescinded.

According to the ICMR report issued in March 1985:

At least in the survivors there is evidence of chronic cyanide poisoning operating as a result of either inhalation of hydrocyanic acid (HCN) or more probably subsequent generation of cyanide radical from the cyanogen pool in gas-afflicted victims. The changes in the urinary thiocyanate and in the blood gas before and after thiosulfate treatment substantiated the findings. While further work on the nature of abnormalities in hemo-

---

[24] INDIAN GAS LEAK = BBC Written Archives Centre. Transcripts Nos. 1618 and 2151 of 03-12-84.
[25] Susanna Dakin, *Bhopal Disaster: a Personal View in Bhopal: From Hiroshima to Eternity,* Ed. S.B. Kolpe, Allied Printing Press, Bombay: 1985, p. 68.

globin brought about by exposure to MIC gas is in progress, the rationale for the use of sodium thiosulfate as an antidote has been established to ameliorate the lingering sickness of gas-affected victims in Bhopal.

The controversy continued and led to a confusing and politically explosive situation, resulting in demonstrations, police beatings, and arrests. Two days after the gas leak, the Central Water and Pollution Board collected air samples near the Bhopal plant for analyses. Using a team of eight scientists, they set up monitoring stations in the most affected areas. Of these, two monitoring stations were placed inside the plant, two in Jai Prakash Colony, two near the Bhopal Railway Station, and one in Amalpura, near Ram Mandir. Air samples near the MIC tank were reported to have 4,533 micrograms of cyanide per cubic meter and dropped to 2,533 micrograms 50 meters away from the tank.[26] Tests for the other sites were negative. This information lent support for the hypothesis that some deaths may have been caused by hydrogen cyanide poisoning.[27]

Although it is well documented in the chemical literature, it is not commonly known that when nitrogen-containing materials like nylons, polyurethane foams,[28] plastics prepared from urea and formaldehyde,[29] ureas, polyacrylonitrile and silk fibers,[30] animal hair and the like are burnt, hydrogen cyanide is liberated as one of the decomposition products. The burning of waste containing any of these materials is likely to produce some hydrogen cyanide gas. In fact, the most common cause of death among victims of house fires is attributed to poisoning by carbon monoxide and hydrogen cyanide present in the smoke. Tobacco smokers also carry small amounts of cyanide in their blood.

In order to obtain expert opinion from specialists in England and the United States, on January 29, 1985, Professor N.P. Mishra, head of the Department of Medicine at Gandhi Medical College, wrote letters to London's Bromptom Hospital and Atlanta's Centers for Disease Control. In

---

26   Report of the Central Water and Air Pollution Control Board (Gas Leak Episode at Bhopal), The Bhopal Tragedy – One Year After, An APPEN Report (Friends of the Earth Malaysia), 1985, pp. 113-118.

27   Ward Moorehouse, M. Arun Subramaniam, *The Bhopal Tragedy. What Really Happened and What It Means for American Workers and Communities at Risk,* Council on International and Public Affairs, 1986, pp. 344-3.

28   K. Ashida, F. Yamauchi, M.Katoh, and T.Harada, *J.Cell. Plast.,*10, No. 4,181-5,194, (1974).

29   V. Andreev and T.I. Sokolova, *Farmakol. i Toksikol.* 16, No. 4, 45-7,1953.

30   K. Yamamoto, *NBS Spec. Publ.* (US), 540,520-7 (1979).

his response of March 1, 1985, A.J. Newman Taylor, consultant physician at Bromptom Hospital, wrote: "It is very unlikely that MIC or its products, methylamine and carbon dioxide would survive in human tissues at two months.... Cyanide is normally present in the body and there are small quantities produced endogenously from constituents of food such as cyanoglycosides, and of course from cigarette smoke." Henry Falk, M.D., chief, Special Studies Branch, Chronic Division Center for Environmental Health, and James Melius, M.D., chief, Health Hazard and Technical Assistance Branch, National Institute for Occupational Safety and Health, both at the Centers for Disease Control, stated that: "We have found no biochemical nor physiological rationale for believing that MIC would be converted *in vivo* to cyanide or to thiocyanate. Looking for cyanide and for thiocyanate as a marker of MIC exposure, therefore, lacks theoretical justification at present. Cyanides are present in small quantities in blood serum, urine, and various organs of normal persons. The amounts detected vary with the tissue tested. Cigarette smokers have higher level of cyanide than do nonsmokers as do persons who consume foods containing cyanides. Thiocyanates produced *in vivo* as a consequence of detoxification of cyanides, naturally occurring or externally derived, can also be detected in normal individuals."[31]

It is known in the chemical literature that when MIC is heated to a very high temperature (427-548°C) in the gaseous state, hydrogen cyanide is one of the several products formed.[32] This information, cited in the MIC Safety Manual, was used by some to assert that the high temperature inside the tank must have caused some MIC to decompose to hydrogen cyanide. As discussed previously, several laboratory replication studies have shown that temperatures inside the tank could not have exceeded 275°C. The gaseous products analyzed (by a combination of gas chromatography and mass spectrometry) from the laboratory simulation experiments also did not indicate the presence of hydrogen cyanide. The extensive studies performed under laboratory conditions, both by CSIR and UCC scientists, have positively ruled out the formation of hydrogen cyanide (HCN) in tank E-610.

---

[31] Letters to Dr. N.P. Mishra from Specialists Abroad on MIC and Sodium Thiosulphate, (Appendix 5.12), *The Bhopal Tragedy One Year After, AN APPEN REPORT,* 1985, pp. 125-128.

[32] P.G. Blake and S. Ijadi-Maghsoodi, "Kinetics and Mechanism of Thermal Decomposition of Methyl Isocyanate," *International Journal of Chemical Kinetics,* vol.14, (1982), pp. 945-952.

Chemically, HCN is known to react with MIC to form a number of products.[33] It is also known to react readily with hydrochloric acid, ammonia, and methylamine – all of which were produced in significant quantities in the tank. These additional competing reactions would have generated another series of HCN-derived by-products. Furthermore, in the presence of hydrochloric acid, HCN is known to undergo acid-catalyzed trimerization (six-membered cyclic compound) to form symmetrical tri-azene.[34] None of the HCN-amines derived materials was detected in the tank residue or in laboratory experiments.

Answers to questions that nagged the doctors and scientists as to why the blood of victims turned bright red, and why some patients apparently responded positively to sodium thiosulfate treatment, may never be known. This is largely attributable to a lack of reliable analytical data recorded soon after the disaster.

However, according to an article published in 1910, entitled "Death Produced by Chloroform,"[35] HCN was identified in two blood samples, one after death by chloroform, and the other after syncope brought on by chloroform. These authors also indicated that when a mixture of chloro-form and ammonia was exposed to an electric arc in the laboratory, it pro-duced HCN; they speculated that a similar reaction could occur inside the body. Given this unconfirmed finding it is possible that along with MIC, chloroform and ammonia also escaped into the atmosphere and these two may have reacted inside the body of some of the victims. Alternatively, the inhaled chloroform may have reacted with the endogenous ammonia inside the body to produce HCN. The supposedly *in vivo* transformation of chloroform into HCN, if validated, may help explain the highly controver-sial issue surrounding some of the deaths in Bhopal. It would also explain the awakenings of many victims after prolonged coma, and the findings in a cluster not far from the plant where the victims "had fallen unconscious with few or no eye symptoms."[36]

---

[33]   K.H. Slotta, R. Tschesche, *Berichte,* vol. 60, 1927, p. 1031.

[34]   Christoph Grundmann, Alfred Kreutzberger, *J. Am. Chem. Soc.,* vol. 76, 1954, pp. 5646-5650

[35]   V. Hancu and V. Gomoiu, *Revista Stiintzelor, Medicale,* Feb. 1910: Abstracted in *Zentr. Biochem. Biophys.*, 10, 413, 1910 and *Chemical Abstracts* No. 2842, 1910.

[36]   See Neil Anderson et. al. in *The Lancet.*

The Singh Commission

In addition to the investigations initiated by the central government through its CBI and CSIR wings, the state government initiated its own commission to determine the cause of the gas leak. By the order of the governor of Madhya Pradesh, issued on December 6, 1984, Justice N.K. Singh, a sitting judge of the Gwalior High Court, was appointed to head the one-man commission.

In a massive 7,000-page document presented to the Singh Commission, with details about the operations of the plant, UCIL rejected the prevailing hypothesis that the gas leak was caused by operational deficiency. This was backed up with the plant performance record for five years. Instead, it argued that it "was caused, very likely, by the deliberate act of some person or persons."

> The MIC unit started working in February 1980, and until the present tragedy, it had operated safely and satisfactorily. This itself is a cogent proof of the efficiency of the plant.... In the rejoinder filed by UCIL vice-president and secretary, Mr. C.P. Lal said the government statement was vague and contained irrelevant inferences.... It has studiously avoided information available to the government that could throw some light on questions involved in the terms of reference. The averments made in the written statement are motivated and appear to have been placed with the objective of creating civil liability.[37]

On December 17, 1985, just as the Singh Commission was finally ready to hold real hearings, after facing several hurdles in setting up his office, the new chief minister, Motilal Vora, announced in the state assembly that the time limit of the commission had expired. Members of the Opposition were surprised to hear that the commission's mandate would not be extended and expressed their strong displeasure by staging a walkout. Apparently, Justice Singh had not even been informed of this decision and only learned of his commission's dissolution through the media.[38] The official reason given by the chief minister for disbanding the commission was that:

---

[37] "UCIL sticks to 'sabotage' theory," *The Times of India,* December 13, 1985, p. 9.
[38] "Panel wound up to 'shield' guilty," *Indian Express,* December 22, 1985, p.1. See also *The Times of India,* December 18, 1985, p. 6.

The State Government did not think it fit to continue the probe by the commission, whose term expired on December 15, as the Center [Government of India] had already set up a commission under Dr. S. Varadarajan.... Besides, there was the Dr. Krishnamurty Scientific Commission and a committee to study safety measures in pesticide, fertilizer and drug industries. The decision to wind up the Singh Commission was taken in the best interest of the gas victims.[39]

Minister of State for Chemicals and Petrochemicals R.K. Jaichandra Singh gave a similar rationalization.[40] According to a senior state government official who did not wish to be named:

The decision had been taken at the insistence of the Government of India's lawyers in USA since they felt that the enquiry's findings might affect the compensation claim of $500 million made on behalf of the victims. If the N.K. Singh Commission...eventually established that the Madhya Pradesh Government, the Union Government and Union Carbide India Limited (UCIL) all shared the blame equally, Union Carbide Corporation (UCC) might have got away with less compensation. In fact, Union Minister of State for Law and Justice H.R. Bhardwaj even suggested that the probe had been withdrawn because 'information submitted there was reaching UCC in America'.[41]

The Indian press was generally critical and reacted angrily at the sudden termination of the Singh Commission before it could finish its investigation. "All this indicates that the authorities were never seriously interested in the commission's work. They had treated it basically as a publicity stunt."[42] A few days later, the CSIR scientists disclosed the results of their studies.

---

[39] "M.P. Govt. commission on gas tragedy wound up," *The Hindu,* December 18, 1985, p. 1. See also *Legal Aftermath,* p. 1152.

[40] "Walkout over Bhopal tragedy panel's discontinuance," *The Statesman,* December 20, 1985, p. 7.

[41] Tavleen Singh, "Ending an Enquiry," *India Today,* January 15, 1986, p. 24. See also *Legal Aftermath,* p. 1240.

[42] *Indian Express,* December 22, 1985, p. 1.

The CSIR Investigation Report[43]

A year after the disaster and nine months after the UCC Bhopal investigation report was made public, Mr. M. Arunachalam, minister of state for industry, presented the CSIR findings to the Indian Parliament. Coauthored by sixteen scientists with principal author Dr. S. Varadarajan, the director general of CSIR, it was structured to include: 1) Operation Faith; 2) a brief chronology of events at the plant on the night of the incident; 3) analyses of the residue samples from tank E-610; 4) results of about seventy experiments conducted in CSIR laboratories; and 5) conclusions.

The laboratory results were basically in agreement with the earlier disclosures by UCC. The cause of the uncontrollable chemical reaction was attributed to the entry of 135 gallons of water. It also confirmed that hydrogen cyanide was not detected in their laboratory studies.

The CSIR scientists also supported the earlier hypothesis promoted by the plant operators, that the water most probably entered through leaking valves. In addition, it alleged that several other factors "probably" aggravated the problem once water entered the tank. Some of these were: 1) Probable contamination by metals from the use of corrosion-prone material of construction, 2) Storage of quantities of unstable and toxic MIC in large tanks rather than in 210 stainless steel drums, and 3) Lack of on-line analyzer/alarm to monitor the quality of MIC and other monitoring instruments. This CSIR Investigation Report will be critically reviewed in the subsequent sections.

The Arthur D. Little (ADL) Investigation Report[44]

In addition to their earlier investigation, which was based on the studies of the tank residue, UCC also engaged the services of Arthur D. Little, Inc. (ADL), one of the most respected international consulting firms, to continue the investigation.

During the course of this investigation, the ruling by the U.S. Court of Appeals ordered the Government of India to abide by U.S. disclosure rules as was expected from UCC – equal access to evidence from both the

---

[43] Since this report was not published, the relevant pages are presented in Appendix B.

[44] Ashok S. Kalelkar, *Investigation of Large–Magnitude Incidents: Bhopal as a Case Study*, London: May 1988.

parties. CBI then made available to UCC lawyers over seventy thousand copies of plant documents and allowed interviews with plant operators. By working jointly with UCC investigators in examining these documents and collecting other information in India, the ADL investigators concluded that they were "virtually certain" that the Bhopal incident was caused by the entry of water into the tank through a hose that had been connected directly to the tank. ADL formally presented its findings at the Institution of Chemical Engineers Conference on Preventing Major Chemical Accidents, held in London in May 1988. The 37-page ADL report included diagrams, photocopies of key documents, and testimonials of plant operators to support their findings.

The investigators concluded that: 1) The water-washing hypothesis was untenable. 2) The last transfer of MIC was from tank E-610 and not from tank E-611, as asserted by the operators and supported by the CSIR scientists, and 3) Some plant documents were tampered with in an attempt to coverup the real cause of the gas leak.

The areas of water-washing activity are depicted in figures 3-4(a) and 3-4(c). Associated with the filters being washed are four 1/2-inch bleeder valves (shown by arrows in Fig. 3-4c). Reportedly, only one of these was plugged and needed cleaning and the other three were not, and were draining freely. The operator attached a 1/2-inch hose to the inlet to wash the blocked filter. According to the ADL investigators the water hose would not have had sufficient pressure for the water to climb 10.4 feet near the point of introduction. The 1/2-inch hose connection used to wash the plugged filters limited the flow to about 10-15 gallons/minute; "the [other] three open bleeder valves would limit the water back-pressure...to no more than 0.7 foot of hydraulic head." It would also require 4,500 gallons of water to fill the 500-foot long piping connecting the storage tanks, with all four intermittent valves fully open, for water to enter freely into the tank.

If any one of the valves was closed it would have stopped the flow of water. (The configuration of the piping and the relative distances are shown in Figures 3-4(a) and 3-5 and the expanded views of the head of tank E-610 and the water-washing area in figures 3-4(b) and 3-4(c) respectively). Unknown to UCC investigators, this test was in fact conducted soon after the incident by CBI along with UCIL engineers, and omitted from the CSIR report. In a one-hour simulation test, water did not even pass even through the very first valve located above the site of water inlet. Furthermore, on February 18, 1985, a hole was drilled at the lowest point along the length of piping to collect any possible trapped water. Several empty 55-gallon drums were made available to collect any water flowing out of the drilled hole. The pipes were dry and "no liquid came out in spite of purging with nitrogen."[45]

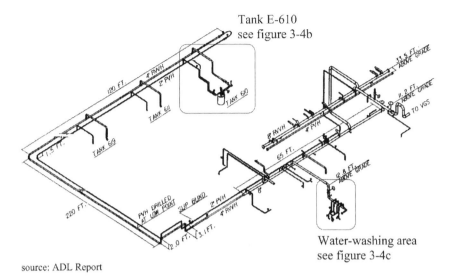

source: ADL Report

Figure 3-4 (a). Diagram showing Tank E-610 with the connecting pipeline to the area of water-washing of clogged valves [Source ADL Report]

[45]   See Appendix A-14 for the CBI authorization letter and Appendix A-15 for the results of the findings.

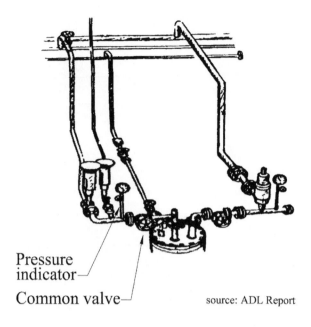

Pressure
indicator

Common valve

source: ADL Report

Figure 3-4 (b) Expanded view of the (above-ground) top of the tank E-610
showing the connecting pipelines, valves, and gauges.

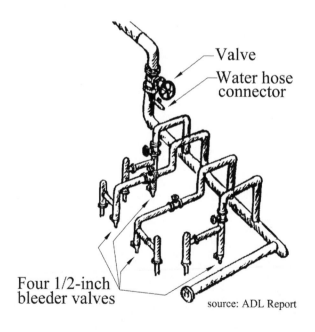

Valve

Water hose
connector

Four 1/2-inch
bleeder valves

source: ADL Report

Figure 3-4 (c) Expanded view of the water-washing area

As discussed earlier, prior to the neutralization of remaining MIC in tank E-611, in preparation for Operation Faith, the contents of the SEVIN feed tank, the carbamoylation reactor and the transfer line (located between the reactor and the MIC storage tanks) were sampled and analyzed. The recovered greenish colored material contained a higher than normal concentration of chloroform along with some solid materials.

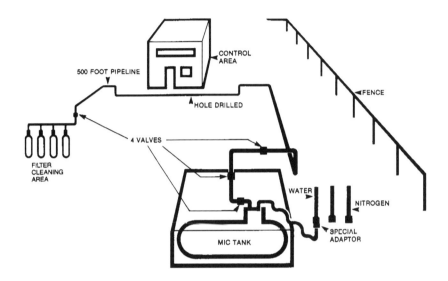

Figure 3-5. Schematic diagram showing the locations of the four valves between the water-washing area and tank E-610. Also the locations of the hole drilled and direct water hose connection to the tank.

Source: Union Carbide Corporation Report

When the MIC stored in tank E-611 was also analyzed at this time, it was found to be of high purity, containing only trace quantities of chloroform. The suspicious green material, and the unusually high concentrations of chloroform found in the feed tank, the reactor and the transfer line, were at the time very puzzling to investigators. Later, when a high amount of chloroform was also detected in the residue of the ill-fated tank E-610, ADL/UCC investigators suspected that the last transfer of MIC was most likely from tank E-610 and not tank E-611.

When the documents were scrutinized more closely, ADL/UCC investigators discovered that data pertaining to the events on the night of December 2 had been tampered with – several pages of plant logs were altered, torn, or missing. One of the tampered log pages indicated the transfer [of MIC] from tank E-611 was made at 10:15 p.m., (which would have been near the end of the second shift), between two third-shift operators – C.N. Sen and M.C. Joshi – who actually did not arrive on site until 10: 45 p.m. Sen supposedly transferred MIC from tank E-611 and Joshi received it at the SEVIN feed tank. The logged time of the transfer was also out of sequence with the remaining entries. The investigators surmised that the originally recorded time was 0:15 to 0:30 but was later changed to "10:15 to :30. " (The entries were also in variance with the twenty four-hour clock convention used at the plant.)[46]

The presence of high concentrations of chloroform in the reaction vessels, the connecting pipe, and the residue in tank E-610 but not in tank E-611, and the altered records of timings, led the investigators to conclude that the last transfer of MIC was made from tank E-610. This was carried out between 12:15 a.m. and 12:30 a.m., roughly fifteen minutes prior to the massive gas emission.

ADL also reported that the operators gave contradictory versions of the events around and during the tea-break period just prior to the gas release. Witnesses from other units reported that the supervisors and the plant superintendent were having tea at the main plant canteen (see Fig. B) when they were told of a small gas leak, which started prior to the scheduled tea break. When questioned, the supervisors were unable to give consistent accounts of their activities during the forty-five minutes preceding the major release of the gas. The operators in the MIC unit also gave contradictory accounts. According to the U.S. investigators, MIC operators and supervisors were aware of the cause of the problem thirty to forty-five minutes prior to the major emission. To forestall the problem they tried to relieve the pressure inside tank E-610 by transferring some MIC out of it into the SEVIN reactor, thereby expecting to remove some of the water as well.

When interviewed a year later, the SEVIN supervisor initially denied entering the SEVIN unit the morning after the accident, but later admitted he had "entered briefly to complete his logs." Prior to neutralization of the remaining MIC during Operation Faith, the same supervisor reportedly suggested continuing the reaction for conversion of MIC into Carbaryl, without the need for analysis of the contents in the carbamoylating reactor.

---

[46] See Appendix A-16 for a copy of the altered page.

The investigators also reported finding a rough sketch on the reverse side of the supervisor's Daily Notes – supposedly scribbled the night of the incident – indicating a connection of a water hose to the pressure indicator (PI) on a tank.

Analysis of the CSIR Report

The media and others readily and uncritically accepted the CSIR investigation report as the authoritative report that explained the cause of the disaster. Because of the limited availability of this document it has escaped close scrutiny by the scientific community at large. Some of the conclusions drawn in this report deserve comment.

1. Stability of MIC: Several statements throughout the report depicted MIC as a very unstable substance that reacts unpredictably and "explosively." After CSIR scientists carried out nearly seventy reactions – as listed in Tables 3.1 and A-3.1 of the Report – not a single blowout or explosion was recorded. The safe handling record of the MIC during its manufacture for many years at the Institute and Bhopal plants and shipments to the various countries is a testimony to its stability and reaction predictability.

2. Other contaminants aggravated the problem: The scientists have argued that the estimated 512 kg (135 gallons) of water was not sufficient to generate the heat and the pressure reached inside the tank and postulated several other "probable" contributing factors – not supported by their experiments. The postulated chemical reactions that occurred in tank E-610, as depicted in Table 3.2 in the Report, (see Appendix B) are presented in an unconventional way. These equations were used for the calculations to estimate the quantity of water that entered the tank.

More specifically, equation (2) is not chemically balanced and consequently the value calculated for the amount of water consumed is understated by 920 kg. Equation (3) indicates that as much as 383.5 kg (844 lbs.) of carbon tetrachloride (CCl_4) was formed in the tank. The conversion of chloroform to carbon tetrachloride under these reaction conditions has no precedence in the chemical literature.[47] Even though lower boiling chemicals including chloroform and dichloromethane were detected in the tank residue and in the replication experiments, CCl_4 was neither detected in the tank residue nor was it analyzed in the residue of the laboratory repli-

---

[47]   Chloroform ($CHCl_3$) boils at 61-62°C and dichloromethane (CH_2Cl_2) at 39.75°C.

cation experiments. Equation (7) indicates that as much as 58 percent of MIC was directly converted to MIC trimer (MICT) independently of the reaction of MIC with water. This amount would represent the total amount of MICT analyzed in the residue. The postulated reaction for formation of MICT exclusively by trimerization by metal contamination, and not by other routes, is not consistent with the results of the experiments recorded elsewhere in the report. In fact, several experiments listed in Tables 3.1 of the CSIR report indicate that as much as 60-84 percent of MICT was produced just by heating mixtures of MIC, chloroform and water[48] or by heating TMB alone or in the presence of chloroform.[49] All the experimental results, both at UCC and CSIR laboratories have indicated that metal contamination, if any, was of little consequence and not the only pathway for the formation of MIC trimer.

3. Volume of MIC stored: The storage of large quantities of MIC in large underground storage tanks was criticized in favor of storage in 210 stainless steel drums of 200-liter capacity. As discussed earlier in great detail, the MIC plant was designed to work by a continuous process in a closed system, with the transfer of MIC and other liquid materials carried out under nitrogen pressure. In such a system MIC can be produced around the clock in three work shifts. This was the preferred technology that UCIL opted to acquire, as was noted in the letter of January 1, 1970 to the Licensing & Progress Section, Industrial Development Internal Trade & Company Affairs (see Appendix A-4.)

Manually filling and emptying MIC drums is suitable for batch-wise operations but not for a continuous production. Moreover, operators would have been exposed on a daily basis to unnecessary high levels of MIC in the process of transferring into and from the drums, requiring continuous use of respirators and various devices to trap the escaping vapors. The logistics of storing hundreds of drums around the plant in a safe manner and at low temperatures during the hot summer months (with temperatures regularly exceeding 100°F) would have been impractical.

All three tanks functioned as expected during the five years the MIC plant was in operation and water had never previously entered the tanks. Despite the massive uncontrolled reaction of December 3, tank E-610 maintained its structural integrity. There was no material evidence to indicate that any contaminant entered the tank other than water. The MIC

---

[48] See experiment 4 in Table 3.1 and experiment 15 in Table A-3.1
[49] See experiment 9 in Table 3.1 and experiment 30 in A-3.1.

stored in the adjacent E-611, of similar design and pipe connections, was found to be pure and free from contaminants.

The CSIR report is significant not only for what reactions were proposed in it, but also for what it failed to report, namely, the two critical tests carried out by CBI and UCIL engineers: The negative results from a one-hour simulation of the water-washing activity, and the absence of any trapped water in the pipeline, which discredited the water-washing and leaking-valves hypotheses.

Interestingly, many of the uncorroborated conclusions listed in the report had been cited earlier in the lawsuit filed by the Union of India in New York in April 1985, eight months before the CSIR report was issued. It is apparent that the chemical reactions postulated in the report were based not on the results of laboratory experiments but in order to rationalize and support the predetermined allegations in the ongoing lawsuit.

The Final Hours

The last batch of MIC produced from October 19 to 22 was collected and stored in tanks E 611 and E-610. The very last fraction collected at higher temperatures, highly contaminated with chloroform, was stored in tank E-610. The MIC plant was then closed and isolated from the rest of the systems. The only activity remaining at the plant was the conversion of MIC to Carbaryl by reacting with alpha-naphthol. A work force of ninety-nine personnel was normally designated for this phase of production.

The assassination of Prime Minister Indira Gandhi on October 31 led to communal riots and a curfew, which paralyzed most of the activities in the city. As a consequence the plant was virtually closed.

Two scenarios were later published to document the activities at the plant starting from the water washing of the clogged pipe. The first by the media, soon after the disaster, was primarily from the perspective of the plant operators, and the other was put forward by the ADL investigators. The following scenario of the events on the night prior to the gas emission was portrayed by the *New York Times*.[50]

On Sunday, December 2, at 2:45 p.m., about 100 workers reported for duty on the eight-hour second shift. Inside the plant pesticide SEVIN was being produced.

---

50   Stuart Diamond, "Disaster in Bhopal: Workers Recall Horror," *The New York Times*, January 25, 1985.

At 9:30 p.m. Rahaman Khan, a plant operator, said that Mr. Gauri Shanker, MIC Supervisor during the second shift, told him "to open a nozzle on the [blocked filter] pipe and put a water hose in to clean the inside." Shanker went along with Khan and stayed there during the procedure. "I connected a hose to the pipe to be cleaned and opened a drain."[51] Then both men left the area with the water hose still connected. "<u>Unattended, the water flowed into the pipe, out pipe drains [three open bleeders] onto the floor, where it entered the floor drain</u>". [Emphasis added].

At 10:30 p.m. workers prepared for a change of shift. The pressure of the tank E-610 was noted to be at 2 psig and was logged. Operators said that the temperature was usually around 22°C, but there is no indication that it was also recorded. At 10:45 p.m. the new shift crew had arrived by company bus and prepared to take over the plant operations, a transition that usually required half an hour. The MIC supervisor for the night shift was Shakil Ibrahim Qureshi, an organic chemist with two years of experience as an MIC supervisor.

Around 11.30 p.m. operators sensed the sharp odor of MIC. V.N. Singh and other operators walked around the MIC structure and spotted liquid dripping from about fifty feet above ground accompanied by yellowish-white gas, and they informed the supervisor. He said he would deal with the leak after the next tea break. Workers continued to inspect the area until tea time at 12:15 a.m. They had tea together in the control room until 12:40 a.m. Five minutes after the tea break ended "the workers began to panic because of the choking fumes and realized that things were out of control." Suman Dey, a senior operator on duty, said: "Things were happening very fast." He glanced at the temperature gauge in the control room. "It had risen above 25°C, the top of the scale." Pressure was rapidly moving towards 40 psi [pounds per square inch]. Dey went to Qureshi's office and told him about the pressure rise. Dey then rushed to the storage tanks. He later recalled standing on the concrete mound over the tanks. "There was a tremendous sound, a messy boiling sound, underneath the slab, like a caldron. The whole slab was vibrating." He started to run but heard a loud noise behind him, and turned back to look to see about a six-inch crack along the length of the concrete. He raced back to tell Qureshi in the control room and saw the pressure gauge again. It was off the scale – above 55 psi. Qureshi ordered all water sources in the area to be shut off and ordered that water be sprayed on the leak. "Someone sounded an

---

[51] See figures 3-4.(a) and 3-4 (c) for a view of the set up.

alarm by breaking its glass, workers said. Dey said he made an announcement on the factory loudspeaker that there was large MIC leak and that people should leave." Dey recalled that workers were running around in panic shouting "massive MIC leak."

At 12:50 a.m., within a minute or so of the alarm, the factory fire brigade arrived and turned on several hydrants. The water spray could reach only 100 feet high. "The gas was escaping from atop a 120-foot stack and was shooting another 10 feet." Dey then turned on the vent gas scrubber to neutralize the escaping gases. "The flow meter indicated there was no caustic soda flowing into the device. The scrubber [VGS] had been under maintenance." [Emphasis added.]

At 1:00 a.m. Qureshi telephoned S.P. Choudhary, the assistant plant manager, at home. Choudhary said to turn on the flare tower – which was designed to burn off the escaping gases. According to Dey, Qureshi hesitated to do so for fear of explosion. He later remembered that a four-foot piece of the pipe of the tower was missing: it had corroded some time ago and had not been replaced.

Around 1:30 a.m., MIC began to engulf the control room area and adjoining offices. Qureshi could not find his oxygen mask. He ran out, scaled a six-foot fence topped by barbed wire, and fractured his leg when he landed outside the plant premises.

At 3:00 a.m. Jay Mukund, the plant manager, arrived at the plant and "sent a man to tell the police about the accident because the phones were out of order." Police Superintendent Swaraj Puri said, "I first learned of MIC, with my lungs and eyes burning, at about 3:30 a.m. when I was informed of it by K.V. Shetty, the plant superintendent for the night shift, four hours after the leak began."

India Today[52] also published a similar version but with slight variations in the timings and details. CSIR investigators only focused on the activities of the control room operator with very few additional details.

The ADL report suggests a strikingly different scenario:

At 10:45 p.m., the shift change occurred. The unit was shut down and it takes at least a half-hour for the shift change to be accomplished. During this period, on a cold winter night, the MIC storage area would have been

---

52   Inderjit Badhwar and Madhu Trehan, "Bhopal City of Death," *India Today*, December 31, 1984, pp. 4-25.

completely deserted. We believe that it was at this point – during the shift change – that a disgruntled operator entered the storage area and hooked up one of the readily available rubber water hoses to Tank 610, with the intention of contaminating and spoiling the tank's contents.... He un-screwed the local pressure indicator, which can be easily accomplished by hand, and connected the hose to the tank. The entire operation could be completed within five minutes...

The water and MIC reaction initiated the formation of carbon dioxide which, together with MIC vapors, was carried through the header system and out of the stack of the vent gas scrubber by about 11:30 to 11:45 p.m. Because the "common valve"...was in a closed position before the incident and the tank held a strong vacuum when it cooled down after the incident, it is clear that the valve was temporarily opened to permit the entry of water. This also permitted the vapors initially generated to flow via...[Process Vent Header] out through the...[Relief Valve Vent Header]. It was these vapors that were sensed by the workers in the area downwind as the earlier minor MIC leaks. The leak was also sensed by several MIC operators who were sitting downwind of the leak at the time. They reported the leak to the MIC supervisor and began to search for it in the MIC structure. At about midnight, they found what they believed to be the source, viz., a section of open piping located on the second level of the structure near the vent gas scrubber. They fixed a fire hose so that it would spray in that direction and returned to the MIC control room believing that they had successfully contained the MIC leak. Meanwhile, the supervisors went to the plant's main canteen on break.

Shortly after midnight, several MIC operators saw the pressure rise on the gauges in the control room and realized that there was a problem with Tank 610. They ran to the tank and discovered the water hose connection to the tank. They discussed the alternatives and called the supervisors back from the canteen. They decided upon transferring about one ton of the tank's contents to the SEVIN unit as the best method of getting the water out. The major release then occurred. The MIC supervisor [Shakil Qureshi] called the MIC production manager [S.P. Choudhary] at home within fifteen minutes of the major release and told him that water had gotten into the MIC tank...

Not knowing if the attempted transfer had exacerbated the incident, or whether they would be blamed for not having notified plant manager earlier, those involved decided upon a cover-up. They altered logs that morning and thereafter to disguise their involvement... .[53]

Entry of water Inadvertent or Deliberate?

All the data presented thus far do not support the postulated hypothesis of an inadvertent entry of water into the tank due to leaky valves. If water was deliberately introduced by an employee, then how was it done and by whom? Much valuable information can be gleaned from various interviews given by the plant personnel to several reporters, and to ADL and UCC investigators.

Just before the first anniversary of the tragedy, Steven Weisman visited the Bhopal plant. During his one-man tour of the Bhopal facilities, the *New York Times* reporter talked to production manager S.P. Choudhary, plant manager J. Mukund, and CBI's chief investigator Zrij Shukla.[54] According to Weisman, the two UCIL managers were eager to talk to a foreign reporter to present their side of the story.[55] This interview took place shortly before UCIL submitted its documents to the Singh Commission in which it challenged the water-washing hypothesis, and before the issuance of the CSIR report. The managers told the reporter the following theory to explain the entry of water:

> ...that it was introduced into the tank deliberately. 'We cannot find any other way it could have happened,' said Mr. Choudhary, who has been working at the plant for six years.... During the tour, Mr. Mukund showed where he said he felt the sabotage could have taken place: a group of six separate pipes leading into the methyl isocyanate storage tank – two for nitrogen and four methyl isocyanate circulation. He said 'it would be easy' to use a hose to connect water from a nearby pipe to the nitrogen pipe or even to a valve on the tank itself.... 'Some of those who studied the accident have suggested that a worker connected water to the nitrogen pipe by mistake.... No employee would confuse these pipes,' he said. 'No one familiar with our color code or who could read would confuse them. But if there was sabotage, this would be the easiest place.'

---

[53] Kalelkar, pp. 26-27.
[54] Steven R. Weisman, "Bhopal a Year Later: An Eerie Silence," *The New York Times*, Dec. 5, 1985, p. 4. See also *Legal Aftermath, Suppl.*, 2, p. 1079.
[55] Personal communication with Steve Weisman.

...he dismissed the suggestion that Carbide employees were too unso-
phisticated to think of the idea of mixing water with methyl isocyanate...
as a way of disrupting the system.... 'All of our employees knew that
water and MIC were not compatible and that mixing them would create
problems...but we don't believe that whoever did it would possibly have
known that this would happen – that 2,000 people were going to die'.

Weisman was then shown the area where the workers were washing
the filter equipment, about two hundred feet from the storage tank. Choudhary said, "the reason he doubted that water leaked from this spot is that
there was not enough pressure for the water to have gone through five
hundred feet of pipe. He asserted that no residual water had been found in
this pipe, and that four other valves were shut tight, preventing water flow
to the methyl isocyanate tank." When Shukla was asked if the cause of the
accident baffled him, he replied: "An angler who is waiting for his fish
shows patience. I am that angler. I am neither bored nor baffled."

Mukund and Choudhary were witnesses to the drilling of the hole in
the pipeline on February 8, 1985, when the pipe was found to be dry. Their
involvement in this critical test is indicated in the notes signed by Mukund and Choudhary as representatives of UCIL and Murari Lal and R.K.
Agrawal of the CBI.[56]

Later, the leaking-valves hypothesis was put to the test in order to
simulate the water-washing operation without the slip-blind. In a one-hour
test no water was found to have leaked past the very first valve, as related
by Choudhary to the *New York Times* reporter. Both of these activities were
conducted jointly by the UCIL engineers and CBI investigators.[57,58] Furthermore, the fact that tank E-610 was found to be below atmospheric
pressure after the gas release indicates that the system was completely
sealed.

UCIL had also presented its case in the 7,000-page document submitted to the Singh Commission claiming that the gas leak was due to the
direct entry of water, probably by a deliberate act and was not connected
to deficiencies in plant operations or maintenance.

---

[56] See Appendices A-14 and A-15 for the notes signed by these individuals.
[57] See also testimony of Bud G. Holman before Hon. John F. Keenan, in U.S.
District Court, Doc. No. 322, MDL 626, January 3, 1986, pp. 5-8.
[58] "Leak due to sabotage:Carbide," *The Times of India,* December 5, 1985, p.
20.

When S. Sundarajan, superintendent of instrumentation of the Maintenance Department, reported to work early in the morning following the incident, he was instructed to check the instruments on tank E-610. He discovered that the local pressure indicator on tank E-610 was missing and brought this to the attention of his supervisor. In statements recorded on video, Sundarajan said, "…so we screwed in another pressure gauge. [He asked the manager] why the pressure gauge is not there, at that time?" He was told, "this is not the time to investigate." Sundarajan said that he also found a hose with running water lying beside the tank man-head.[59] As documented in the ADL report, instrumentation logs seized by the CBI also indicated that the pressure indicator was attached to tank E-610 on November 30, 1984, but was missing when Sundarajan examined it on the morning of December 3.

An off-duty employee from a nearby unit, who reported to work the morning of the accident, stated that he was told "by a close friend of one of the MIC operators that water had entered through a tube that had been connected to the tank." When other witnesses were questioned later, they also recalled that the local pressure indicator was found to be missing after the incident. Another operator on duty that night said that, "shortly after the release had subsided early in the morning, at approximately 3:00 a.m., the workers from other units were discussing the incident in the plant. Two MIC operators told them that water had entered the tank through a pressure indicator."[60]

R.D. Singh worked in the Utilities section, just a few yards away from the MIC plant, and had spent the entire night of the accident at the plant along with his supervisor and the fire truck operator. When interviewed ten years later by an Indian reporter, he said that at 7:00 a.m. he went to the MIC plant and "saw that the concrete cover of the storage tank had cracked and MIC plant manager S.P. Choudhary, a maintenance supervisor and some maintenance workers were working on the tank."[61] Later,

---

[59]   "Unraveling the Tragedy at Bhopal." A 17-minute Video, produced by GFA, Inc., Gittelman Film Associates, Inc, 1989.

[60]   Ashok S. Kalelkar, "Investigation of Large – Magnitude Incidents: Bhopal as a Case Study." London: May 1988, pp. 24-25 (The ADL Report).

[61]   T.R. Chouhan and others. Bhopal: *The Inside Story,* The Other India Press, 1994, p. 107.

when Choudhary was contacted about his activities during the early hours after the incident, he did not respond.[62]

All the evidence and testimonies corroborate the instrument superintendent Sundarajan's statement about the missing pressure gauge on tank E-610. For his nonconformist position and testimony, the government officials subjected Sundarajan to six days of interrogation and intimidation. Allegedly, he was also physically mistreated by Indian authorities and threatened with arrest in a futile attempt to force him to recant his testimony about the missing pressure indicator. According to an affidavit filed by Sundarajan in Indian court, he said that the agent yelled, "Don't you have national pride ...will you sell yourself for money, American stooge?"[63] A CBI spokesman denied the allegations of mistreatment. Sundarajan was later given a new identity and relocated elsewhere.

When interviewed by a reporter on the tenth anniversary of the disaster, Mohan Lal Verma, said that he first learned through the newspapers that UCC had determined the cause of the disaster and blamed a disgruntled employee for it. From the description about the individual, it was apparent to him that he was being framed.[64] Concerning his whereabouts on the night of the disaster and the history of his relationship with the management during the days prior to the disaster, Verma said:

> On 2 December 1984...I punched my card around 10:50 [PM] and reported to the production assistant of the MIC plant. About 11:15 PM, I was sitting in the MIC control room along with my fellow workers.... Generally, when we are free, MIC operators sit in this room. The window of the tea room toward the MIC unit was open. Around 11:30, we felt MIC irritation so we came out of the room to locate the source of the leak.... We reported the MIC leak to production assistant S. Qurashi.... They replied that the MIC plant is down and thus there is no chance of

---

[62] As Production Manager for MIC and Sevin, S. P. Choudhary is a co-defendant in an ongoing litigation in Bhopal District Court. He was contacted by e-mail.

[63] Laurie Hays and Richard Koenig, (contributor, Sudeep Chakravarti), "How Union Carbide Fleshed Out Its Theory of Sabotage at Bhopal," *The Wall Street Journal*, July 7, 1988. See also Interlocutory Application No. 19, filed in Court of District Judge, Bhopal, in Regular Suit No. 1113, February 4, 1986.

[64] T.R. Chouhan and Others, p. 89

leak. They did not take our report seriously, saying 'Koi baht nahin appan chay ke bad dhekhenge' (Okay, no problem, we will see after tea)."[65]

Sitting by the open window in the structure, which housed the 200-ton refrigeration unit, Verma had a direct view of the storage tanks.[66] He was the first to smell the escaping MIC gas and alerted the other operators who initially did not think it was possible as the MIC manufacturing unit was shut down.

Verma, Carbide Worker Token No. 4557, joined UCIL in 1977 and initially worked in the alpha-naphthol unit. When this unit was shut off a number of workers either retired under the voluntary retirement scheme or resigned. Verma chose to stay and was transferred to the MIC unit in September 1983. His discontent and frustrations with the management, in his attempt to attain a certified operator status at the new position, are best described in his own narrative:

My demands for assistance were always refused. In this period, I was asked to take charge when a regular operator was absent from duty. I refused to take charge under these conditions.... For these reasons, management refused to confirm me.... Then, in November 1984, the MIC plant manager S.P. Choudhary told me that if I did not follow all orders, I would be transferred to other units. I told him that I was not refusing any job for which I was confirmed. I would perform any job...if I was trained properly and was receiving proper financial benefits. I told Choudh[a]ry that if they were to transfer me...I wanted it in writing so that I could proceed with a legal response.

After a few days, S.P. Choudh[a]ry took an oral test...and said that if I passed the test, I would be confirmed. I...was able to give a correct reply to every question. Nonetheless, I was given a failure...and told I was not fit for the MIC plant.... They mentioned the transfer [to the SEVIN plant] in their daily notes but did not give me any letter.... The transfer was S.P. Choudhry's way of taking revenge.... Although they announced my transfer on 26 November, I continued to come to the MIC unit.... I went to the MIC unit and sat there because there was no work for me.[67]

---

[65] Ibid. . p. 87
[66] See the plant layout in Figure B.
[67] T.R. Chouhan and Others, pp. 86-89.

When interviewed by another reporter in 1986, Verma complained of his discontent with UCIL management, that he was the only "fifth grade" operator in the MIC plant while the rest of his colleagues had moved to higher positions. He then took up his case to the worker's union. "Although I was fully trained, I was not given independent charge." Verma also confirmed that he had admonished production manager S.P. Choudhary and was expecting his transfer from the MIC unit any time.[68,69]

The general discontent with UCIL management and the involvement of the workers' union in addressing their members' grievances was reiterated by R.K. Yadav, another MIC operator and a union activist:

> Although UCIL was a multinational company, they treated their workers like slaves. They never responded to any problem voiced by the workers. This is why I joined the Union in 1981 and was elected Joint Secretary. The union was called Union Carbide Karmachari Sangh. At first, this union was not recognized, although a majority of workers were with us.... In 1984, our union was finally recognized.[70]

After the disaster, Yadav emerged as a major spokesman for the union and led a number of protest marches. He also disagreed with and questioned the veracity of the ADL and UCC's findings: "I have checked the notes myself...and there is no demotion mentioned. In fact the company couldn't have demoted anyone without consulting the union."[71] Verma also acknowledged to a reporter that he had been frustrated and had protested to his superior for not being confirmed for the job position, and requested that the union take up his cause. "It was sheer mental torture." He said "he was told and that it was announced" of his transfer to the SEVIN unit days before the disaster but was never officially notified in writing. He stated that he was not afraid of the charges that UCC planned to make against

---

[68] N.K. Singh, "Finding a Saboteur," *India Today,* October 15, 1986, pp. 26-27.

[69] A handwritten note obtained from Jay Mukund, supposedly written on Nov. 27, 1984, by A. Venugopal (MIC production Superintendent) to A.K. Chakravarty (Sevin Production Superintendent) stated: "Please note that Mr. M.L. Varma TKNO: 4557 will be reporting in the SEVIN unit from 28/11/84 onwards. He is presently in D Group and will continue in the same group until further information."

[70] T.R. Chouhan and Others, pp. 104-105

[71] Rajiv Dessai, "An ill wind," *Chicago Tribune*, November 30, 1986.

him as he had "the support of the union as well as of the government."[72] About the UCC investigators who interviewed him more than a year after the gas leak, Verma said:

> They asked me about my past history with Union Carbide…[and] used this information against me to construct their sabotage theory…. So, it may be sabotage that caused the leak but not by any worker…. Beyond UCC lies, suggesting that I am to blame, there are other reasons why the sabotage theory is clearly incorrect: it is not possible for any worker to put water directly into the MIC tank as it is a very dangerous job. Further, everyone knows that a MIC water reaction is very dangerous, not just spoiling the contents of the tank. If the leak was caused by sabotage, the culprit is the management who was responsible for overseeing the safety of the MIC plant.[73]

A trade union report also acknowledged that the "Bhopal plant was plagued by labor relations problems and internal management disputes…. At Union Carbide Bhopal there had been conflicts between a union affiliated with the Indian National Trade Union Congress (INTUC) and an independent union over who represented the majority of the workers at the plant."[74]

From Verma's own narrative it is apparent that he was discontented and was perceived by UCIL management as a problem during the days leading up to the gas leak. Since the Government of India's lawsuit was eventually settled out of court without a trial, the key suspect and witnesses were never questioned or cross-examined.

In summary, the missing pressure indicator on tank E-610 marked the most likely place to directly introduce a large amount of water in a short timeframe. Other operators have corroborated Sundarajan's testimony on the missing pressure indicator. The highly publicized alternate route promoted by the plant operators soon after the incident failed to meet the very basic tests.

---

[72] Ibid.

[73] T.R. Chouhan and Others, p.89.

[74] The Trade Union Repot on Bhopal, *The Report of the ICFTU-IEFC Mission to Study the Causes and Effects of the Methyl Isocyanate Gas Leak at the Union Carbide Pesticide Plant in Bhopal, India on December 2-3, 1984*, Geneva: July 1985.

Chemical evidence and altered plant logs indicate that the cause of the gas leak was immediately detected and an unsuccessful attempt was made to transfer MIC to the one-ton feed tank to reduce the rising pressure inside the storage tank E-610. The third storage tank E-619, specially sized and provided for exactly such emergency circumstances, was not utilized, and instead only a ton was transferred – too little to be of consequence.

In a written statement of December 10, 1986 to the Bhopal District Court, UCC reported that in the past there had been numerous minor deliberate mischievous acts at the plant. Cases of "concealment of what had occurred was quite common among the operators," and despite efforts by UCIL plant management, it was often impossible to obtain accurate information about how an incident had occurred.[75] In a letter dated August 28, 1984, Mukund wrote: "It has been observed in the past at Bhopal that after an accident, there is a tendency on the part of some of the persons concerned to withhold information because of misconceptions and unfounded apprehensions regarding the enquiry."[76]

CSIR scientists and CBI investigators chose to ignore all evidence pointing to a deliberate act during their investigation into the Bhopal plant gas leak, and summarily dismissed the sabotage theory.

The surprising discovery of chloroform after the analyses of the contents in the transfer line, the SEVIN feed tank, and the SEVIN reactor prior to Operation Faith, and substantial quantities of chloroform in the residue from tank E-610, provided the chemical evidence that is equivalent to a smoking gun. The ill-fated storage tank E-610 turned out to be the "black box" that helped unravel the true cause of the gas leak and the unsuccessful activities by the employees soon after to contain it. Since the MIC in tank E-610 contained a high concentration of chloroform and the adjoining tank E-611 contained pure MIC, the last transfer had to be made from tank E-610, and not from tank E-611 as asserted by the operators. This corroborating evidence from tank E-611 was just as important in solving the puzzle.

The lowering of all the safety guards at the plant when a substantial amount of MIC was still in the storage tanks was a major management error. If the stored MIC were kept cold, a required safety precaution, the

---

[75]   See also Laurie Hays et al., *The Wall Street Journal*, July 7, 1988.

[76]   Furthermore, he wrote; "it was not uncommon, after such incidents, for master cards and records which might provide evidence…to disappear and, because of such incidents, the plant established a system whereby master cards were prepared in triplicate.

rate of reaction of MIC with water would have been much slower, thereby allowing the employees more time to handle the crisis. The vent gas scrubber and the flare tower, if operational, would also have neutralized a considerable amount of gaseous products before it could escape from the stack. A timely warning to the local residents with information on the wind direction – wisely used by the employees for their own evacuation – would have also minimized the number of the casualties.

The Bhopal tragedy was not initiated by equipment failure but by a deliberate act; it was aggravated by management miscalculations, lapsed safety precautions, and the failure to recognize that well-trained and safety-oriented employees are also critical to the overall safety of a chemical plant.

Original Jehan Numa
Palace in Bhopal which
was bought and razed
by UCIL
(Photo courtesy of
Sonia Jamal)

Baradari – the place
where the wind always
blows – still stands
overlooking the Upper
Lake on the UCIL
grounds

UCIL Research and
Development Technical
Center, Bhopal, built on
the site of the former
palace

Side view of the mounded MIC storage tanks and workers during construction in 1979

Top view of the mounded MIC storage tanks before the eruption

Top view showing the longitudinal crack at the top of the concrete mound over MIC tank E-610 after the eruption

Chapter Four

LITIGATION

Initial Positioning: Moral or Legal Responsibility?

When Warren Anderson, chairman of UCC, heard the tragic news, he immediately announced that UCC would accept moral responsibility for the disaster irrespective of the cause, and promised help as he prepared to leave for Bhopal. He felt he had to show the victims the company's commitment to promptly bring aid and relief support.

Prime Minister Rajiv Gandhi, who was on a campaign tour, changed plans and made a quick stop in Bhopal. He too promised prompt help and rehabilitation to those affected and indicated that the state government was planning to demand compensation from the management of the factory.

When Anderson, Keshub Mahindra, UCIL's chairman of the board, and Vijay. P. Gokhale, UCIL's managing director, arrived in Bhopal on December 7 to personally inspect the site and to control the damage to the company's image, the police stopped them at the airport. They were escorted to a waiting car, whisked away under heavy police escort, and placed under virtual house arrest at UCIL's guesthouse located on the grounds of the Technical Center at Shamla Hills. The three executives were charged under seven different sections of the Indian Penal Code, including criminal conspiracy, culpable homicide not amounting to murder, death by negligence, making the atmosphere noxious to health, and negligent conduct with respect to poisonous substances. About one hundred protestors marched outside the guesthouse, some carrying placards that read "Hang Anderson." The American consul, who had also accompanied the three executives, later remarked, "We have never seen anything like this. We had come here to help and this is what happened."

Politicians on the local and state level immediately began their campaigns, using this arrest to gain support in upcoming elections as well as to distance themselves from the plant and from UCIL, although they had previously been supportive and had profited from their involvement.

Arjun Singh, chief minister of Madhya Pradesh and a candidate for reelection, said, "We are convinced on the basis of facts already available that each one of them have criminal liability...this government cannot remain a helpless spectator to the tragedy and knows its duty towards thousands of innocent citizens"; and the lives of the citizens have been "so rudely and traumatically affected by the cruel and wanton negligence on the part of the management of Union Carbide."[1,2,3]

After being detained for six hours and having posted $2,600 in bail, Anderson was released and ordered by the government to leave the country, on the grounds that "his presence would provoke strong passions." Anderson was flown to New Delhi in a government-provided plane and left the country the following day. "The arrest and detention were the strongest actions undertaken by the Indian government against any head of a foreign company."[4]

According to Talmiz Ahmed, the Indian commercial consul in New York City who also coordinated Bhopal-related matters in the United States for the Indian Government, Anderson had sought assurances from his consulate regarding his safety in India before setting off for Bhopal. They told him that on reaching India he should check in with the officials of the Department of Environment who would be able to assist him. Instead, Anderson went to Bombay "without telling local authorities," and from there traveled directly to Bhopal. "So, in a sense, strictly speaking," said Ahmed, "he violated what we had told him…. There was a warrant in Bhopal naming Anderson and that theoretically he could have been whisked off to the police station instead of the guest house."[5]

The arrest of Anderson and UCIL's top executives was criticized by Pranlal Bhogilal, president of the Indian Merchants' Chamber, as "unjustified and amounted to total disregard for corporate ethics and international business relations." A newspaper editor called it an inexcusable bungle.

The curious circumstances of the arrest and the release six hours later of Mr. Anderson, chairman of Union Carbide Corporation, in Bhopal on Friday show that it was a case of bungling through and through. As Mr.

1   *Capital Times,* Madison, Wisconsin, December 7, 1984, p. 3.
2   "Top Carbide brass held: Anderson released," *The Times of India,* December 8, 1984, p. 1.
3   "Drama at the Airport," *The Hindu,* December 8, 1984. (*The Legal Aftermath of the Bhopal Disaster,* Vol. I, p. 33.)
4   Pat Ohlendorf, "Lingering terror in Bhopal," *MacLean's,* December 17, 1984, p. 28, (*The Legal Aftermath of the Bhopal Disaster, Supplement 2,* Madison, Wisconsin: 1985.)
5   W. David Gibson "How the Indians view Carbide," *Chemical Week,* December 18, 1985, p. 2.

Nani Palk[h]ivala, the eminent jurist, has pertinently pointed out, Madhya Pradesh government cannot possibly justify the arrest of Mr. Anderson – or for that matter, of Mr. Keshub Mahindra and Mr. Gokhale...because the 'country's criminal law requires mens rea or a guilty mind' to be established.[6]

Upon returning to the United States, Anderson held a press conference attended by more than two hundred where he announced that he was treated with respect by the Indian officials and did not feel that he was in danger. He promised to send another million dollars to aid the stricken families "on moral considerations" and that there was no question of criminal responsibility. He added that UCC was eager to pay "fair and equitable" compensation to the relatives of the victims and the injured. At this time UCC also released copies of the 1982 Operational Safety Survey (OSS) report with the comment that they were uncertain whether UCIL had actually corrected all of the deficiencies cited in report.[7] The final progress report from Mukund, dated June 26, 1984, asserted that the only unfinished item from the OSS Action Plan was the item connected with the SEVIN feed tank, and was awaiting delivery of a control valve expected in a month.[8]

On December 12, Ronald Wishart, UCC's vice president for government relations; Robert A. Peck, the U.S. Department of State's deputy assistant secretary for Near Eastern and South Asian Affairs; and James Gustave Speth, president of the World Resources Institute, appeared before the U.S. House of Representative's Subcommittee on Asian and Pacific Affairs of the Committee on Foreign Affairs in Washington. Before the hearings began, New York Representative and Subcommittee Chairman Stephen J. Solarz paid tribute to the many Indians from all walks of life who had risked their lives in the rescue operations: "The names of most of those heroic people may never be known to the world at large, but we are indebted to them for the example of courage and selflessness they demonstrated in caring for their fellow men, women, and children." The congressman wanted to assess the impact of the Bhopal disaster on Indo-American relations, to explore possible measures the U.S. government

---

6   Editorial, *The Times of India*, December 10, 1984, p. 8.

7   J. N. Parimoo, "Carbide shifts blame on Indians," *The Times of India*, December 12, 1984, p. 11.

8   Also cited earlier in "Operation Safety Survey." Letter by J. Mukund dated June 26, 1984.

might undertake to alleviate the suffering of the victims, and to examine the policies and practices of the U.S. government and the multinational corporations in terms of their effects on the countries in which such corporations operate.

Robert Peck informed the subcommittee that the U.S. government had made it clear to the "Indian government of its readiness to respond in a variety of ways, with assistance that the Indian government might identify as useful and appropriate." In addition, the U.S. Embassy in New Delhi had sent a four-person team of disaster relief experts from the Centers for Disease Control in Atlanta to assist and advise on clinical treatment, establish epidemiological surveillance, and assess the overall situation.

Ronald Wishart pleaded ignorance to most of the questions by Solarz on plant safety at Bhopal, responding that "my responsibilities are domestic. If I were to be familiar with that, I am sure I would have to be familiar with those of many other countries."[9] Solarz later visited Bhopal to assess the damage to relations between the two countries and to "demonstrate concern of the Americans and the U.S. Congress over the loss of innocent lives."[10]

On December 14, Anderson and Jackson B. Browning, UCC's vice president for health, safety and environmental programs, also testified before a sub-committee of the House Commerce and Energy Committee.

In New Delhi, V.P. Sathe, the Indian Minister for Petroleum and Chemicals, said "he expected Union Carbide [UCC] to provide the same kind of relief that it would have provided if the accident had taken place in the United States." Raja Nikant Mody, a lawyer who was advising the Indian consulate in New York, recommended that "the complaints shouldn't be filed and heard in India, because there is almost nothing to recover from the Union Carbide subsidary there. They should be here, [in U.S.] against the parent, in accordance with the American scales…and I think there will be sympathy for that because of the loss of so many lives."[11]

---

[9]   The Implications of the Industrial Disaster in Bhopal, India, Hearing Before the Subcommittee on Asian and Pacific Affairs of the Committee on foreign Affairs House of Representatives, Ninety-eight Congress, Second Session, December 12, 1984, pp. 1-4, 55.

[10]   "Solarz apologises to Bhopal residents," *The Times of India,* December 19, 1984, p. 1.

[11]   Tamar Lewin, "Company Is Expected To Face Many Claims," *The New York Times,* Dec. 7, 1984, p. 8.

Only the highlights of the litigation that ensued will be presented in subsequent pages, as the vast subject matter is outside the scope of this book.

Tort Lawyers in Bhopal

The publicity of the disaster, the magnitude of casualties, and the involvement of a multinational U.S. company immediately attracted tort lawyers from the United States and other countries, all interested in claiming their own share of what would surely be a legal bonanza. Among the first to arrive in Bhopal were John Coale and Arthur Lowy, attorneys from Washington, D.C., along with investigator Ted Dickenson. Melvin Belli and scores of other lawyers soon followed.

On their arrival in the capital city and after visiting the worst affected areas and the hospital, Coale told reporters that "the Bhopal case might change the attitude of U.S. companies towards the Third World, if it resulted in financial loss to them." It was also likely, he said "that the company might offer settlement to the affected people in a bid to dissuade them from filing the suit." They then held discussions with Indian lawyers and offered to represent the victims to file lawsuits in U.S. courts.[12] When asked if his trip to India might be interpreted as ambulance chasing, Coale was quoted as replying, "I don't care what they say. If I come from the airport and two days later have seven thousand clients, that's the greatest ambulance chase in history."[13]

Upon arrival in New Delhi and prior to his departure for Bhopal, the flamboyant Melvin Belli – the "King of Torts" – remarked that he was there "to bring justice and money to those poor little bastards who have suffered at the hands of those sons of bitches.... This is an easy one. We'll knock the stuffing out of them. There is no doubt that we will win, for Union Carbide has absolute liability. The only outstanding questions are the amount of the damages – we're going for $15 billion (£12.1 billion) – and the place of the trial. We will try to get the case heard in California. I know my juries there and I like my judges." The American businessman, he said, "is a pretty cruel, unethical customer. He is the son of a bitch. He

---

12 "Two U.S. Lawyers in Bhopal," *The Statesman,* Dec. 10, 1984. Reproduced in *Legal Aftermath*, p. 56.

13 Abbe David Lowell, "Bhopal Tragedy Breeds Legal Disaster," *Legal Times,* Dec. 24, 1984, p. 10. See also *Legal Aftermath*, p. 159.

is concerned only with profit." When he went outside to be photographed and saw a poor Indian woman he gave her a 20-rupee note and told her "it was a Christmas present and that she should buy cigars."[14] He later met with Indian government officials and lawyers. On arrival in Bhopal, he told the reporters at the Bairagarh airport that the latest tragedy in Bhopal was going to be the "last warning to the multinational [corporation] that it could no longer make guinea pigs of innocent human lives." The following day, he held discussions with Attorney General of India K. Parasaran and Chief Minister Arjun Singh. Other teams of American lawyers also arrived at the same time and set up mobile offices across the street from the UCIL plant. It was estimated that over fifty thousand victims signed up during the next few weeks.[15]

On December 7, 1984 a $15 billion lawsuit (Dawani v. Union Carbide Corp., 84-2479) was filed jointly by the law firms of Preiser and Wilson of Charleston (WV); in conjunction with those of Melvin Belli of San Francisco; Waite, Schneider, Bayles and Chesly of Cincinnati; and Michael Tobin of Miami; in the U.S. District Court, Charleston, West Virginia. The petitioners – Sheela Bai Dawani and Rehman Patel of Bhopal – accused UCC of causing the deaths of over two thousand persons, citing negligence in the design and operation of the plant, bad design of the storage tank, and failure to install a computerized early warning system similar to the U.S. facility. Dawani's husband – Ramesh Kumar Dawani – and Patel's wife and son were all killed in the disaster. The attorneys felt that filing a lawsuit in West Virginia was most appropriate because the initial plant designs were done at UCC's Technical Center in South Charleston. Damodar Airan, an attorney of Indian origin and one of the attorneys for the plaintiffs, said: "The case is a class-action suit and all those who were injured or lost a relative as a result of the gas leak can join in suing and if the court awards damages, it would be distributed among them."[16]

Another $20 billion lawsuit was filed in the East District Court in New York by Jay Gould, Federico Sayre, and Ralph Fertiz, from the California-based law firm of Gould and Sayre, on behalf of four Indian citizens.

---

[14]   Trevor Fishlock (report from New Delhi), "Enter justice, in alligator boots and polka-dot tie," *The London Times,* 11 December 1984; See also *Legal Aftermath*, p. 74.

[15]   Lalit Shatri, *Bhopal Disaster, An Eye Witness Account*, Criterion Publications, New Delhi: 1985, pp. 83, 85.

[16]   Arul B. Louis, "Union Carbide sued for $15b World' biggest-ever claim," *Hindustan Times,* December 9, 1984.

These lawyers later arrived in Bhopal on December 11, accompanied by two Delhi-based lawyers. They told the reporters that the case was filed in the United States since UCC was based there and "it was convenient to fight there...as the law of torts has not developed in India."[17] Kenneth Ditkowsky of Chicago filed a third class action lawsuit in the amount of $50 billion in Chicago.

Some lawyers in Bhopal offered potential clients eight U.S dollars to sign up for injury claims, demanding in return full power of attorney to settle out of court and contingency fees of 50 percent, (considerably more than the standard contingency fee of 33 percent in American liability suits.)[18]

According to an Indian reporter, American lawyers were descending on Bhopal like bees to honeysuckle. Within days of the gas leak tragedy they were buzzing about looking for material substantial to file compensation suits in U.S. courts on behalf of the victims and also a cut – as fees – for themselves.

Their early appearance at the scene with promises of enormous compensation had sent hope surging through the gas ravaged localities and the shattered victims. But by fortnight's end the euphoria was dying down and in its place came strong doubts.... The very people who had formed queues to sign forms giving the power of attorney to the Americans just days ago were showing clear signs of hostility.[19]

Ram Gopal Sharma, a local Congress Party (I) leader employed as a mechanical fitter, said that he lost count of the number of lawyers whose forms he had filled out and given power of attorney. When he learned that the lawyers were planning to take a big share of the compensation, he stopped signing and told others about it. Kamta Prasad Vishwakarma, another resident of Jai Prakash Nagar, asked the lawyer to whom he had recently given power of attorney for a receipt. The lawyer, he said, soon became evasive and disappeared.[20]

Bennet J. Bergman, an American attorney who was invited to confer with high-ranking officials from Madhya Pradesh, reported on his return from Bhopal:

---

17 "Second suit filed for $20-billion damages," *The Hindu,* December 12, 1984, p. 1.
18 "India advises gas victims to avoid foreign lawyers," *Milwaukee Journal,* December 31, 1984, See also *Legal Aftermath,* p. 186.
19 Srekant Khandekar, *India Today,* January 15, 1985, p. 100.
20 Ibid

...not only were there makeshift lawyers' stands, similar to what an American child might use to sell lemonade, but I also observed Americans – apparently attorneys – handing rupees to Bhopal residents in exchange for signatures on retainers.... We also observed several instances where United States attorneys were employing local Indians as go-betweens. The Indian associates would sign up the case and pass out rupees while the attorney stayed safely away from the action usually in a vehicle about twenty feet from his accomplice. In one instance, after a period of observation, the Indian associate ran out of rupees and the American lawyer appeared from the car and replenished his supply.... The unethical practices observed by the writer were very disturbing.[21]

The American Bar Association condemned the practice and expressed its strong disapproval of those lawyers for taking advantage of the poor victims and "engaging in practices contrary to the ABA's rules of professional conduct." However, no names were mentioned in this condemnation and the association did not recommend any sanctions.[22]

The mounting complaints about the unfair tactics and unethical activities of the tort lawyers prompted the thirty-five cabinet members of the Madhya Pradesh state government to take action. After a special meeting on December 30, they issued an appeal to the general public "not to enter into individual agreements with foreign lawyers for taking up their suits," and that the state would represent the victims. The American and Indian lawyers reacted angrily and said that they would serve the victims better than the government.[23]

The other important factor in filing the lawsuits in the U.S. was the high filing fees associated with lawsuits in India, with the attorneys paying all costs. Under Indian law, victims have to prove negligence in order to collect compensation, while in the American doctrine of strict liability, they would simply have to show that a defective product had injured them.

By mid-January 1985, a total of 37 lawsuits were filed in the various U.S. Federal courts on top of more than 2,000 cases filed in Madhya

---

21 Bennett J. Bergman, "The Scandal of U.S. Lawyers Seeking Clients in Bhopal," *New York Law Journal*, January 17, 1985, p. 1, col.4. See also *Legal Aftermath* p. 213.

22 "Bar Association Condemns U.S. Lawyers Over Bhopal," *The Wall Street Journal*, July, 10, 1985, p. 12.

23 Robert Reinhold, *The New York Times*, 12/31/84, p. 4, and also *Legal Aftermath*, p. 1

Pradesh. Sixteen additional lawsuits were filed in the State of New York. By October 1985, the number of lawsuits filed in India had increased to 3,981, including lawsuits against the state of Madhya Pradesh and the Union of India. Of these cases, 485 were against the state of Madhya Pradesh and 162 against the Union of India.[24]

Faced with multi-billion-dollar lawsuits and adverse publicity before its culpability could be determined, UCC, as the major shareholder in UCIL, offered to compensate Bhopal's victims on moral grounds through an out-of-court settlement. This was preferable to risking protracted litigation, which would potentially cause greater damage to the company's image and possibly even lead to bankruptcy.

The New York law firm of Kelley, Drye & Warren was retained to work with UCC's in-house lawyers. The company also retained well-known Indian lawyers Fali Nariman and Nani A. Palkhivala, India's former ambassador to Washington. Lawyers from other firms questioned the limited experience of the midsize law firm in defending the liability case of this magnitude. They noted that an earlier major client of Kelley Drye & Warren, faced with a huge financial crisis, had shifted most of its work to a bigger firm. Lawyers for both the plaintiffs and the defendant also criticized UCC for its early mishandling of the crisis by making potentially damaging admissions. One statement, in particular, was significant when UCC reported to the media that safety standards at the Bhopal plant were set by company's headquarters in the United States and were comparable to its West Virginia facility. "We were delighted by their statements," said David Jaroslawicz, a personal injury lawyer who had filed a $20 billion suit against UCC in New York.[25]

On January 24, six U.S. federal judges met in New Orleans to hear arguments on the possibility of combining and transferring all the lawsuits to a single district court. Over sixty lawyers, representing law firms around the country and thousands of clients in India also met before and after the hearings to discuss the strategy. Stanley S. Chesley of Cincinnati indicated preference for the Southern District of West Virginia, since UCC owned a similar plant in that state. Bud G. Holman, representing the law firm of Kelley Drye & Warren in New York, now the attorneys

---

[24]   Holman's testimony of January 3, 1986. p. 9.
[25]   James B. Stewart, "Suits Against Union Carbide Raise Issues for Lawyers, Multinationals," *The Wall Street Journal,* December. 17, 1984, p. 27. See also *Legal Aftermath*, p. 133.

for UCC, pushed for a transfer to New York.[26] On February 6, the Judicial Panel on Multi-District Litigation ruled that all 145 Bhopal suits filed in U.S. federal courts, and involving approximately 200,000 plaintiffs, was consolidated and transferred for pre-trial proceedings before Judge John F. Keenan, in the U. S. Southern District of New York. During this period the government in India, in conjunction with the U.S. lawyers and consultants in India, was preparing to file a lawsuit in the United States.

Bhopal Gas Leak Disaster Act

The legal system in India, while influenced by English common law, has its foundation in the Indian Constitution of 1950. Prior to filing its lawsuit against UCC, the Government of India discussed a number of options. When interviewed by a reporter a year later, R. Panjwani, a senior advocate practicing in the Supreme Court of India, expressed his opinion about the lack of remedy for accidents in the Indian legal system. Under the Fatal Accident Act of 1908, a lawsuit could be filed in India upon payment of 7.5 percent of court fees, whereas:

> In US you have not to pay court fees…you only have to file and demand that you want to have $1 million as compensation…. I was firmly of the opinion that we must file the suit in USA without loss of time, not in the Federal Court, but in the State of California.…

> There were two views before the Government: one was that India as a sovereign country should not go abroad to file a suit. Therefore, it should set up its own tribunal to determine the amount of compensation. I was opposed to such an idea for two reasons. One, we would be governed by Indian law of Torts…. A victim or his relatives would not be able to get more than 1 lakh [100,000] of rupees, or, at the most to be charitable, two lakhs. Because the pressure of Indian industry is so great on the Government of India that if we really set up a tribunal and they set up the principles of awarding compensation on the lines of American law then the entire Indian law of torts changes…[with] far-reaching consequences for which the Indian industry and the Indian government were not prepared…. Therefore the matter was taken up that we should prepare a law

---

26 Frances Frank Marcus, "U.S. Panel Hears Arguments on Bhopal Suits," *The New York Times,* January 25, 1985, p. 9. See also *Legal Aftermath,* p. 237.

that the Government of India shall represent all victims in an American court.... [27]

On February 20, 1985, following the recommendations of Indian Attorney General Parasaran, the president of India, Zail Singh, signed the Bhopal Gas Leak Disaster Ordinance before it was discussed in the Parliament, which was not in session. On March 29, 1985, the *Lok Sabha*, or House of the People, enacted the ordinance into the special law entitled, The Bhopal Gas Leak Disaster (Processing of Claims) Act, 1985,[28] to deal with this unique legal situation. Veerandra Patil, Minister for Chemicals and Fertilizer, in presenting the case for the Bhopal Act to Parliament, argued that the government had three options: to fight the case in Indian courts, in American courts, or go for any compromise which was in the best interests of the disaster victims. Since the president had already signed the ordinance and it was enforceable from that date, the passage of the bill was a formality, pushed through without much discussion so as to meet the filing deadline in the U.S. District Court in New York. Judge Keenan had scheduled the first hearing of the lawsuits filed by American lawyers for April 16.

The Bhopal Act conferred special rights to the central government "to secure that claims arising out of, or connected with, the Bhopal gas leak disaster are dealt with speedily, equitably and to the best advantage of the claimants and for matters incidental thereto." Article 3 of the Act empowered the central government with the "exclusive right to represent, and act in place of (whether within or outside India) every person who has made, or is entitled to make, a claim for all purposes connected with such claim in the same manner and to the same effect as such person." In case of deaths, the spouse, children (including a child in the womb) and other heirs of the deceased were deemed to be the claimants.

The Bhopal Act came under immediate criticism as a means for the government to extricate itself from any culpability. The critics complained, "How can the perpetrator of the crime, the government, become the guardian for the victims of the crime? It is an obvious case of conflict of in-

---

[27] Excerpts from an interview by Claude Alvares with Mr. R. Panjwani, at his residence in New Delhi. on October 31, 1985. in *The Bhopal Tragedy – One Year After, An APPEN Report*, Sahabat Alam Malaysia: (Friends of the Earth Malaysia), 1985, pp. 39-43.

[28] *Gazette of India*, (Extraordinary), Part II, Section 1, dated 29th March 1985, pp. 1-5.

terest and *prima facie* the legislation itself appears to be a denial of due process.... Every action of which any government should be ashamed is concealed by converting it into an official secret to be protected from public scrutiny and exposure."[29] The Bhopal Act was also not well received by the lawyers in India, as it affected all the suits filed by them in India against UCC, UCIL, and the government. With a sweep of the pen the act cast aside hundreds of lawsuits. A faction of American lawyers who had signed up thousands of victims regarded the Bhopal Act as illegal. They complained that the new act deprived the Indian citizens of their right to counsel of their choosing, and set up a possible conflict of interest for the government's failure to enforce safety regulations.

As soon as the Government of India filed its lawsuit in Southern N.Y. District Court, several Indian attorneys, acting in conjunction with their American counterparts, petitioned India's Supreme Court to overturn the Bhopal Act.

> In Charan Lal Sahu v. Union of India, the constitutionality of the Act was impugned before the Supreme Court [of India] on the grounds that the divestiture of the claimants' rights to legal remedy against the multinational for the consequences of carrying on dangerous and hazardous activities 'violates the fundamental rights of equality freedom of occupation, and the right to life and liberty.' The Supreme Court upheld the constitutionality.[30]

The act empowered the government to take over all of the litigation both in India and the USA and combine it into one main lawsuit, which involved the Union of India versus Union Carbide Corporation.

Union of India vs. Union Carbide Corporation

On April 18, 1985, the Union of India filed a lawsuit against UCC in the United States District Court, Southern District of New York, presided by the Honorable John F. Keenan.[31] Shyamal Ghosh - joint secretary to

---

[29] Ram Jethmalani, "The Guilty in Bhopal," *Indian Express,* April 19, 1985, p. 6. Reproduced in *Legal Aftermath*, p. 730.

[30] Douglas Bullis, *Doing Business in Today's India*, Quorum Books, Connecticut: 1998, p. 220.

[31] Union of India v. Union Carbide Corporation, MDL Docket No. 626, 85 Civ. 2696 (JFK).

the Government of India, and the law firms of Robins, Zelle, Larson & Kaplan of Minneapolis, Minnesota and Barrett, Smith, Schapiro, Simon & Armstrong of New York, N.Y. represented the plaintiff. The defendant was represented by O. Jules Romary of UCC and the law firm of Kelley Drye & Warren of New York, NY, and advocates M/s J. B. Dadachanji & Co. of New Delhi, in India.

The Minnesota law firm "pioneered the field of catastrophe law," said Solly Robins, the partner who had cofounded the law firm in 1938. "We have worked on a lot of very complex cases. We thought we could give the Indian government good representation, and I guess they thought so, too." Michael Ciresi, Robins, Zelle's lead attorney, headed the Bhopal team. The 152-lawyer firm with six offices around the country was well known for handling the lawsuits over the Dalkon Shield, the MGM Grand Hotel fire in Las Vegas, Nevada, and the Hyatt Regency skywalk collapse in Kansas City, Missouri, among others.[32] One promotional brochure touted the firm's aggressive style. Facing Robins, Zelle in court is like encountering Genghis Khan on the steppes.[33]

In its complaint,[34] the Union of India's main allegation focused on defective plant design and the storing of unnecessarily large amounts of a poisonous chemical close to populated areas.[35]

As *parens patria* [government as parent], the plaintiff also sought punitive damages for an unspecified "amount sufficient to deter Union Car-

---

[32]   Steven Greenhouse, *The New York Times*, March 12, 1985, p. 25.

[33]   Robert Friedman, "Bhopal Suit Law Firm Is Accused of 3 Cases of Improper Conduct," *The Wall Street Journal,* April 10, 1985, p.1. and also reproduced in *Legal Aftermath*, p. 395.

[34]   Complaint filed by the Union of India in the U.S. District Court, New York: 8th April 1985.

[35]   In addition it also alleged that UCC: 1. Designed, constructed, owned, operated, managed and controlled a chemical plant in Bhopal. 2. Manufactured, processed, handled and stored [MIC] at its Bhopal plant. 3. Warranted that the design was based upon the best manufacturing information available. 4. Had at all material times, an absolute and non-delegable duty to ensure that the said hazardous plant did not cause any danger or damage to the people. 5. Was under a duty to design, construct, maintain and operate its Bhopal plant in such a manner as to prevent the escape of lethal gas from MIC storage tank. The defendant was in breach of this duty. Use of defective instrumentation, safety systems, warning systems, operating and maintenance procedures. 6. Recommended, encouraged and permitted storing MIC in dangerously large quantities. 7. MIC storage tanks were not equipped with dual systems, etc.

bide or any other multinational corporation from the willful, malicious and wanton disregard of the rights and safety of the citizens of those countries in which they do business." In addition, the Government of India sought to recover damages for the cost of its emergency aid relief, medical treatment, food, and rehabilitation to the victims.

While the plaintiff's lawyers used strong language and shrewd tactics publicly, the Government of India and UCC officials were simultaneously conducting private negotiations for an early out-of-court settlement. From the very beginning, Union Carbide publicly accepted moral but not legal responsibility for the disaster and sought an early settlement in the interest of the victims, rather than a protracted court case. The adverse publicity was also demoralizing to UCC employees and affecting the company's business. UCC's worldwide reputation had suffered immensely and the share price had plummeted.

UCC's initial offer of $200 million, payable over a period of thirty years, was rejected by the government as "ridiculously low." At the company's annual meeting, Anderson said that UCC had made a "fair, forthcoming, and comprehensive proposal" to compensate Bhopal's victims and assured that company "stockholders should not take our strong interest in achieving a settlement as an admission of legal liability. The corporation did nothing that either caused or contributed to the accident, and if it comes to litigation we will vigorously defend that position."[36] During this period, both parties resorted to "defensive strategies designed to control damage to their own positions. Each sought to focus public attention away from its own potential responsibilities and to shift the locus of legal and moral blame to other parties. As a result, compensation to the victims remained a low priority."[37]

At the U.S. District Court in Manhattan, Judge Keenan had the enormous task of bringing order to the 100-plus lawyers under the watchful eye of journalists from around the world. At the first pretrial hearing, the judge ordered the lawyers to stop squabbling and laid out conditions as to how he would handle the case stemming from sixty-four competing lawsuits. The confusion and the rift among the lawyers had already widened when the Government of India filed its own lawsuit. The judge gave the lawyers

---

[36]   Thomas J. Lueck, "India Rejects Carbide's Offer," *The New York Times*, 4/25/1985, p. 34 and also in *Legal Aftermath*. p. 414.

[37]   Jamie Cassels, *The Uncertain Promises of Law – Lessons from Bhopal*, University of Toronto Press, 1993.

one week to choose two representatives from their number to serve along with the representative of the Indian government. "If they can't choose, then I will," the judge said.[38] He later named Cincinnati's Stanley Chesley and New York's F. Lee Bailey to serve on the executive committee, with Michael V. Ciresi of the Minneapolis firm of Robins, Zelle, Larson and Kaplan, representing the Government of India. In addition to Chesley and Bailey, Judge Keenan also appointed Jack S. Hoffinger of New York's Hoffinger, Friedland, Dobrish, Bernfeld and Hasen, as New York liaison counsel. The latter had previously offered his services to head up a *pro bono* effort to represent individual plaintiffs.

Recognizing the urgency to provide immediate aid to the victims, Judge Keenan asked the committee to work out an interim relief plan by May 1. He also urged Union Carbide to provide immediately $5-10 million in aid. (This aid offer would not constitute an admission of liability and would be credited against any future settlement.) UCC attorney Bud Holman's initial response was that the best way to help the victims was to settle the case at the earliest date. UCC had made a very generous offer, he said, but it was stalled because the Indian government refused to provide the company with official figures about the number of dead and injured. He also added that he might file a motion to transfer the suits to the courts in India "as the most appropriate tribunal," if the case was not resolved soon. He implied that the Indian government was also partly responsible for the disaster and could therefore become a defendant. When Judge Keenan asked Ciresi if there was any conflict of interest in the Indian government representing the victims, Ciresi replied that the allegations were baseless. It is not apparent if at this early stage the plaintiff's lawyers were aware of the Design Transfer Agreement and the extensive correspondence between UCIL and the various ministries of Government of India disclosed in chapter 2.

On July 31, 1985, UCC moved to dismiss the complaints on grounds of *forum non conveniens,* i.e., that the proper forum for the case was in India and not the U.S. The lawyers for the individual plaintiffs and the Union of India opposed UCC's motion. The Government of India also turned down UCC's $5 million emergency aid offer due to the strict accounting requirements tied to this offer. After a seven-month delay, this money

---

[38] For more details about the court proceedings see Ellain Cates, "100 Lawyers Start The Legal Cleanup," *National Law Journal,* April 29, 1985, see also *Legal Aftermath,* pp. 424-426.

was finally handed over to the International Red Cross to be transferred to the Indian Red Cross. The Indian relief officials were expected to give a simple accounting to the international organization as to how the funds were disbursed. The plan was primarily designed to provide medical aid and other assistance to the thousands of victims still suffering.

Before deciding on whether the case should be tried in the United States or in India, Judge Keenan heard arguments, testimonies, and affidavits from scores of lawyers and witnesses for both the plaintiff and the defendant. Expert testimonies were also heard from a university professor of South Asian Studies, senior advocates before the Supreme Court of India who were experts on India's law and legal system, and a former Indian ambassador to the United States.

In a thoroughly reasoned opinion, on May 12, 1986, Judge Keenan granted the motion to dismiss the suit on grounds of *forum non conveniens*. In his Opinion and Order to transfer the venue of the litigation to India, Judge Keenan cited from the many affidavits and documents submitted by the defendant to counter the plaintiff's allegations:[39]

1. The Court is struck by the assertion that the two agreements (Design Transfer and Technical Services, signed in 1973) were negotiated at 'arm's length' pursuant to Union Carbide corporate policy, and the Union of India mandated that the Government retain 'specific control over the terms of any agreements UCIL made with foreign companies such as Union Carbide Corporation.' (Affidavit Robert C. Brown, at 3-4)...

2. The nature of UCIL's design work is discussed in the affidavit of Ranjit Dutta, who previously held various positions at UCIL and UCAPC. From 1973 through 1976, Mr. Dutta was employed as General Manager of the Agricultural Products division of UCIL. (Dutta Aff. at 2)....

3. Mr. Dutta asserts that the Bhopal facility was built by UCIL over eight years from 1972 to 1980. (Dutta Aff. at 8). He asserts that Union Carbide's (UCC) role in the project was "narrow," and limited to providing "certain process packages for certain parts of the plant." (Dutta Aff. at 9). He continues, stating: Once it did that, it had no further design or engineering role, and that the process design packages, which Union

---

39   N.R. Madhava Menon, (ed). *Documents and Court Opinions on Bhopal Gas Leak Disaster Case: for course onTort II*. National Law School of India, Bangalore: 1991, pp. 47-63.

Carbide Corporation provided, are nothing, more than summary design starting points…. They set forth only the general parameters (Dutta Aff. at 9-12)…

4. According to Mr. Dutta, during the five years between the date upon which Union Carbide submitted process designs, and the date upon which the plant started up, there were only four visits to Bhopal by Union Carbide process design engineers. In contrast, he asserts that ten to fifteen UCIL engineers, working primarily out of Bombay, were involved in the design detailing. (Dutta Affs. at 14 and 16).

5. These UCIL engineers oversaw the 55 to 60 Indian engineers employed by the Bombay engineering firm which performed the detail design work. This firm, Humphreys and Glasgow, submitted designs and drawings to the UCIL engineers for approval. Corrected drawings were returned by UCIL to Humphreys and Glasgow for changes, and sent back to UCIL for final approval. (Dutta Aff. at 19-24).

6. Mr. Dutta alleges that "at no time were Union Carbide Corporation engineering personnel from the United States involved in approving the detail design or drawings prepared upon which construction was based. Nor did they receive notices of changes made."

7. Of the 12,000 pages of documents purportedly seized by the CBI regarding design and construction of the Bhopal plant, an assorted 2,000 are design reports of Humphreys and Glasgow UCIL or other contractors.

8. Mr. Munoz has submitted an affidavit in which he testified that Union Carbide decided to store MIC in large quantities at the Bhopal plant, despite Mr. Munoz's warning that MIC should be stored only in small amounts because of safety. (Memo in Opp. at 15-16; Munoz Aff.). Mr. Dutta, for defendant, asserts that there was never an issue of token storage of MIC at Bhopal, as Mr. Munoz states, and that there is no truth to Mr. Munoz' assertion that he was involved in the storage issue. (Dutta Aff. at 30).)" [Additional information was added in footnote 19 of the Court document. This is shown below.]

9. Plaintiffs state that Warren Woomer supervised the training of UCIL personnel at Union Carbide's Institute, West Virginia plant. According to plaintiffs, 40 UCIL employees were transported to the Institute's fa-

cility for lengthy training (Memo in Opp. at 22). Mr. Warren states in reply that the 40 employees thus trained represented a fraction of over 1,000 employees who were trained exclusively in Bhopal. (Woomer Aff. at 43). In addition, Mr. Woomer asserts that the training at Institute was pursuant to an arm's-length agreement, that UCIL selected the parties to be trained, and that UCIL paid Union Carbide for the training. (Woomer Aff. at 43).

In the final remarks the judge further stated that "the briefs and affidavits contain considerable discussion on the matter of commissioning and start-up of the Bhopal plant. ...However, the Court determines that the Manual regarding start-up was prepared by Indian nationals employed by UCIL." (, Warren Aff. at 48)

(In footnote 19, at the end of the document, the judge also addressed to Munoz's testimony):

"Mr. Dutta asserts that Mr. Munoz was a paid consultant to a member of the Plaintiffs' Executive Committee at the time the affidavit was made. No documentary proof of this assertion has been submitted. (Dutta Aff. 31; Holman Aff. 2 at 18). Moreover, two affidavits submitted on behalf of the defendant state that Mr. Munoz was removed from his position as Union Carbide Corporation Division President in 1978, and is 'extremely bitter as a result of the removal'. (Dutta Aff. at 31. Holman Aff. 2 at 18)."

In his Affidavit to the court, Mr. Holman had testified that "at the time he executed the affidavit – (on January 24, 1985) – Mr. Munoz was a paid consultant... although plaintiffs' papers nowhere mention that fact. Secondly, Mr. Munoz was, in 1978, removed by Union Carbide Corporation from his position as a Division President of the Union Carbide Corporation, and Mr. Rehfield testified at his deposition to both Mr. Munoz' reputation for truth and veracity and to some of the circumstances which preceded his removal."

As general manager of UCIL's Agricultural Products Division, Munoz submitted a proposal on January 1, 1970 to the Licensing & Progress Section, Industrial Development Internal Trade & Company Affairs, to "erect facilities to manufacture up to 2,000 tons of methyl isocyanate and 5,000 tons of MIC based agricultural product.... The MIC unit will be a fully integrated plant operating...under the Union Carbide Corporation process, modified to reduce incidence of exotic materials of construction and imported technology. It will have a capacity of 2,000 tons high purity MIC a year, based on a continuous operation."[40]

This 1970 letter by Munoz to the government ministry is inconsistent with his sworn affidavit submitted to the Judicial Panel on Multi-District Litigation, in which he swore "that only token storage was necessary, preferably in small individual containers based on both economic and safety considerations."[41] A similar allegation was made in the CSIR Report.

The judges of the Second Circuit of the United States Court of Appeals, Mansfield, Pratt, and Altimari, in their judgment of January 14, 1987, also agreed that there was minimum involvement by UCC in the final design and construction of the plan. They ruled that, "Although basic design programs were prepared in the United States and some assistance furnished to UCIL at the outset of the ten-year period during which the Bhopal plant was constructed, the proof bearing on the issues to be tried is almost entirely located in India."

John Macdonald, assistant secretary for UCC, testified in his affidavit that the "Indian government controlled to a large extent the sources of material and equipment used in the construction and operation of the Bhopal plant. Before UCIL could make any purchase abroad, it had to obtain a Capital Goods License from the Government of India. In applying for this license, UCIL was required to demonstrate to the Indian government that the materials and equipment sought were not available from any Indian supplier."[42]

In his concluding statement, Judge Keenan detailed the reasons for his decision to move the lawsuit to Indian courts:

> 1. The Indian courts have greater access to all the information needed to arrive at the amount of the compensation to be awarded the victims.

---

[40] See Appendix A-4 - Letter by E. A. Munoz, January 1, 1970. (Exhibit 3.)

[41] Affidavit of Edward Munoz to the Judicial Panel on Multi-district Litigation, In re Union Carbide Corp. Plant Disaster at Bhopal, India: 1984. MDL Docket No. 626. (n.d.).

[42] Affidavit in support of Union Carbide's motion to dismiss on grounds of forum *non conveniens,* MDL Docket No. 626, Misc. No. 21-38 (J.F.K.) All Cases, United States District Court, Southern District of New York, July 26, 1985, p. 4.

2. The presence in India of the overwhelming majority of the witnesses and evidence, both documentary and real, would by itself suggest that India is the most convenient forum for this consolidated case.

3. No American interest in the outcome of this litigation outweighs the interest of India in applying Indian values to the task of resolving this case.

4. The Bhopal plant was regulated by Indian agencies. The Union of India has a very strong interest in the aftermath of the accident, which affected its citizens on its own soil. Perhaps Indian regulations were ignored or contravened. India may wish to determine whether the regulations imposed on the chemical industry within its boundaries were sufficiently stringent.

5. In the Court's view to retain the litigation in this forum, as plaintiffs request, would be yet another example of imperialism, another situation in which an established sovereign inflicted its rules, its standards and values on a developing nation. This court declines to play such a role.

6. The Union of India is a world power in 1986, and its courts have the proven capacity to mete out fair and equal justice. To deprive the Indian judiciary of this opportunity to stand tall before the world and to pass judgment on behalf of its own people would be to revive a history of subservience and subjugation from which India has emerged. India and its people can and must vindicate their claims before the independent and legitimate judiciary created there since the Independence in 1947.

The consolidated case was dismissed on the grounds of *forum non conveniens* under the conditions that UCC shall:

1. consent to submit to the jurisdiction of the courts of India and shall continue to waive defenses based upon the statute of limitations;

2. agree to satisfy any judgment rendered by an Indian court, and if applicable, upheld by an appellate court in that country, where such judgment and affirmance comport with the minimal requirements of due process; and

3. be subject to discovery under the model of the United States Federal Rules of Civil Procedure after appropriate demand by plaintiffs.

The Government of India initially objected to what it viewed as an unfavorable ruling by Judge Keenan, and appealed to the United States Court of Appeals (Second Circuit). It later reversed its position and accepted the decision.

UCC objected to the third condition imposed by Judge Keenan regarding pretrial discovery, and on July 28, 1986, also appealed before the United States Court of Appeals (Second Circuit). The Appellate Court agreed with the defendant and reversed Judge Keenan's last condition. In his judgment, the Second Circuit Judge Mansfield wrote that:

> ...the district court erred in requiring UCC to consent...to broad discovery of it by the plaintiffs under the Federal Rules of Civil Procedure when UCC is confined to the more limited discovery authorized under Indian law.... Basic justice dictates that both sides be treated equally, with each having equal access to the evidence in the possession or under the control of the other. Application of this fundamental principle in the present case is especially appropriate since UOI [Union of India], as the sovereign government of India, is expected to be a party to the Indian litigation, possibly on both sides.[43]

On April 25, 1987, the Union of India and two days later on April 27, 1987, the lawyers for the individual plaintiffs, appealed to the U.S. Supreme Court, pleading for a reimposition of the conditions of Judge Keenan's order. This request was denied.

Litigation Moves to Indian Court

Union Carbide knew of the possibility of sabotage and should have, but did not, design its plant to cope with that event.

Union of India's Reply to Defendant's Written Statement
(Civil Suit No. 1113/86, (Bhopal)

On September 5, 1986, the Union of India filed a civil suit (Suit No. 1113/86) in the Court of District Judge, Bhopal, against UCC for dam-

---

[43] Judgement of the United States Court of Appeals (Second Circuit), In Re: UCC Gas Plant Disaster at Bhopal, India in December 1984. Docket Nos. 86-7517, 86-7589, 86-7637, Nos. 301,383,496. August Term, before Mansfield, Pratt and Altimari, Circuit Judges, (Decided on January 14, 1987.)

ages caused by the tragedy. Mr. Shyamal Ghosh represented the government through the Joint Secretary of the Department of Chemicals and Petrochemicals. The plaintiff stated that "more than two thousand persons died…and several thousand persons suffered grievous and permanent damage to their person and health…and widespread damage was also caused to the environment in and around Bhopal and to living cattle there." It claimed that deaths and destruction caused by the gas leak "occurred as the result of unreasonable and highly dangerous and defective plant conditions." Some of the forty-nine specific charges were as follows:

1) Defendant Union Carbide recommended encouraged and permitted storing MIC in dangerously large quantities.

2) No intermediate storage facility was constructed between the production plant and the storage tanks, thus creating the potential for a contaminant to enter the storage tanks.

3) The storage tanks were not insulated and the chilling system was defectively designed and improperly maintained.

4) The MIC storage tanks were not equipped with dual temperature indicators to sound alarms and flash warning lights in the event of an abnormal rise in temperature.

5) The emergency relief system was defectively designed and improperly maintained.

6) Defendant Union Carbide failed to provide even basic information with regard to protection against or appropriate medical treatment in the event of MIC exposure.

7) Defendant failed to disclose the internal safety survey of its plant in Institute, West Virginia, dated September 10, 1984, which acknowledged that a runaway reaction in MIC storage tanks could occur.

Defendant Union Carbide failed to provide specifications for determining what constituted either stable of unstable MIC.

Many of the allegations were identical to those cited in the lawsuit filed in the U.S. District Court in April 1985, as well as in the conclusions in the CSIR report of December 1985. In a new claim 27, the plaintiff further adduced that UCC "was under a duty to design, construct, maintain and operate its Bhopal plant with reasonable care so as to protect persons from unreasonable and foreseeable dangers." The Plaintiff pleaded for compensation of an undisclosed sum of money:

> ...for damages for such amount as may be appropriate under the facts and the law and as may be determined by this court so as to fully, fairly and adequately compensate all the persons and authorities, who have suffered as a result of the Bhopal disaster and having claims against the defendant;

> A decree for punitive damages in an amount sufficient to deter the defendant Union Carbide and other multinational corporations involved in similar business from willful, malicious and wanton disregard of the rights and safety of the citizens of India; interest; cost of and incidental to the suit; [and] such further or other reliefs (sic) as this Court may seem fit and proper.

On September 17, 1986, the district court judge in Bhopal ordered UCC "by means of an ad-interim injunction, from creating any change in their financial status...or assets directly or indirectly." This injunction was lifted after UCC assured the court that it would maintain assets of $3 billion in the U.S. until the final settlement of the suit.

On December 10, 1986, in response to the Indian government's civil suit, UCC filed a written statement in the Bhopal District Court as a plaintiff to a countersuit against Union of India and the State of Madhya Pradesh, both as defendants. In a summary of its wide-ranging defenses, UCC charged that;

1) the state government had allowed unauthorized dwellings on government land next to the plant,
2) the central government had significantly influenced the design and construction of the plant,
3) and that both levels of government had to bear the burden of their responsibilities. It also specified in detail how the tragedy was the result of the deliberate introduction of large quantities of water into the MIC storage tank.

In response to UCC's written statement, on January 6, 1987 the Indian government presented additional details to support their earlier allegations and further implicated that "even the conceivability of sabotage was foreseeable to Union Carbide. Thus Union Carbide cannot escape liability even assuming, without admitting, that its improbable and unsupported scenario is true. Union Carbide knew of the possibility of sabotage and should have, but did not, design its plant to cope with that event."

On February 4, 1987, UCC filed a motion to restrain the Government of India and CBI from further harassment of a key witness, S. Sundarajan, instrument supervisor, who had been asked by his supervisor to replace the missing valve on tank E-610 on the morning after the incident.

During that period, reports appeared in the Indian press, which alleged that Judge G.S. Patel himself was a claimant for damages due to the gas leak. On February 24, 1987, Judge Patel was replaced and M.W. Deo was appointed as the new district judge for Bhopal.

On April 2, 1987, the District Court, Bhopal, made a proposal to the "Parties for Reconciliatory Substantial Interim Relief to the Gas Victims," whereby the judge directed the defendant to deposit in Court Rs. 3.5 billion (~$270 million). This sum was to be placed at the disposal of Justice P.D. Mulye, a sitting judge at the Indore bench of the High Court of Madhya Pradesh, also the commissioner for the welfare of the victims. UCC rejected the proposal and appealed to the High Court of Madhya Pradesh in nearby Jabalpur.

On December 5, 1987, the High Court at Jabalpur rejected charges that UCC sought to delay proceedings of Bhopal litigation and directed the parties to cooperate for early out-of-court settlement.

On April 4, 1988, the Madhya Pradesh High Court basically upheld the order by the lower court in Bhopal, but reduced the payment to be made by the defendant to two hundred fifty million rupees (~$192 million). The legal imbroglio was finally settled out of court by the intervention of the Supreme Court of India. Additional information on the court proceedings in India are reported in detail by Claude Alvares, environmental journalist, and Ms. Indira Jaising, a lawyer who represented some of the victims.[44]

---

[44] T.R. Chouhan and Others, *Bhopal – The Inside Story*, The Apex Press, 1994, pp. 113-212.

The Final Out-of-Court Settlement

On February 14, 1989, more than four years after the Bhopal tragedy, the Supreme Court of India ordered UCC to pay $470 million to the Indian government in final and full settlement of the lawsuit. The judges ruled that:

> Having given our careful consideration for these several days to the facts and circumstances placed before us by the parties in these proceedings, including the pleadings of the parties, the mass of data placed before us, the material relating to the proceedings in the courts in the United States of America, the offers and counter-offers made between the parties at different stages during the various proceedings, as well as the complex issues of law and fact raised before us and the submissions made thereon, and in particular the enormity of the human suffering occasioned by the Bhopal Gas disaster and the pressing urgency to provide immediate and substantial relief to victims of the disaster, we are of the opinion that the case is pre-eminently fit for an overall settlement between the parties covering all litigations, claims, rights and liabilities related to and arising out of the disaster and we hold it just, equitable and reasonable to pass the following order.

> We order:

> (1) The Union Carbide Corporation shall pay a sum of U.S. Dollars 470 million (Four hundred and seventy million) to the Union of India in full settlement of all claims, rights and liabilities related to and arising out of the Bhopal Gas disaster.

> (2) The aforesaid sum shall be paid by the Union Carbide Corporation to the Union of India on or before 31 March, 1989. To enable the effectuation of the settlement, all civil proceedings related to and arising out of the Bhopal Gas disaster shall hereby stand transferred to this Court and shall stand concluded in terms of the settlement, and all criminal proceedings related to and arising out of the disaster shall stand quashed wherever these may be pending.

> A memorandum of settlement shall be filed before us tomorrow setting forth all the details of the settlement to enable consequential directions, if any, to issue.

Signed, R.S. Pathak, Chief Justice of India; Justices, E.S. Venkatataramiah;

Raganath Mishra; M.N. Venkatachaliah; and N.D. Ojha

Dated: 14 - 2 -1989.

This order was followed by a supplementary order on 15 February 1989, entitled "Terms of Settlement Consequential to the Orders Passed by the Supreme Court".

Having heard the learned counsel for the parties, and having taken into account the written memorandum filed by them, we make the following order further to our order of 14 February, 1989, which shall be read with and subject to this order:

1. Union Carbide India Ltd., which is already a party in numerous suits filed in the District Court at Bhopal, and which have been stayed by an order dated 31 December, 1985 of the District Court, Bhopal, is joined as a necessary party in order to effectuate the terms and conditions of our order dated 14 February, 1989 as supplemented by this order.

2. Pursuant to the order passed on 14 February, 1989 the payment of the sum of U.S. $470 Millions (four hundred and seventy millions) directed by the Court to be paid on or before 31, March, 1989 will be made in the manner following:

    (a) A sum of U.S. $425 Million (four hundred and twenty five million) shall be paid on or before 23 March, 1989 by Union Carbide Corporation to the Union of India, less U.S. $5 Millions already paid by Union Carbide Corporation pursuant to the order dated 7 June, 1985 of Judge Keenan in the court proceedings taken in the United States of America.

    (b) Union Carbide India Ltd. will pay on or before 23 March, 1989 to the Union of India the rupee equivalent of U.S. $45 Million (forty-five million) at the exchange rate prevailing at the date of payment.

(c) The aforesaid payments shall be made to the Union of India as claimant and for the benefit of all victims of the Bhopal Gas Disaster under the Bhopal Gas Leak Disaster (Registration and Processing of Claims) Scheme, 1985, and not as fines, penalties, or punitive damages.

3. Upon full payment of the sum referred to in paragraph 2 above:

(a) The Union of India and the State of Madhya Pradesh shall take all steps which may in future become necessary in order to implement and give effect to this order including but not limited to ensuring that any suit or criminal complaints which may be filed in future against any Corporation, Company or person referred to in this settlement are defended by them and disposed of in terms of this order.

(b) Any such suits, claims or civil or criminal proceedings filed or to be filed before any court or authority are hereby enjoined and shall not be proceeded with before such court or authority except for dismissal or quashing in terms of this order.

4. Upon full payment in accordance with the Court's directions:

(a) The undertaking given by Union Carbide Corporation pursuant to the order dated 30 November, 1986 in the District Court, Bhopal shall stand discharged, and all orders passed in Suit 1113 of 1986 and/or in revision therefrom shall also stand discharged.

(b) Any action for contempt initiated against counsel or parties relating to this case and arising out of proceedings in the courts below shall be treated as dropped.

5. The amounts payable to the Union of India under these orders of the Court shall be deposited to the credit of the Registrar of this Court in a Bank under directions to be taken from this court.

This order will be sufficient authority for the Registrar of the Supreme Court to have the amount transferred to his credit which is lying unutilized with the Indian Red Cross Society pursuant to the direction from the International Red Cross Society.

6.   The terms of settlement filed by learned counsel for the parties to-day are taken on record and shall form part of our order and the record.

The case will be posted for reporting compliance on the first Tuesday of April, 1989.

Signed, R. S. Pathak, CJI, and Justices Venkataramiah,
Misra, Venkatachaliah, and Ojha
Dated:15 - 2 - 1989

The terms of the memorandum of settlement passed by the Supreme Court were agreed upon by the attorney general of the Union of India and the counsel for UCC and UCIL Ltd., by the joint statement filed in the court.

The parties acknowledge that the order dated February 14, 1989 as supplemented by the order dated February 15, 1989 disposes of in its entirety all proceedings in Suit 1113 of 1986. This settlement shall finally dispose of all past, present and future claims, causes of action and civil and criminal proceedings (of any nature whatsoever wherever pending) by all Indian citizens and all public and private entities with respect to all past, present and future deaths, personal injuries, health effects, compensation, losses, damages and civil and criminal complaints of any nature whatsoever against UCC, Union Carbide India Limited, Union Carbide Eastern, and all of their subsidiaries and affiliates as well as each of their present and former directors, officers, employees, agents, representatives, attorneys, advocates and solicitors arising out of, relating to or concerned with the Bhopal gas leak disaster, including past, present and future claims, causes of action and proceedings against each other. All such claims and causes of action whether within or outside India of Indian citizens, public or private entitles are hereby extinguished, including without limitation each of the claims filed or to be filed under the Bhopal Gas Leak Disaster (Registration and Processing Claims) Scheme 1985, and all such civil proceedings in India are hereby transferred to this Court and are dismissed with prejudice, and all such criminal proceedings including contempt proceedings stand quashed and accused deemed to be acquitted.

Upon full payment in accordance with the Court's directions the undertaking given by UCC pursuant to the order dated November 30, 1986 in the District Court, Bhopal stands discharged, and all orders passed in suit No. 1113 of 1986 and or in any Revision therefrom, also stands discharged.[45]

J. B. Dadachanji	A. Subhashini
For UCC and UCIL Ltd.	Advocate on Record for Union of India
Dated:	15 - 2 - 8

In accordance with Judge Keenan's ruling of May 1986, to comply with the rulings by the Indian courts, Union Carbide Corporation accepted the settlement on February 24, 1989 and paid $420 million and UCIL, the rupee equivalent of $45 million. The sum of $5 million paid earlier by UCC to the International Red Cross was credited towards the final settlement.

This out of court settlement was not well received by the majority of victims and lawyers representing the victims and other interest groups. The amount was considered very low and they accused the central government of capitulating to UCC. Protest marches and burning of effigies continued for a long time, and still continues to a lesser degree, in an effort to pressure the government to change the terms of the settlement.

---

[45]   N.R. Madhava Menon (ed.) *Documents and Court Opinions on Bhopal Gas Leak disaster Case, National Law School of India University, For Course on Tort II*, Bangalore: 1991, pp. 288–291.

Chapter Five

CONCLUSIONS

Bhopal, the capital of the central Indian State of Madhya Pradesh, has become synonymous with the site of the world's worst chemical disaster. The cause of the gas leak that killed and injured tens of thousands of nearby residents on December 3, 1984, has been a controversial issue ever since. For lack of proper documentation and because of the government's control over the investigations that ensued, the full count of the dead and injured will never be known.

Immediately after the gas leak, the Government of India assumed full control of the plant and the investigative process, to the exclusion of others, and drew its own conclusions, designed to influence world public opinion and the negotiations during litigation. It disassociated itself completely from any previous involvement with the UCIL pesticide plant by placing the blame squarely on UCC.

In spite of being hampered by the government authorities in carrying out a normal and open investigation, within three months of the tragedy, UCC investigators disclosed its findings that a large volume of water entered the tank to trigger the uncontrolled reaction and the massive gas leak. This was only possible after the analysis of the sample of residue that was recovered from the ill-fated tank E-610, followed by extensive laboratory experimentation to replicate the complex residue. This information was functionally equivalent to that recovered from the black boxes of airplanes that have crashed. Nine months later, the CSIR scientists concurred with the UCC results, but in addition, postulated several other "probable" contributory factors.

Two hypotheses were postulated to explain the entry of approximately 120 to 240 gallons of water. The first, advanced by the plant operators within days of the tragedy, was the "water-washing" hypothesis. They assumed that during the cleaning of a clogged pipe by the plant operator, who did not take proper precautions, water entered the system. The water then moved along the 500-foot-long pipeline and leaked through all four intervening valves before it entered tank E-610. Since CSIR also supported this route, the hypothesis gained undue credibility, and was widely accepted by the media and most of the authors who wrote about the Bhopal tragedy.

After the U.S. courts ordered the Government of India, as plaintiff in the lawsuit, to abide by U.S. disclosure rules, and UCC and ADL investigators had been given access to plant documents and interviewed plant personnel, they were able to determine that water was added into the tank by a deliberate act.

In fact, two experiments carried out earlier by the CBI and UCIL engineers in order to simulate the "water-washing" hypothesis were not supportive of this mode of entry. In the simulation of the washing of the plugged filter test, the water pressure was not sufficient to rise up even to the first valve located above the point of connection of the water hose. Moreover, expecting the pipe to contain water, a hole was drilled at the lowest point of the piping system, which was found to be dry. The CSIR report ignored these two critical tests, which did not support their arguments.

After the gas leak, all the employees on duty that night asserted that they were using MIC from tank E-611 for conversion to Carbaryl until the time of the gas leak. They claimed that a sudden and unexplained rise in pressure inside tank E-610 gave them no time to control the looming danger. This was proven to be false.

Chloroform, which was used as an inert solvent in the manufacture of MIC, was the clue that cracked the veil of secrecy. This chemical was identified in the residue of tank E-610 as well as in the SEVIN feed tank and the connecting piping. This finding indicated that the last transfer of MIC was actually made from tank E-610 and not from E-611 as asserted by the plant operators. Prior to Operation Faith, as much as 2.5 percent of chloroform was detected in the feed tank and the connecting line to the MIC storage tanks, whereas the MIC in tank E-611 contained only trace amounts of chloroform, consistent with product specifications. This was initially puzzling to the investigators; fearing further eruption within tank E-611, their investigative process focused on neutralization of the remaining MIC. The high purity MIC analyzed in tank E-611 helped discredit the position held by the plant operators and CSIR scientists. Thus the two storage tanks coated in black tar served as the "Black Boxes" of Bhopal.

This finding supports the argument made by ADL and UCC investigators that soon after the plant workers and the supervisors discovered the cause of the problem, a transfer of one ton of MIC was made from tank E-610 into the feed tank. They hoped to remove some water, which, being a little denser than MIC, would be at the bottom of the tank, and thus control the reaction and the rising pressure. When this attempt failed, there was panic and confusion and many fled. After closer scrutiny of the documents provided, the U.S. investigators also uncovered that relevant pages of the log books were altered or removed in an attempt to conceal the real cause of the gas leak and confound the investigators.

When the UCC and ADL investigators disclosed their sabotage theory they did not name the culprit plant worker for legal reasons, but with the information provided, M.L.Verma suspected that he was being targeted. Confident that he had the support of the union workers and the government he denied any involvement and blamed the company for the tragedy. Before the suspected saboteur could be arraigned or interrogated in a trial, the case was settled out of court, preventing a legal assessment of his innocence or guilt.

Small mischievous acts – to get even with the bosses – at industrial plants are not uncommon in India and indeed elsewhere. The UCIL plant had experienced such incidents in the past with little consequence. In this case the "mischief" unwittingly turned into a major calamity. The unprecedented tragedy caused the workers close to the event to distance themselves from the scene and to place the blame on faulty equipment and lax safety practices at the plant. The managers also failed to understand that a well-trained, safety-conscious, and contented work force is a very important element in the overall success and safety of a manufacturing enterprise. They had been fully aware of the grievances and complaints by the employees ever since the death of Ashraf Khan from exposure to phosgene, and knew of the defiant attitude of a frustrated operator, now officially a member of a recognized labor union.

A significant contributory factor and a major setback to UCIL business was the inability of its scientists and engineers to develop a viable domestic manufacturing process for alpha-naphthol compounded by the central government's rigid policies and control over the Bhopal project.

Since the plant was not operating at full capacity and the products were not competitive in the marketplace, the agricultural products business was not profitable. During the months prior to the tragedy UCIL and UCC officials were seriously considering closing the Bhopal pesticide facility. In late 1984 there was a sense of urgency to decide the plant's fate, since the foreign collaboration agreement would expire on January 1, 1985.

Safety guards were lowered or nonexistent after MIC was produced for the last time in October 1984 and stored in tanks E-610 and E-611 for conversion to Carbaryl. The riots following the assassination of the prime minister, and the citywide curfew, left the plant idle for nearly a month.

Nonfunctioning safety-related equipment – not repaired in anticipation of closure and dismantling of the plant – and other cost-cutting measures contributed to the magnitude of the tragedy.

The two MIC tanks were filled beyond the recommended levels in the Safety Manual, leaving very little empty space inside each tank for any corrective action in case of an emergency. A larger space would have slowed the quick pressure increase and allowed for the addition of an inert solvent to moderate the rate of the reaction. More importantly, if MIC had been stored at the recommended lower temperatures, it would also have reduced the reaction rate. The refrigeration system had been shut down as a cost-cutting measure. Also in an effort to save money, the use of electricity was curtailed and ancillary maintenance work, presumed to be non-essential, was not continued. The vent gas scrubber and the flare tower, normally used to destroy fugitive gases during the production of MIC, were not operational on the night of the disaster.

An identical spare tank E-619, provided to contain MIC that did not meet product specifications or to be used in case of pressure buildup in any of the other tanks, was not utilized (apparently this practice was rarely observed). If proper procedures delineated in the MIC Safety Manual were followed, MIC from tank E-610 should have been transferred into tank E-619, which contained only one ton of MIC and could hold as much as half of the contents of the ill-fated tank, up to twenty tons. This would have considerably reduced the pressure in tank E-610 and minimized the volume of gases liberated into the atmosphere. Instead, they transferred only one ton into the feed tank.

When the workers discovered that water had entered tank E-610, they were untrained in relevant emergency procedures and were totally unprepared to deal with a situation of such magnitude.

The numbers of innocent lives lost and of those who suffered long-term injury were also greatly increased by the failure of plant supervisors to inform the police, or to warn the nearby residents of the imminent danger. Plant employees knew the direction that the wind was blowing the gas cloud, but did not notify the authorities, which might have helped to direct the evacuation routes. The middle-of-the-night timing by the perpetrator of the mischief undoubtedly further compounded the confusing situation.

The growth of unauthorized shantytowns and slums on unoccupied public land near construction sites and factories continues to plague India and many developing countries. In the case of the Bhopal plant, workers found it convenient to live close to their workplace, and local governments were either unable or unwilling to face the issue. The slum residents are often potential "vote banks" for aspiring politicians. Earlier concerns expressed by UCIL management to the state government about this potential problem outside the plant premises were ignored. If people had not lived near the plant there would have been fewer casualties.

Early reports by government and media – and from surveys – estimated that the number of deaths ranged between two thousand and three thousand, with thousands more injured. Subsequently, according to several other reports, mostly by activist groups, this number was estimated to be as high as ten thousand dead over a period of several years, all attributed to exposure to MIC gas.

The design technology purchased from UCC was adapted by Indian engineers to suit Indian conditions and to maximize the use of locally available instrumentation and indigenous materials. Indian engineers and consultants built the Bhopal MIC plant, which operated successfully for five years without any significant systemic problems.

In the 1970s, prior to the building of the plant and following government regulations, UCC reduced its equity in the company to 50.9 percent through equity dilution. This was accomplished by selling additional UCIL shares to the Indian public. However it remained a majority shareholder with a controlling interest and proportional representation on the UCIL board of directors. Except for major decisions of strategic importance and annual budgets, which had to be cleared by the UCC management committee at the U.S. headquarters, management of UCIL business and daily operations at the MIC Bhopal plant, and at other facilities throughout the country, were conducted entirely by Indians.

The various deficiencies at the plant, cited by CSIR scientists in their report, are thus not consistent with the history of the MIC plant. The analyses of the causes of the leak and the conclusions drawn in the CSIR report are inconsistent with their own experimental data. These were obviously designed to support the pending lawsuit in the U.S. court. The investigation by the Singh Commission initiated by the state government was aborted just as it began serious enquiry. The Central Bureau of Investigation, which is in possession of all the facts, has not issued a full report except to echo the allegations cited in the CSIR report.

After four years of legal maneuvering the Supreme Court of India ordered Union Carbide Corporation to pay $470 million in an out-of-court settlement. UCC promptly paid the amount.

The true cause of the Bhopal tragedy was determined only because of the significant information contained in the residue of tank E-610, along with the corroborative information from MIC in tank E-611. These studies also provided information about the other gases that might have escaped along with MIC to cause such devastation. It has conclusively eliminated the formation of hydrogen cyanide as part of this gas cloud. The MIC storage tanks turned out to be a unique type of "black box" without which the Bhopal tragedy would have remained unsolved.

Though much has been written on the post-independence industrial policies, the Bhopal tragedy presents an important and unique case study of how the Government of India applied these laws to closely monitoring UCIL's Bhopal pesticide plant. These laws set the terms and conditions of the purchase of technology from foreign companies, extending to details like the terms and conditions for construction of the plant and the tonnage of the product to be produced.

EPILOGUE

With all future litigation against UCC, UCIL, and their employees quashed by the Supreme Court of India, the saga of the Bhopal tragedy did not end there. After a change of government in New Delhi in October 1991 and unrelenting pressure from some groups representing the victims who felt betrayed by the previous administration, the new justices of the Supreme Court permitted the criminal case to be reopened, although they did uphold the $470 million out-of-court settlement. In a lawsuit filed by some interest groups in the Bhopal Magistrate Court, UCC, Warren M. Anderson – who had retired in 1986 – and eight senior UCIL officials were charged with criminal negligence and culpable homicide, the legal equivalent of manslaughter. A warrant for Anderson's arrest was issued in 1992, and since he did not appear before the chief judicial magistrate Anderson was proclaimed an absconder from Indian justice. The Indian government, with elaborate and vague reasoning, ignored the persistent pleas from these groups who sought Anderson's extradition.

In November 1999, a class action lawsuit[46] was filed in the Southern District Court in New York; it charged UCC and Anderson for violating the law on the fundamental human rights of the victims and survivors, environmental law and international criminal law. In August 2000, Judge John F. Keenan dismissed the class action on grounds that the plaintiffs lacked standing to sue and that UCC had fully complied with the February 1989 decision of final settlement by the Supreme Court of India. When appealed, the circuit judges of the U.S. 2nd Circuit Court of Appeals ruled that the district court had properly dismissed the plaintiffs' claims under Alien Torts Claims Act (ATCA), 28 U.S.C. 1350, but erred on dismissing the common-law environmental claims.[47]

---

[46] Lawsuit 99 Civ.11329 JFK) (S.D.N.Y).-

[47] U.S. 2nd Circuit Court of Appeals, BANO V UNION CARBIDE CORPO-RATION AND WARREN ANDERSON, Docket No. 00-9250, November 15, 2001. (ATCA permits aliens to sue corporations for certain human rights violation such as inhumane working conditions, and severe environmental damage, whether committed in the U.S. or abroad.)

In May 2002, the CBI asked the Bhopal District Court to reduce the charges against Anderson from culpable homicide to negligence, which carries a much lower penalty and would not require him to appear in India. The latest announcement shocked the victims and the activist groups, even though similar charges against the UCIL officials had been reduced in an earlier decision by the court. Hundreds of people battling health problems went to New Delhi to ask the government to withdraw the CBI application. Just prior to rendering his decision on August 28 the chief magistrate in Bhopal faced a similar mass demonstration. He sided with the victims. The court cases against Anderson and the UCIL officials are still being litigated and the twenty-one-year-old saga continues.

In April 1985, a team of experts from the International Labor Organization (ILO) made several safety-related recommendations for the entire country. They concluded that the principal elements that needed attention in India were the identification of major hazardous plants, the maintenance of high operating standards, and a competent enforcement authority. The ILO experts also recommended that each plant should have an emergency plan specific for that site.

The Factories Act of 1948, which was based on the British Factories Act and periodically amended, was further amended after the Bhopal disaster. The 1987 amendment set out additional safeguards regarding handling of hazardous substances.

After the CSIR report was presented to the Indian Parliament in mid-December, 1985, Prime Minister Rajiv Gandhi transferred Dr. Varadarajan, director of CSIR and the chief scientist who led the investigation, to the planning commission as a consultant. All the senior staff members at the plant were retired with generous compensation when the plant was closed in December 1985. Jay Mukund, works manager, built a house and settled in the hilly region of South India. S.P. Choudhary, the production manager, has a managerial position with a brewing company. Both are still being tried in Bhopal court on minor charges along with six others, including the chairman of the board and the managing director of UCIL. M.L.Verma and several other plant operators were offered positions with the state government as industry inspectors.

Bhopal was a wake-up call to chemical industries worldwide to do more about the safety at their plants and the surroundings. Many companies voluntarily adopted programs to provide hazard information to nearby residents and their governments, as well as information about toxic materials transported to or from their plants.

In the United States, the Chemical Manufacturers Association adopted a program of Community Awareness and Emergency Response (CAER) in 1986. Two years later it adopted Responsible Care, a comprehensive program of codes of good practice, designed to upgrade chemical industry performance in all aspects of the production and handling of chemicals. During 1990-97, these programs proliferated to other U.S. industrial groups and to more than forty overseas chemical industries.[48]

The Bhopal disaster also prompted the U.S. Congress to enact Title III, the Emergency Planning and Community Right-to-Know Act (EPCRA), as part of the Federal Superfund Amendments and Reauthorization Act (SARA) of 1986. Thereby, the citizens would have the right to know about hazardous and toxic chemicals produced and released in their environment.

The United Kingdom enacted the Protection under the Public Interest Disclosure Act in 1999 to protect workers who disclose serious malpractice in their work environment and deliberate cover-ups.[49]

In November 1994, the Indian Supreme Court allowed the sale of UCIL assets; UCC sold its 50.9 per cent equity to McLeod Russel (India) Ltd. of Calcutta. In December 1994, UCC fulfilled its commitment to the Bhopal Memorial Hospital with about $20 million turned over to the charitable trust in England and an additional $54 million from the sales of UCC shares in UCIL towards the construction of the new hospital and local clinics.[50]

Bhopal had a drastic impact on Union Carbide Corporation, as a company, and on its employees worldwide. It managed to avert a hostile takeover and was forced to sell many of its profitable units. In 1986 it divested from the pesticide business when the wholly owned Union Carbide Agricultural Products Company was sold to Rhone-Poulenc, a French chemical company, and later to Bayer of Germany. Bayer now produces MIC at the Institute plant in West Virginia. Finally, on February 6, 2001, Union Carbide Corporation, once the third largest multinational U.S. chemical company, was merged with Dow Chemical Co. in a $11.6 billion deal.

According to the nongovernmental organization Eklavya, as of August 31, 1994, the final compensation paid to victims amounted to Rs. 305.8 crore ($97.1 million) out of the Rs. 1482 crore ($470 million) paid in the

---

[48] *Chemical & Engineering News,* June 2, 1997, p. 13.
[49] *Royal Society of Chemistry, Professional Bulletin,* No.116, July 2000.
[50] UCC BHOPAL FACT SHEETS, (n.d.).

final settlement (Chouhan et al.) The compensation disbursed amounted to less than the interest earned since the date of the settlement. Each claimant received about Rs. 93,000 ($3,000) for deaths and Rs. 27,000 ($870) on an average for injuries. A sum of Rs.7,000 was deducted from the final payments for the interim cash advances made earlier.

A day before the eleventh anniversary of the disaster, the state government reported that it had spent Rs. 37.75 crore ($11.5 million) in providing public utilities to the affected areas – paving the streets, constructing drains, providing water and electricity – in addition to repairing cremation and burial grounds; that "over 1800 houses have been constructed at Karond Kalan...and over 1574 of these have already been allotted" to the families of the deceased; and that "over 368 victims were trained in different industrial trades in the last two years...and 755 persons" are being trained. Over 152 work sheds had been built at the Govindpura Industrial area at a cost of Rs. 8 crore ($2.5 million).

Just as the Madhya Pradesh government announced the progress made in rehabilitating the victims, the state's English language newspaper in its editorial column described the plight of the victims, the progress made since the tragedy, and the rampant corruption in the administering of aid.

> Until last year, when the city observed the completion of a decade after the tragedy, there was practically no immediate hope on the horizon of saving the gas relief measures from the clutches of the vested interests. And in spite of loud protestations and lamentations in the media, the victims, who were still running from pillar to post to get succor, had nothing but their dejection to count on.... But after 11 years, the tragedy has assumed another dimension, another ugly side has come to light which, in some ways, is even worse than the initial one. It is the corruption, graft and irregularities in general that have turned a human tragedy into a money minting business by unscrupulous individuals. From bogus medical certifications to irregularities of every conceivable to inconceivable kind at gas claim court, it is mostly people with money and the right connections who profited while the genuine sufferers minus the money and/connections continued to languish.[51]

One year after the Bhopal tragedy, the Citizens Committee for Preservation and Rehabilitation unveiled a memorial sculpture in honor of the gas victims. It stands on the edge of the shantytown of Jai Prakash Nagar,

---

[51] Editorial, *Madhya Pradesh Chronicle,* Bhopal: December 2, 1995.

across the street from the defunct Union Carbide plant in Bhopal. This poignant tribute in stone, named *Mamata's Mother,* designed by sculptress Ruth Waterman, a survivor of the Nazi holocaust, portrays a wailing woman fleeing with a limp child in her right hand. Her left hand shields her face and another child clings to the back of her sari. The prevalent sentiment of Bhopal's survivors is reflected in the inscription on the pedestal of the sculpture. "NO HIROSHIMA NO BHOPAL WE WANT TO LIVE" (See the photograph on the next page.) This site has become a central meeting place to commemorate the loss of lives in the tragedy and for annual rallies to honor the dead as well as to criticize the government and denounce and vilify Union Carbide Corporation and its chairman, Warren Anderson. The target company is now Dow Chemical.

In March 1990, addressing the UN-sponsored meeting in New Delhi, Ajit Singh, India's minister of industry, assured the international business delegates that the government was set to make Indian industry more competitive in the world market. He stated his intention "to release Indian industry from unnecessary bureaucratic shackles that may hinder the kind of modernization and growth that we would like. My Ministry is taking steps to ensure that in the future the number of clearances required from the central Government for making industrial investments is kept as small as possible."[52]

In June 2000, the controversial twenty-seven-year-old Foreign Exchange Regulation Act (FERA) was replaced by the Foreign Exchange Management Act (FEMA), designed to be compatible with India's newly evolving pro-liberalization policies. In addition to many other changes to encourage foreign investments, the new law has also lifted restrictions on majority foreign equity holdings in several sectors, and clearance from the central government in the hiring of foreign technicians is no longer a requirement. Today, India is marching along a more progressive path and foreign investments are at an all-time high. Indian industries are competing successfully in the world market and also are investing in other countries.

---

[52]   "Foreign Direct Investment and Technology Transfer in India: Proceedings of the UN Center on Transnational Corporations Round-Table on Foreign Direct Investment and Technology Transfer," New Delhi: 15-16 March 1990, United Nations, 1992, p. 26.

"NO HIROSHIMA NO BHOPAL WE WANT TO LIVE"
"Memorial dedicated to the victims of the gas disaster
Caused by the multinational killer Union Carbide on 2 & 3 December 1984
Nagarik Rahat Purnavas Committee."

[Citizens Committee for Preservation and Rehabilitation]

APPENDIX A

**Primary documents related to the Bhopal pesticide plant.
Reproduced from the archives of United States District Court
Southern District of New York**

A-1: Application for License to build the Pesticide Formulation Plant in Bhopal

UNION CARBIDE INDIA LIMITED

STREET ADDRESS	TELEPHONE : 38-6341 (5 LINES)
5, PARLIAMENT STREET	TELEX : 031-204
NEW DELHI-1	CABLE :UNICARBIDE, NEWDELHI

GENERAL OFFICE
P. O. BOX 533, NEW DELHI-1
INDIA

September 21, 1970

The Secretary
Ministry of Industrial Development
Internal Trade and Company Affairs,
Udyog Bhavan
NEW DELHI

Attention :   Co-ordination & Licencing Progress Section
Subject: COB Licence for Pesticides Formulation Plant – Bhopal

Dear Sir:

We herewith respectfully submit an application, in the prescribed forms, for COB licence for our Pesticides Formulation Plant at Bhopal.

Union Carbide India Limited was granted in December 1966, a Letter of Intent No. A & I-32(14)/66 dated 6.12.1966 by Government of India for the manufacture of SEVIN Carbaryl Insecticide and formulations therefrom. A seeding program was started soon after and a pilot plant on temporary permit No. A & I-32(22)/67 dated 23.11.1967, was installed in 1967 at Trombay for the development of formulations. For various reasons Government of Maharashtra was reluctant to allow us to set up the formulation plant in Trombay area and subsequently we shifted this plant to Bhopal in 1968. This plant is registered with the Director of Industries, Madhya Pradesh and the registration number is DO/BPL/SSI/61/68/4116/ Bhopal dated May 2, 1968. This plant move was also regularized by the Ministry of Petroleum, Chemicals, Mines and Metals vide letter No. A & I-32(22)/67 dated May 6, 1970 and was valid up to July 31, 1970.

Our earlier letter of Intent had lapsed in December 1967 but we have now made a fresh application in February 1970 and this project is under the active consideration of Government of India.

The recent GOI notification has led to the suspension of all temporary permits and requires us to apply now for a COB licence. We, therefore, submit our application for the same and request early grant of the licence so that we can serve the farming community uninterruptedly.

Thanking you,

> Very truly yours,
> UNION CARBIDE INDIA LIMITED
> S/d E. A. Munoz
> Division General Manager
> Agricultural Products Division

Encl: Form "EE"
TR for Rs. 50/-
Balance Sheet

REGISTERED OFFICE; 1, MIDDLETON STREET, CALCUTTA-16

(Court Doc. No 10114808)

A-2: Deed of Lease Between the State of Madhya Pradesh and UCIL

This Deed of Lease is made at this *Tenth* day of *October* 1972 between the Governor of Madhya Pradesh, acting through the Director of Industries (hereinafter called the 'Lessor' which expression shall, where the context so admit, include his successors in office) of the one part and Shri R. K. Dutta, for and on behalf of M/s Union Carbide India Limited (hereinafter called the 'Lessee' which expression shall, where the context so admit, include its successors and permitted assigns) of the other part.

WHEREAS upon the request of the lessee, the lessor has agreed to grant to the lessee, subject to the terms and conditions hereinafter specified, a lease of the piece of land comprising of an area measuring approximately 49.25 acres or thereabout, situated in the Kali Parade Industrial Area of the Tehsil Huzur of the Sehore District, more particularly described in schedule shown hereunder and for greater clearness delineated on the plan hereto annexed and thereon coloured red (hereinafter referred to as 'the said land') for a term of 99 years commencing from *10th October,* 1972 and ending on *9th October,* 2071, for the purpose of construction and establishing thereon a factory for the manufacture of Methyl Isocyanate - based Pesticides and purposes ancilliary thereto (hereinafter referred to as 'the said business').

NOW THEREFORE this deed witnesseth and it is hereby agreed and declared as follows:

1. In consideration of the premium and rent herein reserved and of the covenants on the part of the lessee hereinafter contained, the lessor hereby demises to the lessee the said land for a period of 99 years for holding the same for the purposes of the said business.

2. The lessee shall pay to the lessor for the said land a premium of Rs. 19,700/- (Rupees nineteen thousand seven hundred only) within 30 days of the execution of the deed. During the term of the lease, the lessee shall further pay to the lessor an annual ground rent of Rs1,970/00 (Rupees one thousand nine hundred and seventy only) and such other sum as may be determined in accordance with clause 3 hereunder on or before the 10th of April, of each year.

3. The ground rent of Rs. 1,970/00 per annum shall be liable to be increased on the expiry of 30 years from the date of execution of this deed and also at

subsequent intervals of 30 years, provided that the increase on each occasion shall not exceed one quarter of the rent fixed for the preceeding 30 years.

4 The lessee shall pay and discharge during the term of the lease all assessment rates, taxes and charges of every description whatsoever, now or hereafter to be assessed, imposed or charged upon the said land.

5 The lessee hereby agrees that he shall within a period of three years from the date of execution of this deed:

   i) Construct and establish on the said land a factory for the manufacture of Methyl Isocyanate based Pesticides and allied products as well as structures required for the efficient running of the said business, at his own cost, and

   ii) start manufacture of Methyl Isocyanate-based Pesticides and other allied products in a skillful and workman like manner.

6. The lessee shall submit to the lessor or any officer authorised by him in writing from time to time the plans and specifications for the said constructions for approval of the lessor and the construction shall be in accordance with the plans and specifications as may be approved by the lessor.

7. The lessee shall use the said land and building, structures and works erected or constructed thereon only for the purpose of the said business of manufacturing Methyl Isocyanate-based Pesticides and other allied products and for construction of office, administrative buildings, godowns and shall not use for any other purpose without the previous permission in writing of the lessor.

8. The lessee shall at its own expense forthwith erect and at all times ... and keep in good condition all boundary marks and ... with the boundaries of the said land according to the ... as shown in the plan hereto annexed.

9. The lessee shall keep the said land and buildings erected ... in a condition fit for and ... use expenses effluent ... with underground drainpipe system which may be laid by the State government or the local authority concerned. [Blank spaces are not legible].

10. The lessee shall not sublet, assign or otherwise transfer the said land or any part hereof or any building structure of work constructed thereon for any pur-

pose whatsoever without the previous sanction in writing of the lessor or any officer authorised by him.

11. The lessee shall not encroach upon any land adjoining the said land and in the event of such encroachment, he shall be deemed to be a tresspasser (sic) and liable to be evicted therefrom. The lessor shall be entitled to recover expenses, if any, incurred for eviction of the lessee.

12. While using the said land, if the lessee causes any harm or injury to any person he shall be liable to pay compensation or damages in the same manner as a tenant of land is generally liable to pay.

13. The lessee shall acquire no proprietary right or claim whatsoever over the said land.

14. The lessor hereby covenants with the lessee that the lessee paying the rent hereby reserved and observing and performing the covenants and conditions herein contained and on his part to be observed and performed shall peaceably and quietly possess and enjoy the said land during the term of the lease without any interruption or disturbance of the lessor or any person lawfully claiming under him.

15. In the event of any dispute regarding State Government's title to the land leased out hereunder and/or in the event of such title being found defective, the State Government undertakes to acquire the land and bear the cost of acquisition of land over and above the premium already charged for the land.

16. If the rent hereby reserved or any part thereof shall at any time be in arrears and un-paid for 6 calendar months next after the date whereon the same shall have become due, whether the same shall have been by the lessee of any of the conditions and … contained and the lessee failed to remedy the breach within 6 months of the notice in writing given by the lessor or becomes insolvent or entered into an agreement with his creditors for composition of the industry, the lease will be deemed to have been terminated and the lessor may notwithstanding the waiver of any previous cause or right of re-entry and without prejudice to any right or remedy of the lessor for recovery of rent remaining due under the lease enter upon the said land and repossess the same as if this demise had not been made.

17. On the expiry of the lease period or termination of the lease due to the breach of the conditions of the lease deed, or the transfer of the land or its mis-utilisation by the lessee, the lessor (State Government) will have the right of

re-entry over the land. On such a re-entry, the lessor (State Government) may pay to the lessee the premium/cost of acquisition paid by the lessee at the time the land was leased out to the lessee or the market value, whichever is lesser. The lessor may also pay to the lessee the cost actually incurred on the constructions standing on the land less their depreciated value as determined by the Chief Engineer (B & R), Public Works Department or the market value on the date of re-entry, as estimated by the Chief Engineer, Public Works Department (B & R) whichever is less in case the lessor decides to take possession of the constructions also. In case the lessor does not propose to take over the constructions, the lessee shall be bound to remove them within the period fixed by the lessor. If the constructions are not removed within the period so fixed, the constructions shall lapse to the lessor and no compensation on their account will be payable to the lessee by the lessor.

18. All costs and expenses for preparation, execution and registration of this lease will be borne and paid by the lessee.

19. Any notice required to be made or given to the lessee hereunder shall be deemed to have been duly served on him if sent by the Director of Industries (M.P.) or any other officer authorised by him on this behalf, through post by registered letter addressed to the lessee at the premises of the said business or at registered office of the firm, failing above, if it is affixed at the entrance of the said premise in the presence of two witnesses.

20. Any sum falling due from the lessee under this agreement may be recovered from it as an arrear of land revenue.

SCHEDULE

North:	Western Railway line
South:	Proposed 80 ft. wide road [Kali Parade Rd-see Map]
East:	Chola Road
West:	Existing unit of M/s Shama Forge Co.

In witness whereof the parties hereto have signed this deed on the date and year respectively mentioned against their signatures.

Witness: For and on behalf of the
                                             Governor, Madhya Pradesh, (Lessor)
1.---s/d------------------------   s/d

Appendix A

Asst. Director of Industries

Madhya Pradesh

2.----s/d----------------------- Date: [Not legible]

1.----s/d-----------------------

For and on behalf of the lessee

For UNION CARBIDE INDIA LIM-
ITED

Agricultural & Marine Products Division

2. -----s/d----------------------

s/d

R. K. Dutta

Works Manager - Bhopal Plant

[Editorial Note: Signatures are not legible]

(Court Document Nos. 10124983 to 10124987)

A-3: Application Letter for Allotment of Land for Bhopal Plant

16 September, 1976

The Director of Industries
Madhya Pradesh
BHOPAL

Dear Sir:

Sub.: 1) Allotment of 20 acres of land for effluent disposal pond.

2) Request f or allotment of the balance 2.39 acres of Khasra No. 10.

Please refer to our letter dated 20th August, 1976, on the above and as mentioned in the last para thereof, we now submit herewith necessary application form for allotment of 2.39 acres of land, left out from Khasra No. 10 at Chhola Village. In this connection, we submit the following.

This request of ours is essentially related to our application dated 29th May, 1976, submitted to you, for allotment of additional about 10 acres of land (over and above the 20 acres recently allotted). As explained in that letter, the configuration of the 20 acres allotted to us already (i.e. Khasra No. 10 and 13) is such as to give us a net evaporation surface of only (...) acres, after allowing for the embankments, service roads, safety fencing, etc. In view of the fact that we need a minimum of 20 to 25 acres net evaporation area for disposal of liquid wastes, it is absolutely essential that we are allotted additional 10 to 12 acres of land, adjacent to the plots already allotted. Our above application is already under your active consideration and we have been asked to formalise it through the prescribed application form, along with some other details, which we are furnishing separately today.

As regards the attached application form for 2.39 acres, as you will observe from the enclosed drawing No. CB - GN - 146/0, the share of this piece of land is such that, by itself, it will not be of much use to anyone else since it is a corner of Khasra No. 10, of which a major portion has been allotted to us, it touches the boundary of Khasra No. 9 which we are hopeful of being allotted in due course and on the remaining sides, it is surrounded by other agricultural fields. There appears to be, therefore, no access to this patch of land, except by ourselves.

Because this 2.39 acre area is already in possession of your Department and acquisition and allotment of Khasra Nos. 8 and 9 will take some time, we would request that, in the meantime, this area of 2.39 acres be allotted to us, enabling us to commence the first phase of effluent disposal evaporation pond.

Thanking you.

> Very truly yours
> UNION CARBIDE INDIA LIMITED
> s/d
> C. S. RAM
> WORKS MANAGER

Encl.:   Application form with the drawings.
cc.   The Assistant Director of Industries,
         District Industries Office,
         Bhopal
         with the application form in duplicate and a copy of drawing No. CB - GN-146/0.

         bc.: Mr. R. Natarajan
              Mr. L. J. Couvaras
              Mr. M. H. Sangani
              Mr. P. I. Kabra
              Mr. S. M. Mittal

During a meeting (LJC/MHS/SMM) held on 10th April, 1976, it was decided to move the Govt. for allotment of this 2.39 acres also to us, over and above taking necessary steps to apply for Khasra Nos. 8 and 9. We had, however, not made this formal application since the District Industries Office had already strongly recommended this case to their Head Office. We have now been requested by the Directorate to apply for this land. If we do not, they would be compelled to surrender it to the Govt. since they have apparently no funds to pay for the acquisition charges for this portion (the land having been acquired from the owners under the provisions of the Land Acquisition Act).

During the original acquisition proceedings, the Govt. deliberately acquired this extra area. This was done so as to claim that it was needed for "public purpose" and not for UCIL's needs only. To establish the bona fides of the "public purpose" they acquired the entire two Khasras (10 and 13) amounting to 22.39 acres, saying that the balance would be used for some "public purpose". Unfortunately they did not budget for the required funds for the 2.39 acres portion. If it is surrendered, it will jeopardize the chances of success in their acquiring the additional area now requested by us (i.e. Khasra Nos. 8 and 9). Hence this application.

(Editorial Note: It appears that the last two paragraphs have been added after the main body of the letter was typed.)

(Court documents Nos. 10125012 and 10125013)

A-4: Proposal for Manufacture of MIC-based Pesticides

UNION CARBIDE INDIA LIMITED

STREET ADDRESS   TELEPHONE : 38-6341 (5 LINES)
5, PARLIAMENT STREET   TELEX : 031-204
NEW DELHI-1   CABLE :UNICARBIDE, NEWDELHI

GENERAL OFFICE
P. O. BOX 533, NEW DELHI-1
INDIA

IN REPLYING
PLEASE REFER TO

January 1, 1970

The Licensing & Progress Section
Industrial Development Internal Trade & Company Affairs
Udyog Bhavan
NEW DELHI

Sub: Manufacture of 5,000 tons of Methyl Isocyanate
        based pesticides and formulations therefrom

Dear Sirs:

In 1967, Union Carbide India Limited proposed to the Government to erect facilities for the manufacture of up to 5,000 tons per year of "SEVIN" carbaryl insecticide – a proprietary product of Union Carbide Corporation, New York.

At that time, a letter of Intent was issued and, in anticipation of receiving a manufacturing licence, a large scale technical development and marketing program was initiated. The original project did not prove viable on account of the slower than expected pace of market expansion and the commitment to one single product in an area of rapid technological developments.

The use of agricultural chemicals is justified on economic grounds. The cost to farmers and the return to farmers should exceed a certain ratio before large scale use can be expected. Basic economies of scale must be realized. On the other hand, technological advances in the agricultural chemicals field are taking place at constantly accelerated pace. In the next five year, a substantial replacement of carbaryl by new products providing a better cost/performance ratio is to be expected. Within this period, the market expansion curb might flatten before economic size is reached.

During the last three years, Union Carbide Corporation has made dramatic improvements in the production technology of methyl isocyanate, as exemplified by the announcement made by our associates in early 1969 that the price for this product was being reduced by more than half. Simultaneously, the design of flexible carbamilation unit providing greatly improved efficiencies for a variety of products was perfected and novel carbamate molecules reached the stage of advanced development as agricultural pesticides.

Union Carbide India's proposal corrects the negative factors and takes advantage of Union Carbide Corporation's latest technology to build a viable, up-to-date agricultural chemicals industry in India.

I.   PROPOSAL

To erect facilities to manufacture up to 2,000 tons of methyl isocyanate and 5,000 tons MIC based agricultural pesticides and formulations therefrom.

II. ECONOMICS

The total investment in equipment is estimated at Rs. 41,250,000, Rs. 33,900,000 of which will be indigenously fabricated and Rs. 7,350,000 imported. Practically all the engineering will be done in India. Foreign exchange requirements for overseas engineering is not expected to exceed 4% of the total investment.

A foreign collaboration agreement will be entered into with Union Carbide Corporation. Union Carbide India Limited has negotiated an overall technical service fee amounting to 2% of sales technical material basis for five years renewable and an additional royalty of 3% of sales technical material basis in case of products covered by Union Carbide Corporation patents and for the life of the patents. The carbaryl patent expires in 1972. Patents of all other products being considered at present expire between 1978 and 1980.

Union Carbide India Limited will be free to purchase intermediates wherever it chooses. However, Union Carbide Corporation will endeavor to offer Union Carbide India Limited whenever compatible with lower prior commitments and permitted under antitrust laws or income tax regulations – a subsidized price so designed as to make the landed price in India no higher than the prevalent domestic price in manufacturing countries.

III. CHARACTERISTICS OF THE MANUFATURING UNIT

On a first phase, Union Carbide India Limited proposes to erect MIC, carbamilation, recovery and formulation facilities to react [with] purchased alcohols. The MIC unit will be a fully integrated plant operating with coke, chlorine and monomethylamine as basic intermediates under the Union Carbide Corporation process, modified to reduce incidence of exotic materials of construction and imported equipment. It will have a total capacity of 2,000 tons of high purity MIC a year, based on continuous operation. Commissioning of the unit can take place within 24 months from issue of an industrial licence.

The carbamilation section will be a multi-purpose unit capable of conducting the reaction of MIC with a variety of alcohols. The continuous yearly capacity of this unit will be 5,000 tons per year, carbaryl basis. Maximum capacity for other carbamates will be dictated by technical considerations, among others: speed of reaction and molecular weight. The unit will be initially equipped with recovery systems for temik and carbaryl. Recovery systems for other products will be installed as necessary. Commissioning of the carbamilation unit can take place within 18 months from the issue of a manufacturing licence.

Erection of facilities to manufacture alcohols will be proposed on a case by case basis once economic levels of demand can be predicted and the long range usefulness of the different products has been established.

IV. RESEARCH AND DEVELOPMENT

The pesticide industry in India is based on producing molecules and employing manufacturing processes developed in foreign countries and optimized for foreign conditions. A competitive position in world markets, ultimately a goal of Union Carbide India Limited, requires implementing discovery and process development programs oriented by indigenous economics of production.

Union Carbide India Limited has already established residue analysis, process engineering and product development departments. These Research Groups enable the Company to bring to the commercial stage proven molecules of already established toxicological characteristics.

Integration into toxicology, metabolic research, secondary and primary screening and exploratory synthesis will be taken up progressively as the development of the business permits. The ability of Universities and other Government institutions to provide basic research facilities, particularly in the fields of toxicology and synthesis, will be instrumental in accelerating the viability of the integrated research program.

V. PRODUCT RANGE

The product composition will vary from year to year according to the agricultural requirements of the country, development of infestation patterns, climatic conditions, etc. Intensive research and development activities will undoubtedly lead to the development of better molecules, cheaper, and those that can be economically made with indigenous raw-materials and equipment. Steps towards implementing a basic research and development program have already been taken. In addition to "SEVIN", Union Carbide India Limited is actively developing the following products:

A) TEMIK - A systemic nemetocide/miticide/insecticide. In India it has proved to be useful in increasing yields of tea, potatoes, vegetables, sorghum, tobacco and cotton.

B) TRANID - Specific miticide – useful in complimenting (sic) the spectrum of carbaryl in a variety of crops. Successfully tested in India on tea and mmanu-facturing rights.

C) SIRMATE - Selective herbicide – under testing in India for the last two years for the control of weeds on peanuts, potatoes and rice.

D) UC30044 - Systemic rice insecticide : Expected to replace Sevidol within the next three to four years. It has about three times insecticidal activity and is biodegradable as against the persistent BHC in the Sevidol formulation. Union Carbide India Limited is negotiating world manufacturing rights.

E) UC 30045 – Systemic broad-spectrum insecticide: More active than Sevin against lepidoptera species. Can be applied as a granular to soil to control cotton, sorghum and maize pests.

VI. EXPORT POTENTIAL

In general, manufacturing costs in India are expected to be higher than in U.S.A., Western Europe and Japan. On the other hand, Research and Devel-

194

opment costs are definitely lower than in Western Europe and the U.S.A. and about in line with those in Japan.

Successful competition in "commodity" products, that is, products no longer covered by patents or available from different origins

This is the case of Sevidol in the South East Asia Markets. Union Carbide India Limited has already made distributor contacts in Indonesia and Malaysia, effected sample placements and initiated field testing and market development work. Substantial export orders for Sevidol are expected to materialize during 1970.

The long term export business of Union Carbide India Limited, however, lies with development of "proprietary" products through its own Research and Development efforts. On a first stage, Union Carbide India Limited has selected two patented molecules that Union Carbide Corporation has available for licencing – Tranid and UC 30044. Japanese, Dutch and Israeli companies have expressed interest in acquiring exclusive manufacturing rights. All other factors being equivalent, Union Carbide India Limited as an associated company will be given preference and Union Carbide Corporation has agreed to delay negotiations with third parties for a reasonable period pending issue of a letter of intent by the Government of India.

Tranid is already registered for sales in Italy where a 1,000 ton technical potential is estimated. Additional potential exists in Germany, Chile, France, Australia, Japan and Argentina.

UC 30044 requires considerably more development work, but if present indications are confirmed, it might well become the choice insecticide in the entire rice belt of Asia.

Union Carbide India Limited is an unique position to capitalize these export opportunities because its products carry the name of Union Carbide and possesses access to the Corporation's business intelligence, expertise and marketing facilities al over the world.

The issue of a letter of intent approving, in general, Union Carbide India's scheme for the manufacture of 2,000 tons of methyl isocyanate and 5,000 tons of methyl isocyanate-based agricultural pesticides is respectfully requested.

Very truly yours
UNION CARBIDE INDIA LIMITED
s/d E.A. MUNOZ
General Manager
Agricultural Products Division
EAMunoz/ab
(Court Document EXHIBIT 3)

A-5: Reply from Indian Government to UCIL on MIC-based Pesticides

No. A&I -26(1)/70

Government of India

Ministry of Petroleum and Chemicals

*****

New Delhi, the 13th March, 1972

To

    M/s. Union Carbide India Ltd.,

    5, Parliament Street,

    New Delhi-1 .

Sub:-   Application Serial No. 17/CLP/70 dated 1.1.70 for licence under the Industries (Dev. & Reg.) Act, 1951 for the manufacture of new articles viz. 5000 tonnes per annum of Methyl Isocyanate based pesticides at Bhopal (M.P.).

Sir,

I am directed to refer to your application on the above subject and to say that, the Government are prepared to issue a licence under the Industries (Dev. & Reg.) Act, 1951 to you for the manufacture of 5000 tonnes p. a. of Methyl Isocyanate based Pesticides at Bhopal (M.P.) subject to your finalising arrangements in respect of the following to the satisfaction of Government:-

(1)   That the party will set up indigenous manufacture of Alpha Nepthol.

(2)   Arrangements for foreign collaboration and for import of equipment and plant will be settled to the satisfaction of Government.

(3)   50% of actual production will be reserved for non-associated formulators in the country.

(4)   The distribution of technical material to various formulators will be done by the applicants themselves.

(5)   The Company should bring down their foreign equity participation to the satisfaction of Government.

(6)   The Company shall issue additional equity to the extent of 25% of the cost of the project taking into account such premium as may be allowed on the shares and within such time limit as may be allowed by the Controller of Capital Issues.

197

2. You are requested to confirm acceptance of the above conditions and send (i) within a period of six months form the date of issue of this letter proposals regarding foreign collaboration and (ii) application for import of capital goods and applications for consent of the issue of this letter/ from the date of approval of the terms of foreign collaboration.

3. The letter of Intent will be converted into a licence after the conditions imposed are fulfilled.

4. Your attention is invited to the general guide-lines in the annexure to this letter which should be fully borne in mind.

Conditions (i) to (iii) therein constitute the general policy of Govt. Every effort should also be made to satisfy conditions (iv) and (v).

5. This letter of intent will automatically lapse if, within a period of six months, applications/proposals relating to the conditions mentioned above are not submitted or if, within a period of one year from the date of this letter, an industrial licence is not issued to you unless the period of validity of his letter of intent is, in the meanwhile, extended by Government on a application to be made by you before the expiry of the said period of one year.

6. Please note that this letter of intent does not, in any way constitute an authorisation under the Monopolies and Restrictive Trade Practices Act, 1969. Wherever applicable, such permission or clearance as may be required under the provisions of this Act, should be invariably obtained by the undertaking before instituting any effective steps for implementing the letter of intent.

Yours faithfully,
s/d
(R.J. Bhojwani)
Under Secretary to the Govt. of India

Copy forwarded to:-
1. The Director of Industries, Bhopal.
2. Ministry of Finance (DEA), New Delhi.
3. Planning Commission, New Delhi.
4. Ministry of ID (Deptt. of ID), CLP Section, New Delhi.
5. Department of Company Affairs (CLB), New Delhi.
6. D. G. T. D. (P&I) Directorate, New Delhi.
7. Ministry of Agriculture (Deptt. of Agriculture) New Delhi.

8. Plant Protection Adviser, Room No. 409-410, 'B' Wing, Shastri Bhavan, New Delhi.
9. E & S Division.
10. Guard File.
11. CH/Coord Section.
12. Industrial Licensing Data Unit, Department of Industrial Development), New Delhi.
    (i) the value of fixed assets (Land, Building Rs. 26 lakhs machinery imported Rs. 73.5 lakhs and indigenous Rs. 339 lakhs.
    (ii) the aggregate requirement of foreign Rs. 73.5 lakhs exchange needed for the scheme for machinery.
    (iii) the Business House, if any, to which the applicant firm belongs - Union Carbide U. S. A. 60% shares.

The case was cleared by the L.C. Committee at its 128th Meeting held on 12.10.70.
s/d (U.N. Malik)
For Under Secretary to the Government of India)

ANNEXURE

General Guidelines attached to the letter of intent involving foreign collaboration /capital participation.

(i) Government do not normally favour restrictions on export franchises in the proposals for foreign collaboration, except to such countries where the overseas collaborating parties have licensing agreements for local manufacture. On the other hand, Government would consider favourably proposals of foreign collaboration in which a suitable favoured licensed clause is incorporated in the draft agreement to obtain a process licence, know-how, royalty and research and design assistance.

(ii) Approved /Registered Indian Engineering Design and Consultancy Organisations must be the prime consultants and Government will consider permitting the purchase of only such design and consultancy services from abroad as are not available within the country.

(iii) Proposals for the purchase of overseas technology (process licence fees, know-how, royalty, R & D etc.) must be accompanied by proposals regarding the progamme of further development and improvement of technology in this field (as distinct from analytical or quality control) in the country.

(iv) It is desirable that approved/registered Indian Engineering design and consultancy organisations should be associated right from the start in any evaluation, selection and negotiation conducted for the purchase of overseas technology.

(v) It is desirable that inquiries to overseas parties should be made on the basis of obtaining separate quotations for technology (licence fees, know-how, royalty, R&D assistance, etc.) and design and consultancy services not available in the country.

[Editor's Note: Except for the signatures, the above letter with annexure is reproduced in its entirety, without any change, corrections of typos etc.]

(EXHIBIT 4. Submitted to the U.S. District Court in New York)

A-6: Letter from UCIL seeking permission for visit of Engineers to US

November 24, 1972

Ministry of Petroleum & Chemicals
Shastri Bhavan
New Delhi

Attention: Mr. N. C. Krishnamoorthy, Advisor

Subject: Overseas visit - Engineers of Agricultural
                   Products Division, Union Carbide India Limited

Dear Sir:

This refers to the discussions we had with you regarding the overseas visit of 6 design and production engineers to help the Design Group in the U. S. in the Indianization of the Methyl Isocyanate based project of Union Carbide India Limited. We wish these engineers to be associated from the very beginning of the design and engineering work of the project to maximise indigenous capability in the interest of our country. You will observe that these engineers are visiting for various durations of time ranging from 60 days to 180 days depending upon the process/ processes in which they will be involved. The names of these engineers are shown below against the specific assignments they are required to perform and the cost for stay is also listed.

Mr. U. Nanda: Mr. Nanda will be involved in the design work for the phosgene unit and we believe that this assignment should be accomplished in 90 days time. During his stay Mr. Nanda will visit Union Carbide Corporation's units to familiarize himself with the latest technology and help the design engineers in engineering work to suit the Indian conditions.

Mr. A. K. Mehan and Mr. S. H. Parek: These gentlemen will be involved in the familiarization of SEVIN Carbamoylation units with special reference to Sevin Carbaryl insecticide but also a number of other products based on methyl isocyanate. As in the case of Mr. Nanda their job is to maximize the Indianization of the design work. The duration of stay for these gentlemen is only 60 days each.

Mr. A. S. Ajagonkar and Mr. S. Bandopadhya: These 2 engineers will be involved in the design work of methyl isocyanate units. In view of the complicated technology involved in the manufacture of this product, the duration of their stay will be 180 days each. As is well known, Union Carbide Corporation is the only manufacturer of methyl isocyanate and most engineers are not familiar with this technology; hence extended stay for these engineers to familiarize themselves and be effective in the design work.

Mr. P. G. Shrotri: Mr. Shrotri will be responsible for the instrumentation work. The plant in the U.S. as most plants in that country have a lot of sophisticated instrumentation which can be dispensed with under the Indian conditions, Mr. Shrotri's job will be to evaluate minimum requirements of instrumentation suiting Indian conditions. Mr. Shrotri will be in the U.S. for 60 days only.

Mr. K. D. Ballal: Mr. Ballal is the Production Representative of Union Carbide India Limited and he will be involved in familiarizing himself with all the processes at the plants of Union Carbide Corporation. He will in addition consult with and supervise the work of the other engineers to get maximum mileage out of their stay.

The total cost of the visit for these engineers will be $16,200. As against this if the work was to be done in India we would have to bring in a minimum 2 technicians for a period of about one year and each at a cost of about $50,000 a year considering the cost involved in the movement of their families etc.

It will be therefore observed that it is in the interests of the country to send Indian technicians abroad for training and active involvement in design work.

Very truly yours,
UNION CARBIDE INDIA LIMITED

P. L. JOSEPH

(Court Documents Nos. 10151615-10151616)

A-7: Design Transfer Agreement between UCC and UCIL – (1973)

Only selected paragraphs and Articles II, III, IV, V, VIII, XII, and Schedule A, of the Design Transfer Agreement - and the relevant Articles of the Technical Services Agreement are reproduced. (For complete text see Court documents Nos. 16000860 to 16000893).

DESIGN TRANSFER AGREEMENT

AGREEMENT made as of the 13th day of November 1973 between UNION CARBIDE CORPORATION (hereinafter called "Union Carbide"), a corporation organized and existing under the laws of the State of New York, United States of America, acting by its Chemical and Plastics group, having a office at 270 Park Avenue, New York, New York 10017, United States of America, and UNION CARBIDE INDIA LIMITED (hereinafter called "UCIL") a company incorporated in accordance with laws in India, having its registered office at 1 Middleton Street, Calcutta 16, India:

WITNESSETH

...."WHEREAS, UCIL desires to buy comprehensive information from Union Carbide concerning the manufacture or fabrication and also the installation of capital plant machinery and equipment required for the production of the said carbamate pesticides and Union Carbide is willing to prepare documents (including drawings and the like) containing such information and to sell the same to UCIL.

NOW, THEREFORE, in consideration of the premises and mutual agreements herein contained, the parties hereto have agreed and do hereby agree as follows:"
....

ARTICLE II

2.1 Union Carbide shall deliver the Design Packages described in Schedule "A" to UCIL in accordance with the following schedule:

A. Preliminary Scope Definition Package within thirty (30) days of the Effective Date hereof.

B. Design Report and Equipment Specification Package within nine (9) months of the Effective Date hereof.

2.2 All Design Packages and all information contained therein shall be delivered by Union Carbide in Hong Kong, to a representative or representatives of UCIL acting on behalf of UCIL for that purpose and Title in the Design Packages and all information contained therein shall pass to UCIL forthwith upon such delivery.

ARTICLE III – AMOUNTS PAYABLE

3.1 In consideration of the delivery to UCIL of the Design Packages, as provided for by paragraph 2.2, under this agreement UCIL shall pay Union Carbide, at its office in New York, in the United States of America, a price in the United States Dollars, equivalent to One Million Two Hundred Thirty Seven Thousand and Five Hundred Indian Rupees (Rs. 1,237,500). The said price shall be payable and paid to Union Carbide in the currency of the United States of America, in six (6) equal or nearly equal installments, separated by intervals of ninety (90) days of the effective date of this agreement.

ARTICLE IV – WARRANTY

4.1 Carbide warrants that the Design Packages are the best manufacturing information presently available from or to Union Carbide and that the drawings and design instructions included in the Design Packages shall be sufficiently detailed and complete as to enable competent technical personnel to detail design, erect and commission facilities for the conduct of the Processes. Union Carbide makes no other representation or warranty with respect to the Design Packages delivered hereunder and shall have no responsibility with respect to the use made thereof by UCIL and shall not, in any way, be liable for any loss, damage, personal injury or death resulting from or arising out of the use by UCIL of the Design Packages.

ARTICLE V – CONTINGENCIES

5.1 Neither party hereto shall be liable to the other for any default or delay if caused by Government laws, orders, rules and regulations, strikes, lock-outs or other labour troubles (whether or not within the power of the party affected by such contingencies to settle the same), shortage of man-power beyond the control of the party affected by such contingencies, act or failure to act on the part of the other party, inability to obtain or delay in obtaining transportation facilities, delay of carriers or any similar or different contingencies beyond the reasonable control of the party affected by such contingencies.

Appendix A

ARTICLE VIII – EXPORT

8.1 UCIL is aware of the fact that procurement of the Design Packages by UCIL from Union Carbide is subject to U.S. Government restrictions regarding export of said manufacturing drawings or the intermediate product thereof viz. the carbamate products, directly or indirectly, and UCIL has agreed to such conditions and restrictions as stated hereunder:

UCIL, therefore hereby agrees:

a) to furnish Union Carbide (or cause to be furnished to Union Carbide) upon written request from Union Carbide at any time during the period covered by this agreement such written assurances as may be required under Export Regulations issued by the United States Department of Commerce;

b) that UCIL shall use the Design Packages only in India and that without the prior written approval of Union Carbide, UCIL shall not re-export such Design Packages or the information contained therein in whole or in part, directly or indirectly, to any other country; and

c) that without the prior written approval of Union Carbide, UCIL shall not export the intermediate product namely, Products directly produced by the use of the Design Packages, directly or indirectly to a country which will cause legal embarrassment to Union Carbide under the laws of the United States of America.

ARTICLE XII – MISCELLANEOUS

12.3 Union Carbide shall not be liable for any special, indirect or consequential damages which may be suffered by UCIL, in the course of manufacture or operation of the Design Packages.

SCHEDULE "A"

I. The Design Packages shall contain all such information as is necessary and sufficient to enable UCIL to arrange for the detailed designing, fabrication and installation of the capital plant, machinery and equipment required for:

A. Carbamoylation process based upon Union Carbide technology using a process design scaled to produce 6,500 metric tons of carbaryl per year from 1-naphthol and methyl isocyanate.

B. Methyl isocyanate process from monomethylamine and phosgene based upon Union Carbide technology, scaled to produce 3,200 metric tons per year.

C. Phosgene process based upon Union Carbide technology, scaled to produce 6,200 metric tons per year from chlorine and carbon monoxide.

II. The Design Packages shall include the following information for each of the processes listed in the paragraph I above:
   A. Process Flow Diagrams complete with heat and material balance.
   B. Process and instrument diagrams (P and I) reflecting the proposed control schemes.
   C. Performance specifications and materials of construction of all major and minor equipment from which mechanical design will be developed in India.
   D. Performance specifications of control systems, control schemes and materials from which design will be developed in India.
   E. Valve piping and materials of constructions specifications.
   F. Design criteria and sketches of Union Carbide's proprietary equipment from which mechanical design will be developed in India.
   G. Typical equipment arrangement and unit layout.
   H. Description of special analytical instrumentation and laboratory quality control equipment.

TECHNICAL SERVICE AGREEMENT

ARTICLE II - TECHNICAL SERVICE

"2.1 For the purpose of production and use of Products in India, for pesticidal use, Union Carbide shall, during the period of this agreement, make available to UCIL all such technical services as are generally connected with or specifically pertain to the production and use the Products which may reasonably be required by UCIL for the most efficient use of the production techniques that Union Carbide has developed or may develop in the future in Union Carbide's laboratories, plants and factories for the production and use of the Products as pesticides. Without prejudice to the generality of the foregoing, Union Carbide shall for this purpose, regularly make available to UCIL, from time to time, such technical data and findings of Union Carbide's laboratories which are actually adopted by Union Carbide in the commercial production and use of the Products as pesticides, including, but not limited to operating data and instructions, detailed information as to raw materials, production processes, formulations, formulae and related technical information and such other data as Union Carbide's present and future experience may indicate as being necessary or useful for the production and use of Products as pesticides in India. In furtherance of Union Carbide's obligations to UCIL pursuant to this paragraph Union

Carbide shall deliver to UCIL copies of the documents and reports listed in Appendix "B" hereof within thirty (30) days after the Effective Date of this agreement. All technical data and information furnished by Union Carbide under this agreement shall be the latest and most up-to-date in Union Carbide's possession from time to time. UCIL shall have the right to refer, from time to time, specific problems pertaining to the production of Products to Union Carbide for consideration and advice and also to send to Union Carbide samples of Products manufactured by UCIL for examination, testing and evaluation by Union Carbide of such samples. In addition, Union Carbide shall make known to UCIL, Union Carbide's current production experience for Products by keeping UCIL, informed of all Union Carbide's production processes and working methods insofar as these are applicable to the production of Products by UCIL. With regard to so much of the technical services to be provided under this agreement by way of "documentation" that is to say by means of written instructions and advice, reports, procedures, formulas, drawings and the like, Union Carbide shall be deemed to have discharged its obligations to UCIL under this agreement by properly addressing an envelope or cover containing such documentation to UCIL at its registered office in India and by properly prepaying postal dues in the United States of America and posting the said envelope or cover in the United States of America. PROVIDED THAT nothing contained in this agreement shall be construed as implying any obligation on Union Carbide to supply UCIL with plant design information drawings or other construction data for any plant or equipment which may be required by UCIL for the production of Products or as implying any obligation on Union Carbide to assist UCIL in the procurement, construction or erection of any such plant or machinery.

2.2 Upon request of UCIL, in writing, Union Carbide shall provide training and instructions for technical personnel of UCIL, at Union Carbide facilities in the United States at such times and such periods of time as are mutually agreed upon by the parties, during the term of this Agreement at no cost to UCIL, other than the salaries, maintenance and travelling expenses of any such personnel of UCIL so assigned for training purposes.

2.3 Upon request of UCIL in writing, Union Carbide shall provide for one or more Union Carbide Technical Specialists at Union Carbide's discretion to visit UCIL facilities in India for project implementation, training and instruction for technical personnel of UCIL at such times and for such periods of time as are mutually agreed by the parties during the term of this agreement. For such technical assistance UCIL shall pay Union Carbide immediately upon receipt of invoice therefor, One Hundred Fifty Dollars

($150.00) United States of America funds per man for each day spent away from their usual place of employment plus the cost of travel for all such employees sent to India, plus reasonable living expenses. UCIL shall secure at its own expense, from Governmental Authorities of India such authorizations as may be required for Union Carbide's Technical Specialists to enter into and remain in India in order to provide technical assistance to UCIL as provided in the Article 2.3.

2.4 Upon request of UCIL in writing Union Carbide shall undertake to perform in the United States such specific research, development and/or engineering assignments relating to Products, their production (including engineering and equipment design) use and sale as are specifically agreed upon at a price and subject to such other terms and conditions as the parties shall mutually agree upon.

2.5 During the term of this agreement, Union Carbide will supply UCIL full details of future significant improvements relating to the production of Products which Union Carbide may acquire through operation or development work in Union Carbide's facilities in United States of America and from there will furnish UCIL such information as may be needed by UCIL to adopt any of such improvements in connection with the production and use of Products in India.

2.6 Nothing in this agreement, or in any document ancillary to this agreement, shall be interpreted as granting to UCIL any right or license under any patent now or hereafter owned or acquired by Union Carbide.

ARTICLE V – AMOUNTS PAYABLE

5.1 In consideration of the Technical Services rendered by Union Carbide under this agreement, UCIL shall pay Union Carbide a remuneration (hereinafter called "royalty"), computed at the rate of two and a half per cent (2 1/2%) on the ex-factory selling price of products sold by UCIL.

ARTICLE VIII – WARRANTY

8.1 Union Carbide warrants that the technical service to be provided by Union Carbide hereunder shall be the best technical service available from Union Carbide at the relevant time. Union Carbide makes no other representation or warranty with respect to the technical service and shall have no responsibility with respect to the use made thereof by UCIL and shall not in any way be liable for any loss, damage, personal injury or death resulting from or arising out of the use by UCIL of such service.

[Editor's Note: Other Articles in the Agreement address the issues of record keeping, taxes, exports and other contingencies caused by Governmental laws, etc.

Both the Agreements are signed by E.A. MUNOZ, in New Delhi, on behalf of UCIL on November 13, 1973.]

(From Court Documents Nos. 16000860-16000893 as Exhibit 6.)

A-8: Letter from Government of India for expediting MIC Project

No. L- 36016/2/75 - Pest
Government of India
Ministry of Chemicals and Fertilizers

New Delhi, 19th May, 1976

M/s Union Carbide India Limited
5 Parliament Street
New Delhi

Subject: Implementation of the MIC Based
Pesticides Project at Bhopal

Dear Sirs:

I am directed to refer to your letter dated 10th March, 1976 on the above subject and to say that as requested by you this Ministry have already taken up the matter with the Ministry of Finance for expediting necessary action on your request for approval of terms and conditions of the loan.

As pointed out during the discussions held in this Ministry on February 27, 1976 it is of utmost importance that your MIC Project should be implemented without delay. You are, therefore, requested to take effective steps to ensure expeditious implementation of this project within the schedule already indicated by you. In this connection this Ministry would like to receive from you quarterly reports indicating the progress achieved during the quarter, impediments, if any encountered in maintaining the requisite progress and the steps taken /being taken to overcome them and completion of the project as per schedule. I am to request that the first Report for the quarter ending 30th June 1976 may please be sent by the first week of July, 1976. The reports for the subsequent quarters may be sent to this Ministry in the first week of October, January and April.

The receipt of this letter may please be acknowledged.

Yours faithfully,
(K. P. Srivastava)
Deputy Secretary to the Govt. of India
(Court Document No. 10114862)

210

Appendix A

A-9: UCC Specifications for MIC Storage Tanks

II - 8
SS - 4534 - E - 610/1/1
March 5, 1974
Sheet 1 of 1

4534 - E - 610
4534 - E - 611
4534 - E - 619 - MIC STORAGE
TANK (3 Required)

Drawings:	DS - 4534 - E - 610/1/1
	DS - 4534 - E - 610/2/1
	DS - 4534 - E - 610/3/1
	DS - 4534 - E - 610/4/1
	DS - 4534 - E - 610/5/1
	DS - 4534 - E - 610/6/0
Service:	Lethal
Location:	Outside
Nominal capacity:	15, 000 gallons
Nominal diameter:	96 in. (8 ft 0 in.)
Length of cylindrical portion:	40 ft 0 in.
Design pressure:	40 psig
Max. temperature at design pressure:	121°C (250°F)
Max. vacuum:	Full Vac
Emergency vacuum relief:	Not required
Specific gravity of operating liquid:	0.9599 (20°C)
Min. design temperature:	-15°C
Air test:	Required
Material of construction:	Type 304 SS
Corrosion allowance :	None
Corrosion test specimens:	Not required
Valve and piping specification:	Process: 6E62
Flanges:	300 lb ANSI

Construction:	Per UCC Std. Spec. COP-1-72 and ASME Code, Section VIII/I Other requirements. Full Radiograph.
Manway:	24 in. Required with cover
Vessel support:	See notes below
Clips:	4 clips, 304 stainless steel, to connect anodes to tank
Painting or pro tective coating:	See Notes 5A and 5B

NOTES:
1. This is a horizontal mounded tank. Bottom of tank to be 4 ft below ground level 2 ft earth fill at top of tank.
2. Seismic intensity for Bhopal (M.P.) India VI Modified Mercalli, corresponding to a horizontal Seismic acceleration range of 5-175 CM/Sec^2 or an average acceleration of 40 CM/Sec^2 . Wind velocity: 80 MPH max
3. Aprrox. 1 ft layer of sand under tank.
4. See drawings for concrete covering and sealing details.

II - 9
SS - 4534 - E - 610/2/1
March 5, 1974
Sheet 2 of 2

4534 - E - 610
4534 - E - 611
4534 - E - 619 - MIC STORAGE TANK (cont'd)

Notes: (cont'd)

5. Coating & Cathodic Preparation:

    A. Coating Coal tar enamel, glass reinforced after each application of enamel; two coats required, 15 mils thickness each for a total thickness of 30 mils minimum (glass reinforcing applied after each coat while coating is still tacky). See applicable parts of specs. UCC MOC - 148 and UCC MOC -160, which are attached.

B. Cathodic Protection

1 Eighteen (18) anodes required
Suggested brand: High potential magnesium anodes such as 17 lb
GALVOMAG, manufactured by Dow Chemical Company.

2. All anodes to be spaced 4 ft (min.) to 5 ft (max.) from tank.

3. All anodes to be buried in vertical position with the anode center at the
same depth as the horizontal center line of the tank; however, top of anode will be at least 2 ft below the surface of the ground.

4. All leads from anodes to be buried except where the leads come above
ground at the test stations.

C. Reference Specifications:

1. For test stations involved in cathodic protection layout:
UCC Std. ELC - 77

2. For attachment of anodes: UCC Std. ELC - 76.

A-10: Letter from UCIL about Discontinuing Manufacture of alpha-Naphthol.

July 2, 1970

Adviser
Ministry of Petroleum, Chemicals,
Mines and Metals,
Department of Chemicals
Shastri Bhavan
New Delhi 1

Kind Attention: Mr. L. Kumar

Subject: Serial No. 17/CLP/70
Application under the Industries (D&R) Act,
1951 for the manufacture of Methyl Isocyanate
based pesticides and formulations thereon.

Dear Sir:

This is to confirm our discussions of June 24, 1970 regarding manufacture of alfa naphthol by Union Carbide India Limited. The following facts should be carefully considered:

(1) The only large use of alfa naphthol in the world is the manufacture of Sevin insecticide.

(2) Sevin insecticide has been in the market for over twelve years. Substantial replacement of Sevin should take place within next five to eight years. In fact, we are in possession of several replacement molecules already. These are phenol, benzil alcohol and iso-propanol based. None of these require alfa naphthol.

(3) Unlike manufacture of Beta naphthol, which is a simple, straight forward process, production of <u>high grade</u> alpha naphthol <u>at a reasonable cost</u> requires elaborate, expensive equipment, particularly in the alfa naphthol refining and by-product recovery steps. For this reason, a alfa naphthol plant cannot be economically converted to production of beta naphthol as suggested. In fact,

214

once replacement of Sevin takes place most of the investment made in alpha naphthol facilities would be lost.

It is our educated conclusion that, within the present state of the art and in view of the uncertain long term usefulness of this intermediate, erection of alfa naphthol facilities in India would amount to wasting of foreign exchange resources of the Country and the capital of this Company. Should any other concern in India be able to produce Sevin grade alfa naphthol at a reasonable cost, we would be happy to enter into a supply contract.

Again our feeling is that the best interests of the Country and the Company will be served by accelerating the replacement of Sevin by newer, non-naphthol based pesticides through our internal research and development efforts.

Very truly yours
UNION CARBIDE INDIA LIMITED
S/d
E. A. MUNOZ

Copy to :
Deputy Secretary
Ministry of Petroleum, Chemicals,
Mines and Metals, Dept. of Chemicals,
Shastri Bhavan,
New Delhi 1
Attention: A. Satyanarayam

Under Secretary
Ministry of Petroleum, Chemicals,
Mines, and Metals, Dept. of Chemicals,
Shastri Bhavan, New Delhi 1
Attention: Mr. . J. Bhojwani

Plant Protection Adviser to the
Government of India
Ministry of Food, Agriculture, C.D. & Coop.
Directorate of Plant Protection, Quarantine & Storage
N. G. IV, Faridabad
Attention: Dr. K. D. Pabaria

Assistant Development Officer
Insecticides Directorate
D.G.T.D.
Odyog Bhavan, New Delhi 1
Attention: Mr. K. D. Sharma
B.C.C.   G. R. O. K. K. SAHNI [Handwritten entry]

(Court Doc. Nos. 10114323 and 10114324)

A-11: Letter from UC Eastern to UCIL on Dismantling of MIC Facility

UNION CARBIDE EASTERN, INC.
(INCORPORATED IN U.S.A.)
16TH FLOOR, NEW WORLD OFFICE BLDG.,(EAST WING)
24 SALISBURY ROAD, KOWLOON, HONG KONG
TEL: 3-7313333, TELEX:43449 HX
CABLE ADDRESS: UNICARBIDE
P.O.BOX 98616, T.S.T.POST OFFICE
KOWLOON, HONG KONG

R. Natarajan   October 26, 1984
VICE PRESIDENT

Mr. K. S. Kamdar
Union Carbide India Ltd.
15, Mathew Road
Bombay 400 004
INDIA

Dear Kishor,

The following subjects came up during the recent WAPT meeting.

1) There is a possibility that a MIC facility will be installed in Brazil and there is an equal possibility that a Carbamoylation facility will be installed in Indonesia. The question came up whether economically the MIC facility and the Carbamoylation facility in Bhopal could be dismantled for shipment to these countries. There was some thought expressed that since the labour cost in India was low, such a move could be effected in a viable manner. I would appreciate if you would assign people from inside or outside and provide me with a feasibility report and cost involved in such an undertaking. I would also appreciate your responding to me on the time that you would require to have such a report made.

2) We discussed Paushak's capability to product (sic) Carbaryl and how they claim to be capable of producing 1000 tonnes with an investment of $2MM with their own MIC and Naphthol. This attracted a lot of attention in view of UCC's general belief that such an endeavour would require a lot higher investment. UCC expressed an interest to determine whether Paushak has some

technology that is worth buying. Is there a way for you to ask Paushak to let your engineers visit their plant on the basis of this interest, and also seek their views on whether they would let UCC visit their facility on the basis.

3) WAPT asked me whether UCIL had considered eliminating their sales and marketing organisation in Ag Products and establish a relationship with companies such as Rallis to take your entire formulation production for marketing. I need your views as well as the economics/improvement in performance that would result from such a move.

4) WAPT feels strongly that UCIL should seek assistance from APC to make a last ditch effort in getting Temik widely registered. They are willing to form a high level professional group seasoned in technical details and registration matters who would be happy to visit India and make appropriate presentations to support your Temik registration efforts. Please advise me a suitable timetable. I am also telexing BP (B.P. Srivastava) in the States for his views with a copy to you.

Best regards,

s/d

R. Natarajan

RN/pp   cc: Mr. V. P. Gokhale

(Court Document Nos. 10114506 f/g)

A-12: Telex Reply from UCIL on Dismantling of MIC Facilities

[COPY OF THE TELEX FROM K. S. KAMDAR TO R. NATARAJAN]

ZCZC
EHK ENY
BOM 1OC4 11/13/84

TO;   R. NATARAJAN - UCE HK

       R. NATARAJAN - ENY (C/C MS CHRIS DUFFY - DANBURY)

CC: V P GOKHALE - UCIL BOM

RE: YR LETTER OCTOBER 26 AND OUR TELEPHONE CONVERSATION ON NOVEMEBR 9.

1.   WE HAVE ASSIGNED UMESH NANDA TO MAKE THE ESTIMATE ON DISMANTLING AND SHIPMENT OF THE MIC AND CARBAMOYLATION FACILITIES. THE DISMANTLING ESTIMATES WILL TAKE THREE WEEK. IT SHOULD BE READY BY NOVEMBER 30. THE SHIPMENT ESTIMATES WOULD PERHAPS PROVE TO BE DIFFICULT. HOWEVER WE WILL TRY OUR BEST. ASSUMING THE SHIPMENT ESTIMATE TO TAKE TWO MORE WEEKS, WE SHOULD HAVE THE DESIRED INFORMATION BY DECEMBER 14.

THE WRITTEN DOWN VALUE OF THE SEVIN UNIT IS LOW WHEREAS THE SAME DOES NOT APPLY TO THE MIC UNIT. IN THE FIRST PASS IT WOULD APPEAR THAT THE SHIPMENT OF THE CARBAMOYLATION UNIT DOES NOT LOOK IMPRACTICAL. HOWEVER THE SHIPMENT OF THE MIC UNIT IS A QUESTION BECAUSE OF THE HIGH CORROSION AT SEVERAL POINTS AND SOME TALL COLUMNS, WHICH MAY PERHAPS NEED SOME REWORK AT THE OTHER END.

WE ARE ALSO RULING OUT THE POSSIBILITY OF EXPORTING UTILITY EQUIPMENT AS WELL AS THE GENERAL SUPPORT STRUCTURE FOR THE FACILITIES.

2.   REGARDING UCC'S INTEREST IN PAUSHACK'S TECHNOLOGY, I HAVE NOT BEEN ABLE TO CONTACT THEIR CHAIRMAN AS HE

IS ON TOUR. THEY CLAIM TO BE ABLE TO MANUFACTURE 1000 TONNES WITH THEIR OWN MIC AND NAPHTHOL MAY NOT BE CORRECT AS THEY HAVE REQUESTED US TO GIVE THEM SOME IMPORTED ALPHA NAPHTHOL. THEIR OWN COST OF ALPHA NAPHTHOL IN INDIA IS REPORTED TO BE OF THE ORDER OF USD 6 TO 7 PER KG. TO THE BEST OF OUR INFORMATION THEY DO NOT HAVE A SEPARATE MIC FACILITY BUT RESORT TO IN-SITU REACTION WITH NAPHTHOL. I WILL CHECK WITH PAUSHAK WHETHER THEY WOULD PERMIT A VISIT TO THEIR FACILITIES. IN EARLIER DISCUSSIONS WITH THE CHAIRMAN, PAUSHAK HAD INDICATED THEIR CAPACITY TO BE ONLY 500 TONNES OF CARBARYL.

3. THE QUESTION OF FINDING A THIRD PARTY TO HANDLE OUR SALES HAS BEEN EXAMINED A NUMBER OF TIMES. WE HAVE APPROACHED RALLIS INDIA AND THEY HAVE DECLINED TO TAKE OVER OUR SALES. 1984 SALES EXPENSE IS RS. 14.6MM WHICH IS 7.4 PCT OF OUR NIFS AND OUR 1985 ESTIMATE IS 13.6 MM WHICH WOULD BE 6.2 PCT OF OUR NIFS.

    IF A THIRD PARTY IS INVOLVED, THE SAVINGS IN THE SELLING EXPENSES WOULD BE RS. 4.5 MM, AS A COMMISSION WILL HAVE TO BE PAID IN ADDITION TO THE NORMAL TRADE DISCOUNT, TO THE THIRD PARTY SALES AGENCY.

    FURTHER SUCH AN AGENCY WOULD NOT TAKE MUCH INTEREST IN PUSHING OUR PRODUCT AS THEIR OWN AND THIS WOULD THEREFORE TEND TO DEPRESS THE VOLUME FURTHER.

    THERE IS ONLY ONE MORE PARTY, VIZ. COROMANDEL INDAG, WHO WOULD PERHAPS TAKE SOME INTEREST IN TAKING OVER SALES OF OUR PRODUCTS. HOWEVER, WE HAVE NOT YET APPROACHED THEM. WE PLAN TO DO SO SOMETIME DURING DECEMBER DURING MY PLANNED VISIT TO MADRAS.

4. REGARDING TEMIK REGISTRATION, ON A FIRST PASS GOI OFFICIALS HAVE DECLINED THEIR INABILITY TO TAKE ADVANTAGE OF OUR INVITATION TO VISIT THE U. S. A. AND TO SEE FOR THEMSELVES THE WIDESPREAD USE OF TEMIK IN USA.

    I HAVE DIRECTED BPS (B.P. SRIVASTAVA) TO SEEK THE ENDORSEMENT OF THE REGISTRATION COMMITTEE OF GOI TO HEAR A PRESENTATION MADE BY UCAPC EXPERTS. THE OUTCOME IS NOT

YET KNOWN. HOWEVER, WE ASSURE YOU THAT WE WILL TRY
OUR VERY BEST TO USE THE ASSISTANCE OFFERED BY UCC.

REGARDS KS KAMDAR – BOMC12 / NNNN
(Court Documents Nos. 10114506 b/c/d)

A-13: UCIL Telex with Cost Estimate for Dismantling MIC Units

'.!.'.!! { This message was
not transmitted

TELEX

Raome —
9/12/84

FROM : KS KAMDAR   NOVEMBER 29, 1984

TO   : R NATARAJAN - UCE HK

AA   PRELIMINARY COST ESTIMATE HAS BEEN PREPARED FOR DISMANTLING
      AND SHIPPING SEVIN AND CO/MIC UNITS FROM BHOPAL TO OVERSEAS
      LOCATIONS. ESTIMATE IS ON IV QR. 1984 BASIS WITH AN ACCURACY
      OF PLUS/MINUS 25%

BB   ALL MAJOR AND MINOR EQUIPMENT, ELECTRICALS, INSTRUMENTS,
      VALVES, EXOTIC MATERIAL PIPING CONSTITUTE THE SHIPMENT.
      UTILITIES, GENERAL FACILITIES, STRUCTURES AND CIVIL ARE NOT
      INCLUDED.

CC   ESTIMATE (RUPEES THOUSAND)

UNIT	DECONTAMINATION & DISMANTLING	PKG	INLAND TPT & DOCK CHGS	CONTIN- GENCY	TOTAL FOB BOMBAY
CO/MIC	2590	5650	2580	1080	11900
SEVIN	860	1900	860	380	4000

					15900
					======

DD   BOOK VALUES OF TWO UNITS :

	ORIGINAL VALUE RS.M	NBV DEC. 1983 RS.M
CO/MIC	57333	39234
SEVIN	15509	8424
T O T A L	72842	47658
	=====	=====

Raau —

101145C6 !

EE   PREVALENT OCEAN FREIGHT CHARGES FROM BOMBAY TO SURABAYA PORT FOR SEVIN UNIT ARE ESTIMATED AS US $ 249 M, AND THAT FOR CO/MIC UNIT TO MEXICO PORT AS US $ 1400 M. THESE DOLLAR VALUES ARE BASED ON CURRENT CONVERSION RATE OF US $ 1.00 = RS.12.20.

FF   ABOVE ORDER OF MAGNITUDE FIGURES MAY BE USED TO STUDY PROJECT ECONOMICS. SHOULD THE PROPOSAL APPEAR PROFITABLE THEN WE WOULD NEED TO REFINE ESTIMATE TO ARRIVE AT A BETTER ACCURACY.

REGARDS.

A-14: CBI Letter instructing UCIL to drill hole in MIC piping for water test

To   8th February, 1985

    Mr. J. Mukund
    Works Manager
    Union Carbide India Limited,
    BHOPAL

Sub: <u>Case 3/4 CIU(1), New Delhi</u>

Dear Sir:

In order to determine whether there is any liquid in the
section of PVH header running on the pipe rack between
the MIC storage area and the manufacturing units, you are
hereby instructed to drill or cut a hole in this section
of pipe, since it does not have any flanged joints or
bleeders. Every attempt should be made to collect the
total ixxuxixxx quantity of liquid which may be found
in this pipe which should be carried out in the presence
of CBI representatives. Samples of liquid, if found,
should be preserved for analysis.

                                    Yours faithfully,

Received 2 PM
8/2/85
J. Mukund

                                    (MURARI LAL)
                                    SP/CBI, New Delhi
                                    Camp: Bhopal

Source: ADL Report

A-15: CBI / UCIL Signed Memo documenting MIC Pipe-draining attempt.

MEMO

Today,i.e. on 8th February, 1985, in the presence of
S.P., CBI; Mr. J. Mukund, Works Manager, Mr.S.P.Chaudhury,
Production Manager and another operator, an attempt was
made to drain out liquid, if any, in the PVH Header near
MIC Structure on the pipe-track after drilling a hole
in the side PVH at the lowest point.

After the hole was drilled, no liquid came out inspite
purging the PVH header. With nitrogen.

Certain valves in the storage area which had been sealed
by the CBI had been re opened for this operation and
re-sealed by CBI. A detailed statement prepared by UCIL
is also enclosed.

S.P. Chaudhury
Production Manager-UCIL
8/2/84

R.K. Agrawal
SI / CBI / SPE/J8P
Camp: Bhopal

8.2.1985

A-16: Copy of Altered Log Sheet of MIC Transfer

Source: ADL Report

A-17: UCIL Letter detailing problems with alpha-Naphthol Manufacture

December, 10, 1982

.... Aghoramurthy*
Adviser
Deparment of Chemicals & Fertilizers
Shastri Bhavan
New Delhi

Dear Sir:

We thank you for the courtesy extended to our representatives when they met you on December 8, 1982 to appraise you of the operational and process difficulties faced by us in the manufacture of Alpha-Naphthol, leading to the temporary closure of this unit.

In terms of Industrial Licence C:IL: 409: (75) dated October 31, 1975 we have established facilities for manufacture of Methyl Isocyanate and Alpha Naphthol - intermediates required for production of Carbaryl Technical. We commenced commercial manufacture of Carbaryl Technical in the Year 1977 based on imported intermediates, meeting the country's total requirement. With the help of our collaborators we successfully commissioned the MIC Unit in February, 1980 and import of this item ceased thereafter.

In the manufacture of Alpha Naphthol, however, we are facing severe operational and process problems and have not been so far successful in producing this item to the requisite specification at a reasonable cost. In our application dated January 1, 1970 for issue of a Letter of Intent for manufacture of MIC based Pesticides, we had indicated that erection of facilities to manufacture alcohols (such as Alpha Naphthol) would be proposed only after economic levels of demand could be predicted and the long range usefulness of the different products had been established. We conveyed our apprehension that production of Alpha Naphthol would require elaborate expensive equipment particularly in the refining and by-product recovery steps and that in view of the uncertain long term usefulness of this intermediate, erection of expensive facilities for the relatively small quantity of alpha Naphthol required in India would amount to wasting the resources of the country and the capital of the Company. Government, however, insisted on our manufacturing Alpha Naphthol locally and imposed a condition on the Industrial Licence stating "the applicant Company will set up indigenous manufacture of

Alpha Naphthol". Since the "tetralone process" used by UCC is highly capital intensive (estimated investment for the 5000 tonnes Naphthol we require is Rs. 40 crores) and cannot be economically scaled down to the level of UCIL's requirements of Alpha Naphthol, we went to work to develop a process locally for the manufacture of Alpha Naphthol. We opted the sulfonation route using Chlorosulfonic acid as the Sulfonating agent, which was piloted in part during 1972-74. Based on these studies a commercial scale plant was built with a capacity of 5000 tonnes per annum at a cost of nearly Rs. 5 crores. In late 1977 this unit was started up but had to be abandoned after 6-7 months of trials because of serious problems in trying to attain design efficiency and capacity. Severe operating problems were encountered at various points including filter plugging. ODCB loss from the system, tar formation in fusion, naphthol loss in decanting the salt waste and poor yields in the refining step. Only about 15 tonnes of Alpha Naphthol could be made in the plant at that time.

Certain process and equipment changes were made as a part of a de-bottlenecking program, most significant being the adoption of a water-extraction route to separate naphthalene sulfonic acid from ODCB instead of the earlier filtration step. This was done at an additional cost of Rs. 1.7 crores. The modified plant was started up in May, 1982. The results now indicate that the mechanical performance of the unit is greatly improved (although the average capacity achieved so far is only about 20% of design). However, after spending close to further Rs. 2 crores we find that the Beta content in the Alpha Naphthol produced cannot be brought down below 6-8% at this time. Although we have produced 198 tonnes of this item, the Beta content caused operating problems and imposed a severe cost penalty in the subsequent Carbamoylation step to make Carbaryl Technical which has to be completely devoid of any Beta isomer. The Beta content in Naphthol imported from USA is 0.5% which purity level is essential to make Carbaryl.

The unpredictable and inexplicable excursions into high Beta-Naphthol operation has forced us to shut down the Alpha Naphthol plant and we are presently taking proper measures to purge and seal the unit so as to minimize corrosion. We believe that it is necessary for us to go back to basics, starting from scratch and to re-examine the process, identifying the causes for these excursions and to re-design the plant. It is estimated that it will take us at least two years to complete the experiments in the laboratory on a bench scale and subsequent piloting to identify the causes of off-spec. excursions and to develop production processes which will assure specification product. We have asked UCC's assistance to sort out the process problems. Simultaneously, we also propose to seek help from National Laboratories such as RRL [Regional Research Laboratory]- Hyderabad, NCL [National Chemical Laboratory]- Pune and CSIR in developing alternate processes, if found necessary. Meanwhile, we seek your support in allowing import of Alpha Naphthol to produce Carbaryl Technical to meet the country's requirement.

Very truly yours,
UNION CARBIDE INDIA LIMITED

KUMARARASWAMI*

(* The first names were partially masked in the document submitted to the court.)

(Court Document Nos. 10151492-10151493)

A-18: Progress Report Letter from UCIL

?.11.1972

Ministry of Petroleum & Chemicals
Shastri Bhavan
New Delhi-1

Attention: Mr. R. Grover
               Deputy Secretary
               Subject: Methyl Isocyanate Pesticide Project

Dear Sir:

We are pleased to submit below progress report on the subject project for which Letter of Intent was issued to us on March 13, 1972.

We have successfully negotiated the purchase of 55 acres of land at Bhopal for the project. Copy of a letter allotting us the land by the Madhya Pradesh Government is attached for your information.

A contract has been signed with an Indian company Messrs. Tata Consulting Engineers to study, define and prepare estimates for utilities and general facilities at Bhopal for the subject project. The work in this regard has already been started by the consulting engineers and two of our engineers have been stationed in their offices for day to day coordination.

Union Carbide India Limited recently deputed an Indian Project Coordinator to the U.S. for discussions to finalise the basic design for the plant suited to the Indian conditions with a special reference to minimise foreign exchange components of the project. Foreign collaboration agreement is currently being discussed with the principals and hope to be finalised soon.

We have already interviewed and selected a number of design and construction engineers including the construction manager for the project. Efforts are also being made to recruit qualified and experienced Indian engineers presently residing in U. S. and Canada. We are also pleased to state that the pilot plant for Alpha Naphthol designed and constructed by Union Carbide India Limited at Bhopal, is in full operation for collection of engineering data, for scale-up for the main project.

We have recruited additional senior chemists and engineers in our R & D group to increase our capability to develop indigenous know-how wherever possible.

We trust the above information gives you an idea of the speed with which we are moving towards the implementation of this project. We shall be sending similar reports to you from time to time to keep you advised of the progress.

Very truly yours,
S/d
C. L. DHAWAN

Encl: as above

cc:	Mr. L. Kumar, Advisor
	Ministry of Petroleum & Chemicals
cc:	Directorate General of Technical Development
	Attention: Mr. B. Shah, Advisor
bcc:	Mr. P. L. Joseph – GRO; Mr. J. S. McGee – DGO; Mr. M. E. Hitchcock/
	Dr. P. C. Banerjee – BGO; Mr. R. K. Dutta - Bhopal

(Court Document Nos. 10151617-10151619)

A-19: Relevant Sections of the Foreign Exchange Regulation Act

THE FOREIGN EXCHANGE REGULATION ACT, 1973 (FERA)

(RELEVANT SECTIONS ONLY)

28. Restrictions on the appointment of certain persons and companies as agents or technical or management advisers in India

(1) Without prejudice to the provisions of section 47 and notwithstanding anything contained in any other provision of this Act or the Companies Act, 1956, a person resident outside India (whether a citizen of India or not) or a person who is not a citizen of India but is resident in India, or a company (other than a banking company) which is not incorporated under any law in force in India or in which the non-resident interest is more than forty per cent or any branch of such company, shall not, except with the general or special permission of the Reserve Bank,-

   (a) act, or accept appointment, as agent in India of any person or company, in the trading or commercial transactions of such person or company; or

   (b) act or accept appointment, as technical or management adviser in India of any person or company; or

   (c) permit any trade mark, which he or it is entitled to use, to be used by any person or company for any direct or indirect consideration...

29. Restrictions on establishment of place of business in India

   (1)   Without prejudice to the provisions of section 28 and section 47 and notwithstanding anything contained in any provision of this Act or the provisions of the Companies Act, 1956, a person resident outside India (whether a citizen of India or not) or a person who is not a citizen of India but is resident in India, or a company (other than a banking company) which is not incorporated under any law in force in India or in which the non-resident interest is more than forty percent or any branch of such company, shall not, except with the general or special permission of the Reserve Bank,-

(a)   carry on in India, or establishment in India a branch, office or other place of business for carrying on any activity of a trading, commercial or industrial nature, other than an activity for the carrying on of which permission of the Reserve Bank has been obtained under section 28; or

(b)   acquire the whole or any part of any undertaking in India of any person or company carrying on any trade, commerce or industry or purchase the shares in India of any such company.

(2) (a)   Where any person or company (including its branch) referred to in sub-section (1) carries on any activity referred to in clause (a) of that sub-section at the commencement of the Act or has established a branch, office or other place of business for the carrying on of such activity at such commencement, then, such person or company (including its branch) may make an application to the Reserve Bank within a period of six months from such commencement or such further period as the Reserve Bank may allow in this behalf for permission to continue to carry on such activity or to continue the establishment of the branch, office or other place of business for carrying on such activity, as the case may be.

5.   Every application made under clause (a) shall be in such form and contain such particulars as may be specified by the Reserve Bank.

6.   Where any application has been made under clause (a), the Reserve Bank may, after making such inquiry as it may deem fit, either allow the application subject to such conditions, if any, as the Reserve Bank may think fit to impose or reject the application:..."

Government of India
Guidelines For Administering Section 29 of FERA 1973.
Applicable to Branches of Foreign Companies

(Only relevant categories are reproduced below.)

"CATEGORY

I. Industrial Activities

> (c) Indian companies having more than 40% foreign shareholding and branches of foreign companies having a valid Industrial licence and engaged in production of items not specified in Appendix I of Industrial Licensing Policy, 1973 but engaged in the manufacturing activities which need sophisticated technology.

PROPOSED ACTION

2   The extent of foreign shareholding in the existing Indian companies will be considered on merits of each case subject to the conditions that they will increase within a specified period, Indian participation to not less than 26% of the equity of the company.

3   The branches of foreign companies will be required to convert themselves within a specified period, into Indian companies with Indian participation of not less than 26% of the equity of the company.

> (iii) In determining whether a technology is sophisticated or not, Department of Science and Technology will be consulted and consideration will be given, inter alia, to aspects such as (i) whether the technology is used for the manufacture of products which would otherwise necessitate imports, (ii) whether the discontinuance of the manufacture of products with the technology would have adverse effect on the economy, etc.

CATEGORY

Indian companies having more than 40% foreign shareholding and branches of foreign companies engaged in manufacturing activities.

Appendix A

PROPOSED ACTION

4   Such Indian companies will be required to bring down, within a specified period, foreign shareholdings to the level of 40%.

    (ii) The branches of foreign companies will be required to convert themselves into Indian companies having foreign shareholding not exceeding 40%, within a specified period.

    (iii) Alternatively, they will be required to change, within a specified period, their character from existing manufacturing activities in the areas specified in Appendix I of Industrial licensing Policy, 1973 or engage themselves in predominantly export-oriented industries (minimum exports being 60% of total production)..."

APPENDIX B

Selected Sections of the CSIR Report - The Government of India's Council of Scientific and Industrial Research

REPORT ON SCIENTIFIC STUDIES ON THE FACTORS RELATED TO BHOPAL TOXIC GAS LEAKAGE

December, 1985

This Report results from Studies by

Dr. S. Varadarajan; Dr. L.K. Doraiswamy; Dr. N.R. Ayyanga r; Dr. C.S.P. Iyer; Dr. A.A. Khan; Dr. A.K. Lahiri; Mr. K.V. Muzumdar; Dr. R.A. Mashelkar; Dr. R.B. Mitra; Dr. O.G.B. Nambiar; Mr. V. Ramachandran; Mr. V.D. Sahasrabudhe; Dr. S. Sivaram; Dr. M. Sriram; Dr. G. Thyagarajan, and Dr. R.S. Venkataraman

CONTENTS

236

TABLE 3.1

REPRESENTATIVE LABORATORY EXPERIMENTS WITH MIC & DERIVATIVES

Expt No.	Reactants	Reaction Temp.°C	Time (Minutes)	GLC of Acetone Extract (Approx %)
1.	MIC+H_2O+trace HCl	Rose 23 to 28	6	Not analysed. Temp. rose from 23° to 28°, remained at 28° for 15 minutes and started decreasing.
2.	MIC+H_2O+trace HCl	1. Rose 23 to 29	3-5	Residue was a solid mass which analysed for DMU, TMB and MICT qualitatively.
	+ trace $FeCl_3$	2. 29 to 31	60	
		3. 31 to 45	in a few minutes boiled off	
3.	MIC+$CHCl_3$+H_2O	100	40	DMU (7), MICT(5), TMB (84)
4.	MIC+$CHCl_3$+H_2O	190	40	DMU(3), MICT(60), TMB (36) Dione (Trace)
5.	MIC+$CHCl_3$+H_2O	200	15	DMU (1), TMB (54), MICT (45), Dione (0.5).
6.	MIC+$CHCl_3$+H_2O	250	45	TMU (2), DMU(14), MICT (41) TMB (2.5), DMI (6) Dione (3).
7.	TMB+MIC+$CHCl_3$	240	40	TMU (1), DMU (4.5), MICT (80) TMB (3), DMI (6), Dione (5).
8.	TMB + $CHCl_3$	245	45	TMU (2.5), DMU (40), MICT(6) TMB (4), DMI (9), Dione (2).

9.	TMB	250	45	DMI (4), Dione (nil), TMB (1)
				MICT (29), DMU (61), TMU (trace)
10.	DMU	280	45	DMU (100)
11.	DMU+MIC+CHCl$_3$	250	45	TMU (3), DMU (13), MICT (52)
				TMB (8), DMI (4), Dione (2)
12.	TMU+MIC+CHCl$_3$	251	45	TMU (10), DMU (1.5), MICT (47), TMB (3.5), TRMB (2), DMI (12), Dione (2).
13.	MICT+CHCl$_3$	280	45	MICT (100)
14.	MICT+CH$_3$NH$_3$Cl	300	45	MICT (100)

TABLE 3.2

MATERIAL BALANCE

Chemical Reaction	Product	Kg. Mole (Kg)	MIC consumed Kg.	Water consumed Kg.
1	2	3	4	5
MIC+H$_2$O —> MMA+CO$_2$	MMA	4.17 (129)	237.7	75.0
MIC+H$_2$O—> DMI+TMA+ DMA+NH$_3$+CO$_2$	DMI	17.04 (2675)		
	TMA	7.17 (423)	3792.2	277.4
	DMA	5.47 (246)		
3 MIC+H$_2$O+2CHCl$_3$ —> Dione+ 2HCl + CO$_2$ +CCl$_4$	DIONE	2.49 (391)	425.8	44.8
2 MIC+H$_2$O —> DMU+CO$_2$	DMU	1.83 (161)	208.6	32.9
3 MIC+H$_2$O —> TMB+CO$_2$	TMB	0.81 (117)	138.5	14.6
3 MIC+2H$_2$O —> TMU+NH$_3$ +2 CO$_2$	TMU	1.87 (191)	319.8	67.3
3 MIC ———> MICT* [*MICT for MIC trimer]	MICT	40.72 (6964)	6964.0	-
			12086.6	512.0

Overall reactions

$$212.03 \text{ MIC} + 28.45 \text{ H}_2\text{O} + 4.98 \text{ CHCl}_3 \longrightarrow 4.17 \text{ MMA} + 17.04 \text{ DMI} + 7.17 \text{ TMA}$$
$$+ 5.47 \text{ DMA}$$

$$+2.49 \text{ Dione} + 1.83 \text{ DMU} + 0.81 \text{ TMB}$$

$$+1.87 \text{ TMU} + 40.72 \text{ MICT} + 4.98 \text{ HCl}$$

$$+2.49 \text{ CCl}_4 + 4.64 \text{ NH}_3 + 28.45 \text{ CO}_2$$

5.0   AN ANALYSIS OF THE EVENT:

1.   ...MIC readily undergoes chemical reactions with explosive violence, which produce a large amount of heat, and allow a large portion of stored liquid MIC to vapourise. This is inherent to the nature of the material. Neither the precise conditions under which such run-away reactions could be initiated in MIC nor its manner of prevention are well known.

2.   ...From the examination of the tank residue and from the conditions of formation of the residue, it is surmised that the temperature reached in the bulk storage tank may have been around 250°C. The total energy balance on the tank also indicate that the probable temperatures would be in the range of 200 to 250°C...

3.   ...The chemical analysis of the tank residue clearly shows the evidence of entry of approximately 500 kg. (1100 lb) of water. The fact that the tank 610 was not under pressure of nitrogen for approximately two months prior to the accident also indicates that conditions existed for entry of contaminants such as metallic impurities through the high pressure nitrogen line...

4.   The hydrolysis of MIC with about 500 kg.(1100 lb) of water by itself and in the absence of other contaminants is not expected to lead to thermal run-away conditions. The presence of this quantity of water would have possibly resulted in reaction with about three to four tonnes of MIC, generation of carbon dioxide, breaking of the rupture disc and release of CO_2...

5.   The presence of trace amount of metallic contaminants derived from the material of the tank or its attachments or from extraneous sources, may not necessarily initiate a violent reaction under dry conditions. Small amounts of local trimerisation may take place, as noticed throughout the pipelines

and plant. However, the ingress of water, would provide for active species of initiator to be generated and distributed in the liquid.

6.   … Once initiated, the trimerisation reaction rapidly led to a temperature increase leading to levels as high as 250°C with autocatalytic and auto-thermal features. At these high temperatures, secondary chemical transformation occurred leading to the complex mixture of products actually found in the tank 610 residue.

7.   … A detailed analysis indicates that water entry through RVVH/PVH lines is quite likely. It has been reported that around 9.30 P.M. on 2 December, 1984, an operator was clearing a possible choke of the RVVH line downstream of phosgene stripping still filters by water flushing. Presumably the 6" isolation valve on the RVVH was closed but a slip blind had not been inserted. Under these conditions when the filter lines are choked, water could enter into RVVH, if the 6" isolation valve had not been tightly shut or passing…

8.   … Opportunities for intrusion of water, alkali and metal contaminants into tank 610 thus existed from 22nd October, 1984 and into tank 611 as well during 30th November to 1st December, 1984, when there was negligible positive nitrogen pressure in these tanks.

9.   It was entirely unnecessary to provide facilities for storage of such large amount of MIC in tanks. The quantities stored were quite disproportionate to the capacity of further conversion of MIC in downstream unit. This permitted MIC to be stored for months together without appreciation of potential hazards.

10. … The rapid rise in temperature and violent reactions that occurred necessitate the onset of metal ion catalysed polymerisation. The presence of chloroform has no influence whatsoever in initiating or accelerating the run-away reactions. The chloroform present was involved in chemical transformations when the temperature had risen above 200°C at which stage all the water would have already been consumed by reactions.

11. … The quantum of toxic leakage by violent chemical reaction is not related to the amount of metal and water which initiate the reactions but to the quantity of MIC stored in a single container. If 42 tonnes of MIC had been stored in 210 stainless steel drums of 200 litre capacity each, as alternative to a single tank, there would be no possibility of leakage of more than one fifth of a tonne and effects of even such a leakage could be minimised by spray of water or alkali.

12. In retrospect, it appears the factors that led to the toxic gas leakage and its heavy toll existed in the properties of the very high reactivity, volatility and inhalation toxicity of MIC. The needless storage of large quantities of the material in very large size containers for inordinately long periods as well as insufficient caution in design, choice of materials of construction and in provision of measuring and alarm instruments, together with inadequate controls on systems of storage and on quality of stored materials as well as lack of necessary facilities for quick effective disposal of material exhibiting instability, led to the accident. These factors contributed to guidelines and practices in operation and maintenance. Thus the combination of conditions for the accident were inherent and extant. A small input of integrated scientific analysis of the chemistry, design and controls relevant to the manufacture would have had an enormously beneficial influence in altering this combination of conditions, and in avoiding or lessening considerably the extent of damage of December, 1984 at Bhopal.

APPENDIX C

C-1: A Chronicle of Significant Events

THE HISTORY OF UNION CARBIDE INDIA LIMITED (UCIL)

1905   Union Carbide made its first venture in India under the name "National Carbon" with a total sales amounting to less than Rs 500.

1926   The Eveready (India) Company commenced manufacturing batteries in the Canal Road Works, Calcutta, with an installed annual capacity of 6,000,000 cells.

1934   The Eveready Company (India) Ltd. was incorporated as a private company on November 12th.

1935   Installed capacity of the Canal Road works was increased to 15,000,000 cells/year.

1936   United Battery Distributors Ltd. was formed and appointed as sole selling agents for Eveready Company (India) Ltd.

1940   Camperdown Works, India's first modern battery plant was established in Calcutta with an annual capacity of 40,000,000 cells/year. Capacity was increased to 100,000,000 in 1948

1941   United Battery Distributors merged with Eveready Company (India) Ltd. and changed its name to National Carbon Company (India) Ltd.

1949   Camperdown Works installed Manganese crushing and grinding Mill.

1952   A second Battery Plant was established in Madras.

1954   Industrial Products division was established.

1956   National Carbon Company (India) Ltd. was converted to a public company and on January 11 it offered 800,000 shares to the Indian public. A Zinc rolling mill, the first in India was completed in Kidderpore.

1958   The Eveready Flashlight Case Plant was inaugurated at Lucknow.

1959   National Carbon Company (India) Ltd changed its name to Union Carbide India Limited

1961   The Carbide Chemicals Company (CHEMCO), a division of UCIL began operations at Trombay Island, Bombay.

1962   Film and Pipe manufacturing unit goes into production.

In response to India's need during war with China, UCIL worked around the clock to produce an uninterrupted supply of batteries for the defense forces. Again in 1965 UCIL provided special batteries to meet defense forces requirements.

1965   Carbon Products Company commenced operations to produce cinema carbons and midget electrodes.

1966   India's first Naphtha cracker was installed at CHEMCO, thus pioneering India's petrochemical industry.

1967   The Third Battery Plant, the company's most modern, was set up in Hyderabad.
The Agricultural Chemical Division was established.

1970   UCIL's Pesticides Formulation plant went into production in Bhopal.

1971   Marine Products Division started operations with the purchase of two fishing trawlers, "Sunita Rani" and Lakshmi Rani".

1973   The foundation stone for the Research and Development Center in Bhopal was laid. The two crore rupees Research Center was inaugurated on January 2, 1976. Another two crore Electro-chemical Research Center at Calcutta was inaugurated on March 24, 1976

1977   The Carbamoylation Unit to produce Carbaryl (Sevin) insecticide went into production at the Bhopal manufacturing facility

1980   The MIC plant went into production at Bhopal.

1984   UCIL celebrated fifty years since it was incorporated as a company.

On December 2-3, 1984, a large quantity of water got inside an MIC storage tank and caused a massive emission of toxic vapors. Over two thousand people were killed and the Bhopal pesticide plant was closed permanently.

1994   Union Carbide Corporation completed the sale of its 50.9 percent interest in UCIL to McLeod Russel (India) Ltd of Calcutta for the rupee equivalent of ninety two million US dollars. Part of the proceeds was used to build and operate a hospital in Bhopal.

Reference: UCIL Chronicle of Events – (n.d.).

C-2: Operating Divisions of Union Carbide India Limited

AGRICULTURAL PRODUCTS DIVISION

Products & Services
Agricultural Products including Fungicides, Miticides, Herbicides,Nematocides, SEVIN insecticides, SEVIMOL insecticides, SEVIDOL insecticides, TEMIK insecticides, SIRMATE insecticides.

Manufacturing Unit
Bhopal
Research & Development Center
Bhopal
Sales Offices
Ahmedabad, Bangalore, Calcutta, New Delhi, Guntur, Indore, Pune, Secunderabad.

CARBON, METALS & GASES DIVISION

Products & Services
NATIONAL Cinema Carbons, FETLARC ouging Electrodes, EMMO Photoengraver Plates, Zinc Addressograph Strips, Electrolytic Manganese Dioxide, Stellite hardfacing rods, electrodes, castings and components. Process Carbons and FETLARK Welding and Cutting Equipment, Carbon Electrodes and calot and zinc strips for batteries.

Manufacturing Units
Calcutta, Madras, Thane.

Sales Ofices
Bombay, Calcutta, New Delhi, Madras, Secunderabad.

BATTERY PRODUCT DIVISION

Products & Services
EVEREADY and NATEX brand Batteries, EVEREADY COMMANDER, JEEVAN – SATHI Torches, Lanterns, Torch Bulbs and Mantles.
Manufacturing Units
Calcutta, Hyderabad, Lucknow, Madras. Research & Development Center Calcutta

CHEMICALS & PLASTICS DIVISION

Products & Services
NION CARBIDE Polyethylene Resins, Polyethylene films, Acetic Acid, Butyl Alcohol, Butyl Acetate, Ethyl Acetate and 2-Ethyl Hexanol.

Manufacturing Unit
Bombay.

Sales Offices

Ahmedabad, Bangalore, Bombay,
Calcutta, Cochim, New Delhi,
Gauhati, Jabalpur, Jaipur, Lucknow,
Madras, Patna, Secunderabad.

Sales Offices

Bombay, Calcutta, New Delhi,
Kanpur, Madras.

MARINE PRODUCTS DIVISION

Products & Services

Commercial fishing, processing and
export of marine products.

Manufacturing Unit

Visakhapatnam.

(Information taken from Annual Report 1981 Union Carbide India Limited)

C-3: Union Carbide India Ltd. – Union Carbide Eastern Reporting System.

UCIL's reporting system - within the Agrochemical Division - and UCE- and the managerial responsibilities at the various levels

During the period immediately prior to the tragedy, Jaganath Mukund, Bhopal Plant's General Manager reported to Kishor S. Kamdar, Vice President UCIL Agricultural Products Division based in Bombay. K. S. Kamdar reported to V. P. Gokhale, Managing Director of UCIL, who in turn, reported to the Board of Directors of UCIL. The Board of Directors comprised of officers from UCIL, government controlled financial institutions (shareholders) and Union Carbide Eastern. Union Carbide Eastern (UCE), an arm of Union Carbide International, a wholly owned division of UCC, was responsible for overseeing UCC's 50.9 percent equity interest in UCIL. (See figures 2-1 and 2-3 for organizational charts).

R. Natarajan, Vice President of UCE (resident of Hong Kong) and a member of UCIL Board of Directors, was the individual responsible for overseeing UCC's interest in Agricultural Products Division. UCE also provided advice and assistance to UCIL. For a listing of names of UCIL's Board of Directors and the years served on the Board during the early 1980's, see Appendix C-4.

V. P. Gokhale, K. S. Kamdar and K. Ramachandra, Vice President and Treasurer of UCIL communicated with Vice Presidents D. Parrish and R. Roeder, Treasurer and Controller of UCE respectively, on UCIL's finances and capital expenditures.

T. N. J. Raman, General Manager of Personnel of UCIL, reported annually to J. Stahl, UCE's Director of Employee Relations, statistical information about plant personnel and staffing.

T. L. Vashi, Safety Manager of UCIL reported statistical information on lost workdays, etc. in the area of safety and health at UCIL to J. Stahl.

Communications concerning plant operations, on a highlight basis was from Gokhale and Kamdar to R. Natarajan, R. E. Brindley, F. J. Costello, R. Roeder and D. Parrish, all at UCE based in Hong Kong.

R. Natarajan, D. Parrish, R. Roeder and J. Stahl reported to A.W. Lutz, Chairman of UCE. Lutz reported to the members of the Board of Directors of UCE and also communicated with J. M. Rehfield, Executive Vice President of UCC. Stahl had a functional relationship with UCC's Employee Relations Department and Jackson Browning, UCC's Director of Safety, Health and Environmental Affairs.

Besides overseeing UCC's interests in UCIL business, the various Vice Presidents at UCE also had coordinating roles for the various product lines in the Eastern region and as such were also members of the world-wide business teams for those lines. Natarajan had such a role for Agricultural Products in the eastern region, which included UCIL.

(Ref. UCC's Response to Plaintiff's First Combined Set of Interrogatories and Requests for Admissions, MDL Docket No. 626 Misc. No. 21-38 (JFK) 85 Civ. 2696 (JFK) All Cases. pp. 3-4).

C-4: UCIL Board of Directors for the years 1982-1984

Keshub Mahindra Chairman #	1966-1984
J. B. Law * Vice-Chairman (deceased)	1975-1984
W. R. Correa (UCIL)	1977-1983
A.M. M. Arunachalam #	1970-1984
V. P. Arya (UCIL)	1973-1982
R. E. Brindley, Jr.*	1979-1984
V. P. Gokhale (UCIL)	1980-1983
N. N. Lahiri #	1981-1984
Bhaskar Mitter #	1966-1983
R. Natarajan*	1977-1984
J. M. Rehfield**	1973-1984
J. N. Saxena #	1979-1983
M. G. Skelsey	1980-1983
A. W. Lutz* (replaced J. B. Law)	1984
F. J. Costello*	1983-1984

* Also served as Board of Directors of UC Eastern.
** Executive Vice President UCC. Also member of UCC Management Committee.
# Non-executive members representing the public shareholders.

(Source:UCC's Response to Plaintiffs' First Combined Set of Interrogatories and Requests for Admissions. MDL Docket No. 626 Misc. No. 21-38 (JFK) 85 Civ. 2696 (JFK) All Cases.)

APPENDIX D

Information Sheet

D-1: Methyl Isocyanate (MIC) Fact Sheet

Chemical Formula : CH_3NCO Molecular Weight 57.05

Physical Properties: [#]

Boiling Point	39.1°C (102.4°F)
Specific gravity	0.9599 (8.0 lb. per gal.)
Vapor Pressure at 20°C	348 mm.Hg
Solubility in water at 20°C	about 6.7% by weight
Solubility of water in MIC at 20°C	about 1.2% by weight
Critical Pressure	55 Atm.
Heat of Vaporization at 1 atm.	223 Btu per lb
Heat of Combustion at 25°C	8,041 Btu per lb

Toxicity: Rat Inhalation. IDLH -   20 parts per million (ppm)

(Immediately Dangerous to Life or Health)*

LC_{50} value/ Time   5 ppm /4 Hr[1]

11 ppm /4 Hr[2]

(IDLH: This concentration represents a maximum level from which one could escape within 30 minutes without any escape-impairing symptoms or any irreversible health effects).

251

Studies on Humans:

The OSHA standard for permissible exposure limit (PEL) during an 8-hour work-shift is 0.02 ppm in air. This is equivalent to 0.05 milligrams of MIC per cubic meter of air.

At 0.4 ppm, four individuals tested experienced no odor or irritation of the eyes, nose or throat. At 2.0 ppm, they still could not detect any odor but there was irritation of the nose and throat and tearing of the eyes. Those conditions were more marked at 4.0 ppm, and at 21 ppm the exposure was unbearable.[3]

\#   Methyl Isocyanate Manual, Union Carbide Corporation, Publication No. F-41443A –7/76, p.2.

*   F.W. Mackison (ed.), NIOSH/OSHA Pocket Guide to Chemical Hazards, Pub. No. 78-210, 4th. printing, 1981.

R.J. Lewis, D.V. Sweet (eds.), Registry of Toxic Chemical Substances, DHHH(NIOSH), Pub. No. 84-101,1984.

1.   Kimmerle and Eben, 1964.

2.   D.E. Dodd, E.H. Fowler, W.M. Snellings, and I.M. Pritts, Acute Inhalation Studies with Methyl Isocyanate Vapor, Fundam. Appl. Toxicology, (1985).

3.   Occupational Health Guideline for Methyl Isocyanate, National Institute for Occupational Safety and Health, <http://www.cdc.gov/niosh/pdfs/0423.pdf>. See also Pushpa S. Mehata, Anant Sunder J. Mehta and Arjun B. Makhijani, Bhopal Tragedy's Health Effects, A Review of Methyl Isocyanate Toxicity, J. Am. Med. Assoc,. 264, 1990, pp. 2781-2787.

D-2: Glossary

Aldicarb: An oxime carbamate with systemic properties, also discovered by UCC.

Baradari: An ornate Mogul-design pavilion with twelve doors – "a place where the wind always blows." The one on Shamla Hills is by the lakeside.

Carbamoylation: A process by which alpha-naphthol is converted to Carbaryl (SEVIN- insecticide), by reacting with MIC. Other types of carbamate insecticides may be prepared by a similar process.

Carbofuran Phenol: A related chemical intermediate which could also be reacted with MIC to produce another carbamate insecticide (Carbofuran) having a different spectrum of insecticidal properties.

Carbofuran: Another carbamate insecticide (described above) discovered by two other chemical companies and is also effective against rice and other pests.

Cathodic Protection: Special external protection around the storage tanks in order to prevent corrosion

Commissioning: Prior to starting a new unit (e.g. MIC), it has to be thoroughly and methodically checked out with an inert material like water. This involves checking that the gaskets (seals), pumps, instrument calibration and every piece of equipment is properly installed. Each step of the commissioning process is set forth in a detailed manual specifically for that particular unit. UCIL employees had to prepare such manuals for the Carbon monoxide unit, phosgene unit, MIC unit and the other units on site.

Congress Party: Indian Political Party in power in 1984 and since independence.

Core Sample: A cylindrical, cross-sectional sampling of the residue settled at the bottom of tank 610. This was obtained by forcing a hollow tube to the bottom of the tank and entrapping the material inside the tube.

Crore: 100 lakhs or 10 million rupees. Lakh is equal to 100,000 rupees. The exchange rate gradually changed from $1 = Rs. 7 in 1966 to Rs.12 to 14 in 1984.

Diluent: A solvent used to dilute a more concentrated mixture.

Distilled/Distillation: A process of separating liquid components from a mixture by taking advantage of the differences in their boiling points.

Exothermic: Chemical reaction that liberates heat.

FAS: Free Alongside Ship.

Feed Tank: An intermediate tank to hold a predetermined amount of MIC before it is introduced into the Carbaryl reactor. Same as Carbaryl Charge Tank.

Flare Tower: A tall cylindrical steel structure designed to destroy the escaping gases at high temperatures. (On the night of December 2, 1984, the flare tower was out of service since a 4-foot section of the structure was disconnected).

Flow Indicator: An instrument that measures and displays the flow of a gas or liquid.

Formulate or (Formulation): To convert the manufactured material into market-able products for a specific end use by mixing with appropriate inert ingredients. Sevin is sold in the diluted form as a sprayable liquid or dust.

Header: A pipeline used as a collection or distribution system in a chemical plant.

Homologs: Higher members of the same family of compounds.

Hydrolysis: A reaction of the chemical with water.

Intermediate: A substance that is further reacted to produce another compound. Like Alpha-naphthol and MIC, which are intermediates required to produce Car-baryl..

IRR: Internal Rate of Return. A method of analyzing a project's viability from its rate of return on investment.

LD_{50} values: Lethal dose required to kill 50 percent of the population. Acute oral $(AO)LD_{50}$ values are for white rats. For example, if the AO $LD_{50} = 100$ mg/kg, it indicates that if 100 mg were administered orally to a population of rats each weighing a kilogram, then there is a high probability that half or 50 percent of these rats would die.

Appendix D

Acute dermal AD values are when the material is applied on bare skin, usually a rabbit.

Naphtha: Flammable petroleum based oil.

Naphthalene: A white crystalline solid obtained from coal tar. Used in the manufacture of Carbaryl, as well as in the manufacture of dyes and drugs.

NIAT: Net Income After Tax

Off-specification: Containing more or less than the specified amount of the impurities in a product.

P.L. 480: Public Law 480 – also referred to as "PL 480" and "Food for Peace." It continues to be the primary U.S. overseas food assistance program.

Polymerization: A process of joining together many units of a reactive molecule.

PPM: Parts per million. Equivalent to 1 milliliter in 1,000 liters or 1 second in 11.6 days.

Process Vent: The vapor and gas released from a vessel to a vent header in the normal course of maintaining the vessel at a selected pressure.

Pyrethroids: A novel class of synthetic insecticides modeled after the natural pyrethrins.

Pyrolyzer: A unit of the chemical plant wherein the methylcarbamoyl chloride intermediate is converted into MIC and hydrogen chloride gas by the application of heat.

Reactor: A vessel in which a chemical reaction is carried out.

Refined: Purified. A product that meets the specifications.

Rupture disc: A graphite or metal disc placed between two adjoining pipeline flanges to prevent any flow of gas until a predetermined pressure causes it to burst.

SEVIN Reactor: A reaction vessel of certain capacity used to react alpha-naphthol (or related intermediates) with MIC to produce Carbaryl or other carbamates.

Slip blinds/lines: A metal disc inserted between two adjoining pipeline flanges to prevent the flow of liquids through the pipeline.

Solvent: A liquid used to dissolve other substances.

Specification: A list of maximum and minimum levels of components permitted in a material.

Swadeshi: Indigenous or homegrown. A movement started by the Indian National Congress in the 1930's under the leadership of Gandhi to urge city-dwellers to develop a habit of consuming Indian rather than foreign products. To also wear cloth spun by villagers using the spinning wheel (Charkha).

Technical Grade: Material produced in the plant with a high concentration of insecticide before it is formulated.

Thermal Stability: The stability of a material to heat.

Transfer Line: The pipeline to transfer MIC from the MIC storage tanks to the Feed Tank for conversion to Carbaryl.

Trimerization: A process by which three molecules of a same compound join together to form a different compound. (Three molecules of MIC react to form the cyclic MIC trimer).

Vent Gas Scrubber (VGS): A device used to neutralize (or scrub off) the escaping upward-moving reactive gases (e.g. MIC, phosgene and acids) with a downward flowing caustic solution. (On the night of December 2, 1984, the scrubber was not in operation).

WAPT: World Agricultural Products Team

INDEX

ISBN 141208412-1

Made in the USA
Lexington, KY
20 October 2011